T5-CVQ-803

JAMES PLAYSTED WOOD has served in the editorial, marketing research, and circulation departments of national magazines and has written for a number of them. He joined The Curtis Publishing Company in Philadelphia in 1946 where he served in various posts until 1962. During this period he worked closely with many of the principal Curtis editors. Mr. Wood worked first on newspapers and in book publishing in New York City, and completed his graduate work in American literature at Columbia University. He taught for some years at Amherst College, and is the author of many books, including *Magazines in the United States* and *The Story of Advertising,* both published by The Ronald Press Company.

THE
CURTIS
MAGAZINES

JAMES PLAYSTED WOOD

THE RONALD PRESS COMPANY · NEW YORK

Copyright © 1971 by
THE RONALD PRESS COMPANY

All Rights Reserved

No part of this book may be reproduced
in any form without permission in writing
from the publisher.

VR

Library of Congress Catalog Card Number: 78–13774
PRINTED IN THE UNITED STATES OF AMERICA

Z
473
.C98
W6

*To friends with whom I
worked at Curtis in Philadelphia*

180936

George Horace Lorimer once gave an excellent description of the magazine publishing business when he described it as purely a business of buying and selling brains. . . . In no other human activity may one be so absolutely sure that sins of commission will find one out, he argued. They are printed for all the world to read. On every issue of a periodical there is a plebiscite to determine its worthiness or unworthiness, whether it shall be encouraged to continue or forced to suspend. Consequently, no business so quickly succumbs to dry-rot, to apathy or content.

 . . . [magazine] publishing is a business that, in all its essentials, is literally pulled out of the air, leaving nothing behind it except a memory, some presses which deteriorate from the moment the wheels are first started and some type which becomes battered from the first time it is used. . . .

A publisher's entire stock in trade is under his hat. . . . unless, under his leadership, the men in his offices can again and again make a new thing that will reflect ever-changing yet eternally changeless human nature, the publisher is a bankrupt.

EDWARD W. BOK, *A Man from Maine,* 1923.

Preface

Cyrus Hermann Kotzschmar Curtis was the prototype of an American idol and ideal, now a folk hero of the past, the self-made man. He created the mass magazine and mass advertising. The editors he selected were strong men of strong convictions, strongly marked individuals with a touch of greatness. Edward Bok made the *Ladies' Home Journal* "The Bible of the American Home," and George Horace Lorimer made *The Saturday Evening Post* "An American Institution" and for many years an accurate reflection of American life.

These three men made The Curtis Publishing Company the largest and most successful periodical publishing house in the world. Socially, economically, even politically sometimes, its magazines were a pervasive and nearly inescapable force. They influenced the life of the nation and the lives of countless individuals in it. They provided sound information and bright entertainment. They helped to form and guide popular taste. Curtis, Bok, Lorimer, and those who worked with them or wrote for them or drew or painted for them knew the exhilaration of triumph and the rewards, power, and glory of sustained success.

Neither they nor the public or even Curtis competitors could foresee any valid reason why the triumph and success should not continue forever. Cyrus Curtis and his aides had built substance into the structure and performance of The Curtis Publishing Company. There was about it the aura of stability and the illusion of permanence.

After a longer period of dominance than most men or institutions enjoy, the permanence proved transient and the stability unstable. The position of the major Curtis magazines was challenged by many forces. For reasons which this book attempts to trace, signs of weakening showed. Decline set in.

The flux of failure accelerated toward what could only be a dismal end. When that end was reached for *The Saturday Evening Post*, the story of the Curtis magazines assumed the outline of an ascending and descending life curve that is almost classical.

In general, quickness is more significant than the terminal date on a tombstone or laboratory reports after postmortem examination. This book concentrates on the life, not the death, of the essential Curtis. It is journalistic history and biography, the story of a publisher, his executives, editors, writers, and illustrators who created something that had distinct identity and pervasive force.

For the greater part of a century the Curtis magazines were an essential part of their time. The *Ladies' Home Journal* under Curtis, *The Saturday Evening Post,* and *Country Gentleman* acted upon people and events. They helped to form and sustain the ideas and the tastes of several generations of readers. In this way the Curtis magazine story is central and important social history.

As such it is addressed to the general reader. The forces that affected The Curtis Publishing Company and killed *The Saturday Evening Post* affect him. The book is particularly addressed to professionals in and students of public communications in all of its many forms. The Curtis accomplishment and what happened to the Curtis magazines are of peculiar and vital concern to them.

My sincere thanks go to former Curtis officials, editors, writers, and artists for information and illuminating discussion. Once again, I thank Elizabeth Craig Wood for her help in checking manuscript and proofs but, as always, more for creating the atmosphere which makes it possible for me to write anything at all.

JAMES PLAYSTED WOOD

Springfield, Massachusetts
December, 1970

Contents

1   CYRUS HERMANN KOTZSCHMAR CURTIS 3
2   EDWARD WILLIAM BOK 15
3   THE *Ladies' Home Journal* 21
4   PURCHASE OF *The Saturday Evening Post* 33
5   GEORGE HORACE LORIMER 40
6   THE NEW CURTIS BUILDING AND A NEW MAGAZINE ... 53
7   ADVERTISING—COMMERCIAL RESEARCH 62
8   THE CURTIS MAGAZINES AND WORLD WAR I 81
9   *The Saturday Evening Post* OF THE 1920's 90
10 THE CURTIS STRONGHOLD 110
11 THE CURTIS TRUST 121
12 *The Saturday Evening Post* AND THE NEW DEAL . 128
13 THE SECOND GENERATION 141
14 RESURGENCE OF THE *Ladies' Home Journal* 154
15 NEW EDITOR AND NEW *Saturday Evening Post* ... 164
16 READER TRAFFIC 176
17 *Holiday* 183
18 DYNASTIC CHANGE 193
19 POSTWAR *Post* WRITERS AND EDITORS 207
20 DEATH OF *Country Gentleman* 215
21 NEW MEN, NEW VENTURES 226
22 COMPETITIVE MAGAZINE RESEARCH 235
23 THE NEW *Saturday Evening Post* 244
24 THE SEA CHANGE 255
25 THE CIRCUS—MAXIMUS 263
26 LAST ACT 271
27 CONCLUSION 282
    BIBLIOGRAPHICAL NOTE 291
    INDEX 293

THE
CURTIS
MAGAZINES

Chapter I

Cyrus Hermann Kotzschmar Curtis

Cyrus H. K. Curtis had his portrait painted in 1906 when he was 56 years old. The artist was Irving Ramsey Wiles, and the portrait hung in Lyndon, the Curtis mansion in Wyncote, a few miles north of Philadelphia. When the mansion was razed, the portrait was sent to The Curtis Publishing Company on Independence Square in Philadelphia and hung in the office of the company president.

A more familiar portrait of the founder and publisher of the Ladies' Home Journal and the modern Saturday Evening Post was painted in 1926 by R. I. Partington, an English artist who had his studio on Sansom Street in Philadelphia. It was hung in the Curtis board room, and a number of copies were made to hang in the Curtis branch advertising offices. These were impressive quarters in Philadelphia, New York, Chicago, San Francisco, Cleveland, Detroit, and Boston.

One day in the late 1940's Mrs. Mary Curtis Zimbalist—who had been Mary Louise Curtis, then Mrs. Edward Bok, and who was principal stockholder, director, and a vice president of The Curtis Publishing Company—stopped unannounced in the Boston office. Its executives had not yet returned from lunch. She said that she would wait. A young girl substituting for the receptionist during the lunch period greeted her pleasantly and saw that she was comfortably seated.

3

Mrs. Zimbalist sat looking up at the portrait of her father. White hair parted in the middle above a narrow face, classic nose, high forehead, large dark eyes, neatly trimmed white beard; it was the unexpressive face, controlled, a little watchful of the handsome successful man. The portrait gave no indication, of course, that he was tiny. Curtis stood only five feet and four inches high. The standup collar, rich dark cravat, edge of white waistcoat, and the rich background of the seated figure bespoke opulence, but they could hardly indicate the scope of the subject's publishing accomplishment.

Noting the direction of the visitor's gaze in the quiet outer office, the girl at the desk spoke up cheerfully.

"We don't know who he is," she said. "We call him Monty Woolley." The white-bearded Yale drama coach who had become a stage and motion picture star was at the height of his popularity.

Few except the daughter and only child who was looking at the portrait of her father knew much more of the real man. Certainly Edward W. Bok, who when he was 60 wrote the biography of his father-in-law, then 73, knew little except the surface of the man—or, if he knew more, was careful not to say it. That would be unlike Bok, who usually told everything he knew or thought he knew.

Cyrus Hermann Kotzschmar Curtis was quietly intent and not given to self-revelation. He planned, organized, delegated responsibility, and went on his way—usually to plan, organize, delegate, and wait for more success to come. Except, perhaps, in the intimacy of his family, he saw no need for other expression of his thoughts, if he had them, or his emotions, if he felt them. He valued his privacy. To help his eager biographer he explained, "I was born. I'm not dead yet. That's all there is to it."

Edward Bok wrote a biography of the man to whom he owed his millions and his editorial reputation. He told the story of from rags to riches, of the poor but honest boy who through his own efforts rose to fame and fortune. Cyrus Curtis had all the Christian virtues: ambition, energy, determination, thrift, generosity, courage, love of dogs and music, and the golden touch.

Bok was not being hypocritical. In that day you wrote a biography to praise someone who deserved the praise, and by the standards both men knew and understood and shared with men of their generation Cyrus Curtis did. *A Man from Maine* is a hymn to Curtis and a hymn to business, the kind of business achievement which brings wealth, power, estates, and a yacht. Bok had lived the American dream through Curtis who first realized the dream for himself.

Cyrus Curtis was born at the corner of Brown and Cumberland Streets in Portland, Maine, June 18, 1850. The family was downeast Yankee and had been for generations. The German middle names given the child were those of a Portland organist and composer to whom the father was devoted. The boy went to school in time, did the chores, ran errands, and played on the ocean shore with his dog. He grew up like any other boy in Portland, but there was one difference. He dreamed early of becoming a great merchant, and he had initiative. He became a newsboy under difficulties. As he was undersized, the other newsboys beat him up. Curtis defeated them by his first display of business acumen. He collared a market for himself by taking copies of the *Courier* to the Civil War soldiers at nearby Fort Preble where the men were so glad to get the paper they often gave him a nickel instead of the paper's three-cent price. This strategy brought the boy to the attention of the business manager of the *Portland Press* who paid him $2 weekly to serve two paper routes with the privilege of selling additional copies on the side. Curtis had to serve his routes, sell his extras, then get home for breakfast at seven and school at nine.

He had made his start with ink and paper and went on. In Boston for $2.50 he bought a small hand press and set up as a printer. He charged ten cents a hundred for visiting cards. Job work led to the more ambitious periodical publishing. Cyrus H. K. Curtis, editor and publisher, issued his first four-page *Young America,* April 12, 1865. Cover price was two cents. Subscription rates were ten cents a month or 25 cents by the quarter. This enterprise ended when, along with the family home, it was burned out in the Portland fire of July 4, 1866.

Curtis seems to have finished grammar school. By age 16 he was a combination errand boy and clerk in the dry goods store of Leach, Bartlett, and Parker for $3 a week. He carried bundles and waited on customers. More important, he read and thrilled to the business stories of Richard B. Kimball. They reinforced his ambition to succeed as a merchant, and he felt he was under way when he moved to the dry goods store of George R. Davis and Company in Boston for $10 a week.

Less than a year later Cyrus Curtis abandoned dry goods forever and returned to his first love. In 1870 he went to work at 25 per cent commission as an advertising solicitor for *The Traveller's Guide*. In 1871 he went to the *Boston Times* in the same position. In 1872 he moved to the *Boston Independent*. Before the end of 1872 he and a fellow worker who promised to invest money in the enterprise but never did, ventured a paper of their own, *The People's Ledger*.

Three years later, still struggling with the *Ledger*, which he had taken over completely, Cyrus H. K. Curtis married Louisa Knapp, who had been secretary to the physician husband of Julia Ward Howe. Their daughter Mary Louise Curtis was born in Boston, August 6, 1876.

Because he could get it done more cheaply there, Curtis moved the printing of *The People's Ledger* to New York. Then he found he could get it printed for $1,500 a year less in Philadelphia. He liked Philadelphia and believed that he, his wife, and their infant daughter could live there on the $1,500 saved. The Curtises moved there before the year was out, found living quarters, and Curtis rented an office for his paper at 713 Sansom Street from which he continued to issue his paper for two years.

Philadelphia was the home of printing and publishing. Scores of small weeklies came out there, among them The

Saturday Evening Post. Any paper had a chance in Ben Franklin's town, but the competition for readers and advertisers was sharp. Curtis sold *The People's Ledger,* which soon went out of business, and settled for a job and a sure income. He became advertising manager of the weekly edition of *The Philadelphia Press* at $15 a week and a 25 per cent commission on all the advertising he could obtain for it.

Cyrus Curtis came into publishing through advertising. He believed in what he sold, and he had learned the value of unrelenting promotion. He promoted the weekly *Press* energetically through direct mail, stressing the importance of Thomas Meehan who wrote its agricultural and horticultural department. Meehan was surprised to learn of his hitherto unsuspected fame and value, but Curtis was pressing for rural and small town readers. Circulation rose, and the advertising came in.

Mrs. Curtis's sister had married, obviously better than she. She was the wife of a banker of Leominster, Massachusetts. Curtis was beginning to do well on the *Press,* but when Hamilton Mayo and his wife came to Philadelphia on a visit, the brother-in-law was unimpressed. He shook his head and advised Curtis to start a business of his own so that he could keep not just a percentage but all of the profits. He did better than that. He lent Curtis $2,000, and Curtis started *The Tribune and Farmer,* a four-page weekly selling for 50 cents a year.

Most people lived on farms or in villages or small towns in the 1880's. They distrusted city slickers. Boston, New York, and Chicago were the places where fast-talking dude drummers came from. Farmers' daughters were not safe anywhere in the land. After the evening chores were done, the farmer wanted a paper he could trust to read by the light of his oil lamp. Curtis got Meehan as editor and writer, hired a one-room office at the corner of Fifth and Walnut Streets for the editor, himself, and one clerk. He featured Meehan's articles on his front page, promoted vigorously, and solicited advertising busily. In lieu of $800 he owed him he gave an advertising agent part interest in *The Tribune and Farmer*. The agent wanted to exploit it through a get-rich-quick subscription scheme, but Curtis demurred. He was always honest, and he was always far-sighted.

He began to run a "Women and Home" department which he pasted up from clippings. His wife ridiculed it. She told him that women were not like that; neither were their homes or their interests. To prove her point she took over the new department and built it into a full page. It was so well received that Curtis decided to make it a monthly supplement to give away with *The Tribune and Farmer*. When that proved successful, he decided to make it a separate paper and sell what had been the supplement at a subscription price of 50 cents a year. With Louisa Knapp Curtis as editor, this first eight-page women's magazine was readied for December, 1883.

The printer's composing room foreman asked Curtis what to set as title for the new paper. Curtis said, "Call it anything you like. It's sort of a ladies' journal." The foreman had *The Ladies' Journal* set in large black capitals at the top of the front page with "And Practical Housekeeper" in much smaller capitals below. Between the words "Ladies'" and "Journal" he ran an elegant embellishment. It was an artist's rendering of the women of a farm family embroidering and sewing, children on the floor and in a rocking chair, a tall grandfather's clock in the background. Under this in black capitals almost as large as the intended logotype was the word "Home." Women who wrote in asking subscriptions to the magazine which was just for them actually gave it its name by calling it the "Ladies' Home Journal."

Cyrus H. K. Curtis, a 12-year-old newsboy who had hoped to become a merchant, was 34 years old with a history of consistent effort for small success behind him when, with money borrowed from a brother-in-law, a suggestion from his wife, and almost by accident he started the Ladies' Home Journal.

The first number of the eight-page monthly, all black and white on paper a little better than newsprint, with steel engravings for illustrations and ornaments, contained the first installment of a serial story. It had articles on flower culture, fashion notes, and advice on the care of children. It carried instructive pieces on cooking, needlework, and handicrafts. The magazine was practical, entertaining, but unpretentious. There were far more elaborate women's magazines being published.

Founded in Philadelphia in 1830, edited for years by the formidable Sarah Josepha Hale (in an off moment she wrote "Mary had a little lamb"), *Godey's Lady's Book* was still going strong. It was the *Vogue* of its era, the arbiter of fashion with Emerson, Longfellow, Holmes, Hawthorne, Harriet Beecher Stowe, and even Edgar Allan Poe for contributors. The even older Graham's Magazine, founded as *The Casket* by Samuel C. Atkinson and Charles Alexander, publishers of The Saturday Evening Post, was a literary monthly with a deliberate, strong appeal to women readers. It used many women writers, many sentimental love stories, the verse of the prolific Mrs. Lydia Huntley Sigourney, and every issue a fashion plate in competition with *Godey's*. In 1840 Charles Jacobs Peterson, an early *Graham's* editor and part owner of The Saturday Evening Post, founded the *Lady's World*. Edited for almost a half century by Peterson, it became *Peterson's Magazine* in 1848. Cheaper, with a larger circulation and greater influence than *Godey's*, *Peterson's* was still flourishing when the Ladies' Home Journal made its first modest appearance in 1883.

Godey's, *Graham's*, and *Peterson's* with their elaborate fashion plates, some in black and white, some hand-colored, were regular-sized magazines, booklike in appearance. They purveyed literature, art, and culture as well as high fashion. Philadelphia had these three strongly established women's magazines when the far simpler Ladies' Home Journal with its appeal to humbler women ventured to seek female favor. It also had competition from out-of-town women's papers resembling it. *McCall's* had been started as *The Queen* in 1870 and the *Woman's Home Companion* in Cleveland in 1873.

As Louisa Knapp, Mrs. Cyrus H. K. Curtis proved that she had been right in ridiculing her husband's clumsy efforts in the women's page of his *Tribune and Farmer*. She knew what ordinary women liked, and women responded by liking it. She gave them a strong, sensible, and attractive periodical. Louisa Knapp was the first and only sole woman editor of the Ladies' Home Journal. Cyrus Curtis had found an editor and a good one. He ceased trying to be an editor at all. He became the businessman he had always wished to be and, above all else, he became an advertising man. Curtis always described himself as an advertising man. He never claimed to be anything else.

He had learned his lessons painfully but well on *The Traveller's Guide*, the *Boston Times*, the Boston *Independent*, with his *People's Ledger*, then on the *Philadelphia Press*, and with his *Tribune and Farmer*. He knew the pitfalls, but also he understood the possibilities. Early indication of the success of the Ladies' Home Journal reinvigorated him. His imagination fired, he took on a confidence, showed a courage, even a daring, he had not hitherto displayed. Honest, simple, direct, he gambled everything. Soon the $2,000 he had borrowed from Mayo was petty cash to the debts he risked.

It had taken five years to get the *Tribune and Farmer* up to a circulation of 48,000. The Ladies' Home Journal reached 25,000 the first year. One day The Curtis Publishing Company would fight bitterly against cut-rate subscriptions and insist on adherence to published rates, but Cyrus Curtis started out with bargain offers. He continued to charge 50 cents a year for single subscriptions to the Ladies' Home Journal but fulfilled club orders for four or more subscriptions at half price. By this means he quickly doubled the Journal's circulation to 50,000 paid.

Curtis was his own space salesman. He sold both the idea of advertising and all that it could accomplish for the advertiser and his conviction that the Ladies' Home Journal with its fast-growing circulation was the place for the smart manufacturer and merchant to advertise. He believed completely in what he preached. He practised it by spending $400 through the Philadelphia advertising agency of N. W. Ayer & Son to advertise the Ladies' Home Journal in three different publications. As he insisted to Journal advertisers, he saw this not as money spent but as money invested. When this first advertising brought in subscription money, he invested it in more advertising through Ayer. Within six months the circulation of the Ladies' Home Journal doubled again to 100,000. Six months later it was 200,000. Few magazines of the time had circulations approaching anywhere near this figure.

Now Cyrus Curtis really had something to sell to advertisers. He confronted them with a large and widespread market of women readers who purchased necessities and luxuries not only for themselves, but also for their entire families. Every one of his 200,000 subscriptions represented a buying household. Curtis rented larger quarters at 427 Arch Street, opposite the Christ Church Burying Grounds, where Benjamin and Deborah Franklin lie, to house his growing editorial, advertising, and circulation promotion and fulfillment business.

Cyrus Curtis understood one advertising fundamental well. There must be value in the product advertised, and that value must be maintained. Product improvement must follow promises made in the advertising. To insure this for the Journal he early established the Curtis policy of seeking out popular big-name authors. He wrote them letters asking them to contribute to the Ladies' Home Journal. He went to Springfield, Massachusetts, and persuaded the popular "Marion Harland," wife of a minister there, to sell him one of her stories for $90. When he returned in triumph to Philadelphia, his editor–wife was horrified at the enormous expenditure.

Curtis proved to her that his strategy was correct. A manufacturer of egg beaters admired Mrs. Harland's writing with commensurate extravagance. Curtis sold him $90 worth of Journal advertising space and paid for the story. Curtis tried to get Rose Terry Cooke, Elizabeth Stuart Phelps, and Mrs. A. D. T. Whitney, but all of these popular women writers had other commitments, and they had never heard of the Ladies' Home Journal. He scored a coup with the famous author of *Little Women*. He promised Louisa M. Alcott that he would give $100 to her favorite charity for a one-column article.

Cyrus H. K. Curtis.   Courtesy of Wide World Photos.

When the article came to Arch Street it was almost two columns in length, so Curtis gave $200 to the charity. Surprised and pleased by this unusual generosity from a publisher, Miss Alcott told other writers, and they began to submit their writing to the Ladies' Home Journal.

Shrewdly, Cyrus Curtis began to consolidate his gains. He advertised a list of well-known authors who were appearing or would soon appear in the Journal. He abolished his cut-rate subscriptions and raised his advertising rates. Circulation continued to climb. Then Curtis decided on the riskiest of magazine publishing risks. He would double the size of his magazine and at the same time double its subscription price. Knowing that he would lose many subscriptions which he would have to replace through hard and expensive promotion, Curtis went to N. Wayland Ayer who had virtually created the legitimate advertising agency business. Wealthy, a large breeder of registered Jersey cows, about to add the presidency of the Merchant's National Bank of Philadelphia to his other interests, Ayer was also a devout churchman. For 50 years he was superintendent of the Sunday School of the North Baptist church of Camden, New Jersey, and for many years he was president of the Northern Baptist Convention. A churchman too and strict in his business ethics, Curtis had built a home in Camden and took the Market Street ferry across the wide Delaware every day to his Arch Street office. Although Ayer was slightly older, the two men were friends. Curtis had paid his first advertising bills promptly. His credit and his reputation were good. Curtis now asked Ayer for $200,000 in advertising credit, and Ayer agreed. He did more.

He went with Curtis to ask credit from Crocker, Burbank and Company of Fitchburg, Massachusetts, who supplied the paper on which the Ladies' Home Journal was printed. The Crocker, Burbank people demurred. Ayer asked Curtis to leave the hotel room in which they were meeting for a few minutes. When he returned he found that the paper manufacturers had granted him a $100,000 credit. Though he did not know it at the time, Ayer had guaranteed his notes.

Curtis weathered losses in subscriptions and advertising caused by the rate increases, but it took money to do it. Instead of $200,000 he spent $310,000 in advertising, and Ladies' Home Journal circulation rose to 488,000—nearly a half million, a huge, an almost incredible figure for any periodical in 1889. In six years' time Cyrus H. K. Curtis, until then just another of the crowd of editor–publisher hopefuls whose journalistic ventures seldom lasted long, had built the woman's page of a now defunct farm magazine into a powerful monthly. Out of practically no business he had created Big Business, and Curtis loved Big Business. Almost incidentally he had created the mass magazine, the large-circulation magazine conceived and published primarily as an advertising medium through which sellers could reach a mass market of buyers.

Now came the great change on the Ladies' Home Journal. Mary Louise Curtis had grown to be 13 years of age. She complained that whenever she wanted her mother she found her too busy with pencil and paper to pay much attention to her. A little conscience-smitten, Louisa Knapp recognized the justice of the charge. She relinquished her editorship, and in October, 1889, Cyrus Curtis hired a 26-year old employee away from the New York publishing house of Charles Scribner and Sons. Curtis could hardly have realized then that the real story of the Ladies' Home Journal and The Curtis Publishing Company was only just about to begin.

Chapter 2

Edward William Bok

When Edward William Bok was born to a family of modest wealth and social position in Helder, the Netherlands, October 8, 1863, he weighed 14 pounds and had a very large head, facts which he considered important enough to report with considerable pride 62 years later. Before he was two years old he stared Prince Otto Eduard Leopold von Bismarck completely out of countenance, proving that the Prussian chancellor finally met his match. Brought to the dinner table for display by his parents, the 20-month old child fixed unblinking wide eyes on Bismarck, who sat still for the inspection, then completed his conquest by spilling a glass of wine on the awesome guest by whom he was not awed at all.

Bok was watched over by his governess Antje and adored by his maiden Tante Katrien. He was never ill as a child. He was made hardy, he felt, by the winds of the North Sea and vital by the interest and curiosity that marked him from the first. As Bok says over and over again in talking of himself with unflagging interest in several books, he never knew the meaning of fear.

Misfortune struck when Edward Bok was seven years old. The family lost its money. Rather than attempt a fresh start in Holland, his father decided to emigrate, and Edward Bok, his mother, father, and older brother landed in New York, September 20, 1870. His crushed father was unable to adapt to plebeian circumstances in the new world and took a clerical job with the Western Union Telegraph Company in Manhattan. The family lived in Brooklyn where Bok's mother, used to servants and the amenities of life, was quickly broken in health by the hardships of housekeeping.

Bok and his brother entered public school in Brooklyn. They soon learned English, and Edward Bok took readily to American ways. In *The Americanization of Edward Bok*, third-person Pulitzer Prize autobiography of 1920, he tells in detail of his boyhood, which was really much like that of any other Brooklyn boy of the time, and of the family struggles. Bok coasted on a Flexible Flyer, hunted tinfoil in the streets, helped with the housework, went to Sunday School, and searched for scraps of kindling in a nearby lumber yard. He yearned "to be somebody" and "to do something."

Bok did not learn his push and self-confidence in America. He brought them with him. He was the born go-getter. Often he protests to himself and his readers that it was never selfishness or the desire to push himself forward but the wish to know, to grow, to succeed which motivated him. Whatever their source, his self-assurance and lack of the ordinary inhibitions worked from his early years.

His father gave him a diplomatic appointment signed by Bismarck and one of Bismarck's calling cards with which to start an autograph collection. Unlike most small boys, Bok did not start with his uncles, aunts, and schoolfellows. He started at the top, where he felt he belonged, and he went at his tuft-hunting scientifically. He looked up likely autograph prospects in *Appleton's Encyclopedia*, then wrote them as an inquiring and appealing little Dutch boy seeking under difficulties to further his education. He asked questions about some incident in the great man's life or about his ideas on some subject or his favorite poem. Instinctively he used flattery as approach and a charming diffidence. Soon he had captured John Greenleaf Whittier, Thomas Hardy, Mark Twain, Harriet Beacher Stowe, Lew Wallace, Paderewski, Cardinal Newman, Eugene Field. . . .

The boy did not stop with writing. He screened the New York newspapers for news of the arrival of the great, then presented himself at their hotels as the earnest Dutch boy bravely fighting adversity and wishing only to follow their example to greatness and success. He bearded President Rutherford Hayes, then having captured a President, caught a king in the person of King Kalakaua of what were then called the Sandwich Islands. He wrote General Grant. Grant asked him to call, then took him to dinner at the Fifth Avenue Hotel. Bok talked to Jefferson Davis and corresponded with General William Tecumseh Sherman. This early acquaintance-ship with famous authors and public figures, the noteworthy and the newsworthy, would stand the later editor in good stead.

At 13 Bok left school and went to work. His father got him a job as office boy with a desk next to his in the Western Union offices. The boy started in 1876 for $6.25 a week. Each morning he walked to the ferry to save the carfare. He got the driver of a dray to take him across, thus saving another three cents, and the truckman drove him up Broadway to the Western Union building, saving him another carfare. A waiter gave him the leftovers from the private dining room in which officers and executives of Western Union lunched. In this way Bok and his brother, who was earning the same salary, could turn over almost all of their $12.50 each week to help support the family.

At Western Union, Bok found more celebrities. Thomas Edison was in and out. So were Jay Gould and other success-ful men. It was success Bok worshipped and was determined upon. He began to study shorthand at the Y.M.C.A. Because the course moved too slowly for him, he took additional eve-ning courses at a Brooklyn business school. Soon he was re-porting speeches for the *Brooklyn Eagle* and, if they were big enough to warrant his attention, meeting the speakers. He multiplied his conquests by taking a trip to Boston, Cambridge, and Concord where, using his ingenuous approach, he met and talked with Holmes, Longfellow, Thoreau, Emerson, and the rest and carried home his trophies.

At 18, against the advice of Jay Gould from whom he took dictation and who prophesied a great future for him in Wall Street, and turning down a pressing invitation to enter the theatrical world to which he was attracted, Bok left Western Union. His departmental employer there, Clarence Cary, got him the job, and Edward Bok went to work as a stenographer with the book publishing firm of Henry Holt and Company.

Bok went to church and Sunday School in Brooklyn's famed Plymouth Church and became intimate with its even more famed pastor, Henry Ward Beecher, through offering to help him with his correspondence. He became one of Beecher's youthful confidants, and Beecher left his lasting mark on Bok's moral and ethical code as well as on his journalistic career.

Bok remained at Holt only two years. In 1884, again with the help of Clarence Cary, he went as a stenographer to Scribner's. With both publishers he learned the uses of publicity and advertising, knowledge which would stand him in good stead. Scribner's, though, was not enough to satisfy his ambition. On the side he became an entrepreneur. With the same mixture of native intelligence, quickly learned skills, ambition, and effrontery, he embarked on several journalistic ventures, all of them successful. With a friend who had had some publishing experience he began to print and solicit advertising for theatre programs. In 1884, with the same associate, he started *The Philomathean Review*, an organ for the debating society of Plymouth Church. Obtaining financial backing from wealthy members of the Plymouth Congregation, notably Standard Oil's Rufus T. Bush, they expanded this into *The Brooklyn Magazine*. It became *The American* when Bok and his partner sold it to Bush for his son and, after Bush sold it, the *Cosmopolitan*, of which Bok was several times offered the editorship.

Out of these experiences Bok stumbled on the idea of syndication. He and Colver started with the sermons of Henry Ward Beecher, to whom they guaranteed $250 a week, then

Edward W. Bok. Reprinted by special permission.
© 1953, 1957 The Curtis Publishing Company.

drew on the writers whom Bok had captured in his autograph
hunting for additional contributions which they could sell to
a number of newspapers. Bok opened an office for his syndicate and made his brother, William J. Bok, partner and manager. He hired the popular Ella Wheeler Wilcox to write a
weekly article and thus established the first syndicated women's
page in American newspapers. Using his New York publishing contacts, he began to write book reviews and syndicated
these as "Literary Leaves" to papers in Boston, New York, Cincinnati, and Philadelphia.

Bok's energy and enterprise were boundless, and he capi-
talized on everything in sight. Henry Ward Beecher was just
about to celebrate his 40th anniversary as minister of the
Plymouth Church, and Brooklyn planned a giant observance.
Bok decided to solicit congratulatory letters from the great of

the world to be bound into a presentation volume. With the ready consent of the Beecher family, Bok sent out his requests. The correspondence was well under way when Beecher died, March 8, 1887. Bok then decided to finish his work and publish the results.

His *Beecher Memorial*, "Contemporaneous Tributes to the Memory of Henry Ward Beecher, Compiled and Edited by Edward W. Bok," was privately printed in Brooklyn, copyrighted by Bok, in 1887. Bok contented himself with a brief note in the front matter acknowledging the cheerful willingness of his many distinguished contributors, who certainly were a mixed lot. Presidents, poets, ministers, humorists, educators, and multi-millionaires mingled with radical statesmen, atheists, scientists, and inventors—Whittier, Edwin Booth, John C. Fremont, Hayes, Cleveland, John Burroughs, Andrew Carnegie, Robert Ingersoll, Charles Stewart Parnell, Joaquin Miller, William E. Gladstone, Bill Nye, Louis Pasteur, Alexander Graham Bell, Baron Bernhard von Tauschnitz, Charles Dudley Warner. . . . When Henry Ward Beecher "passed away"—Bok never said "die"—Bok made invaluable additions to his already strong list of promotable contacts.

He was a success at Scribner's, with his syndicate, his "Literary Leaves," and his first book. There was every indication that he would soon do even better. The world was his oyster, and he had the shell open wide enough so that he knew he could easily pry it the rest of the way. He hesitated when Cyrus H. K. Curtis offered him the editorship of the Ladies' Home Journal. It meant leaving the literary and publishing world of New York in which he had begun to establish himself.

Bok did not hesitate long. In six initial years Louisa Knapp Curtis had firmly established the Ladies' Home Journal. Nearly a half million women and their families were reading it eagerly every month. The Journal's momentum was gathering speed; so was that of Edward Bok. Curtis felt that if he could combine the dynamic Journal with the aggressive Bok there would be no limit to the possibilities. Bok came to the same conclusion, and both men were right.

Chapter 3

The Ladies' Home Journal

When Edward Bok took office in Philadelphia, October 20, 1889, the event did not go unnoticed. Curtis and Bok promoted it as loudly and as widely as they could. Edward Bok was the youngest and highest paid editor of any woman's magazine in the country. He was unmarried. He was 26 years old. This was news, and it was also ridiculous. The press made the most of all the humor and derisive wit they could squeeze out of the situation. That this brash youth dared become editor of what was already the largest woman's magazine was deliciously absurd. Bok would be the butt of endless jokes for years to come. That was all right with Bok and all right with Curtis. It was publicity and the kind of publicity that would make the curious buy copies of the Journal to find out just what the heralded young editor was accomplishing or how big a fool he was making of himself.

Bok gave them all the help he could. He forswore the anonymity usual with magazine editors who preferred to center attention on their productions and decided to impress his personality openly on the pages of the Ladies' Home Journal and the minds of its readers. They could not think of the Journal without Bok or Bok without the Journal. Bok wanted to become the consort of American womanhood. He invited the confidences of the feminine heart and tried to make them think of the Ladies' Home Journal as an intimate. He adopted many devices to insure two-way communication, what later editors would call "reader rapport," between women, all women, and the Journal.

Edward Bok first appeared in the Ladies' Home Journal as a literary gossip writer. His syndicated "Literary Leaves" was in the issue for September, 1889, and it was packed with juicy bits: General Grant's family had thus far received $90,000 from the sale of the general's "Memoirs"; Mark Twain's *Connecticut Yankee in King Arthur's Court* would be out in December; William Dean Howells had moved back to Boston from New York; Robert Louis Stevenson was in Samoa and did not plan to return to the United States for another six months; Jean Ingelow was unwell; E. P. Roe's widow was living in New York. Bok was back in October with an article, "Forgotten Graves of Famous Authors" and in December with "Gladstone's Love for Reading" and "Bismarck's Literary Tastes."

All this was very cultural, but with Bok's name listed on the masthead as editor for the first time in January, 1890, came Bok in another and more characteristic guise. He appeared as "Ruth Ashmore" in "Side Talks to Girls." He advised girls to learn to say no. "There is in that little word much that will protect you from evil tongues." He warned them not to give their photographs to every Tom, Dick, and Harry. In a later "Side Talk" Bok warned girls against dancing. "It's all very well to say there is no harm in dancing. There isn't. But there is harm in having about you, a sweet, pure girl, kept as much as possible from the wickedness of the world, the arm of a man who may be a profligate, and not possess the first instinct of a gentleman."

Letters poured in to "Ruth," their writers baring their young hearts and asking advice, so Bok turned the column over to a woman writer and went on to bigger and better things. William Dean Howells was recognized as the leading novelist of the day. Bok already knew him through his autograph hunting. He bought serial rights to *The Coast of Bohemia* for the Journal and contracted in advance for the novelist's autobiography. He arranged to publish a new story by Rudyard Kipling. The Dutch boy's penchant for big names was now part of the Journal editor's natural approach. Flattery had always been a basic weapon in his armory. He used it lavishly on his women readers. He wooed them with Laura Jean Libbey, Ella Wheeler Wilcox, and Mrs. Lyman Abbott, wife of Beecher's successor at the Plymouth Church. He had Mamie Dickens write "My Father As I Knew Him." This led to series of series of pieces by eminent women or women with eminent connections: "Unknown Wives of Famous Men," "Unknown Husbands," "Famous Daughters of Famous Men." He devoted most of an entire issue to contributions by the daughters of Hawthorne, Harrison, Howells, Greeley, Sherman, Gladstone, Jefferson Davis, and others.

At the same time Bok established more features which would reinforce the emotional ties between his magazine and its readers. Mrs. Margaret Bottome held heart-to-heart talks with girls in every issue. She urged them to bring all their problems to her. They were assured repeatedly that everything they wrote would be held in the strictest confidence. Every letter was answered. Some were discussed in the Journal's columns, but the most intimate were never published.

Bok reached for the best-known writers. He made profuse use of illustration. He instituted novel features. Inventive, imaginative, he had his self-confidence for chief asset but softened it. He asked the advice of his readers about what they liked and disliked, what they wanted to see in *their* magazine. At the same time he was unrelentingly didactic.

Cyrus Curtis cooperated perfectly by letting Edward Bok alone. This is not a negative but a positive virtue in a publisher and one few can observe. June 25, 1891, Curtis formed The Curtis Publishing Company with a capitalization of $500,-000.[1] He retained majority control and with the circulation

[1] The company underwent several reincorporations and slight name changes. July 3, 1900, The Curtis Company of New Jersey was formed. July 24, 1907, this was succeeded by Curtis Publishing Company incorporated in Pennsylvania with capitalization of $2,500,000, doubled in 1910. In 1911 the name was changed back to The Curtis Publishing Company. July 6, 1914, Curtis Publishing Company was organized with a capitalization of $10,000,000 which was raised almost immediately to $25,000,000. It became The Curtis Publishing Company again December 24, 1921, and stayed with its original corporate title from that date on.

of the Ladies' Home Journal leaping ahead, used the money thus obtained to buy presses and lease a new Curtis Building at 421-423 Arch Street in Philadelphia.

By 1893 the Ladies' Home Journal was a magazine of 34 over-sized pages with a fully illustrated cover. Mrs. Lyman Abbott was writing "Just Among Ourselves" for every issue. In April there were six pages—another Bok innovation—of sheet music, Reginald de Koven's "Magnolia Blossom Waltz." The Christmas issue that year had "The Manhattan Beach March" by John Philip Sousa as well as a story, "The Pioneer Christmas" by Hamlin Garland. It was in 1893 that Bok, stern and fatherly this time, felt impelled to take a stand. Too many women were going into office work, and he knew he should warn them.

> The atmosphere of commercial life has never been conducive to the best interests of women engaged in it. The number of women in business who lose their gentleness and womanliness is far greater than those who retain what, after all, are woman's best and chief qualities. To be in an office where there are only men has never yet done a single girl any good; and it has done harm to thousands . . . I know whereof I speak, and I deal not in generalities.

Two years later the Ladies' Home Journal went to 48 pages including covers. The whole of the December, 1895, cover was given to James Whitcomb Riley's "At the Gate" with five vignettes of country life in black and white. Inside the issue President Benjamin Harrison wrote on "This Country of Ours." Three serials were running: Kipling's "William the Conqueror"; Mary E. Wilkins's "Neighborhood Types"; and Mary Anderson de Navarro's story of her life on the stage. The music this time was "Jesus, the Very Thought of Thee," and the prize illustrations were Kate Greenaway drawings which, on a visit to England, Bok had persuaded the shy artist to contribute to the Journal. There was a sermon, "The Passion of Money-Getting" by the Rev. Charles H. Parkhurst, D. D.

Bok had now started a new and important service. Each issue of the Ladies' Home Journal contained the plans and drawings for a new house. In this issue they were those for a suburban home which could be built for $3,500. Cyrus Curtis had said early of his magazine, "We propose to make it a household necessity—so good, so pure, so true, so brave, so full, so complete that a young couple will no more think of going to housekeeping without it than without a cookstove." Bok was realizing his employer's objective and adding purposes of his own.

As commercially minded as any publisher could wish his editor to be, as opportunistic as he was, Edward Bok yet had a concomitant idealism. As its original subtitle had read, the Ladies' Home Journal was still the "practical housekeeper." There were the recipes, the fashions, the sewing, knitting, and crocheting instructions. These were the staples in any woman's magazine. Bok was also intent on raising the standards of American taste in domestic architecture, interior decor, art, music, literature, and morals. His magazines was practical, literary and aesthetic, but, above all, unflinchingly moral by the standards of Henry Ward Beecher and Edward Bok.

Ruth Ashmore held her own along with Kipling, ex-Presidents, and popular women novelists. In 1895 she was answering the questions of "Grace G.," "Inexperience," "Homoselle," and hundreds of others. She advised Henrietta A., "I can only suggest that you write to the friend who behaved coldly to you and find out if any one has been trying to make mischief between you." She assured Annie H. that when a gentleman took her to a place of amusement he expected to pay the carfare. She comforted Lizzie about a matter of etiquette. "Melons are usually eaten either with a fork or a spoon; a knife is never offered with them." Ruth had to be firm with Madge and Others. "I must ask my girls not to request that I recommend a depilatory. I do not know of any that are quite safe."

In January, 1896, Bok extended his ministry. He gave advice to young men in his lead editorial. He was reaching for male as well as female readers. Men and boys as well as women and girls could enjoy Frank R. Stockton's "The Widow's Yarn" in this same number, but the appeal of Isobel Mallon was strictly feminine. In "For His Highness the Baby" she wrote:

Your baby is the most lovely that was ever born, but do not let strangers, in their desire to express their admiration of it, kiss the little lips that cannot object, or clasp tightly in their arms the little body that is, as yet, so tender.

Big names, stories of the great that let readers share in the glamor of the larger world, stories of women preeminent through their accomplishments were a Bok specialty, but sometimes the big names were surprising.

In November, 1896, the Ladies' Home Journal carried a stirring article, "When Jenny Lind Sang in Castle Garden." Its author was A. Oakey Hall. A graduate of New York City University and Harvard Law, Hall had been a New Orleans newspaperman before he became a notorious Tammany mayor of New York. Supposedly his initial and middle name on a document gave rise to the "A-Okay" phrase of approval. Hall was tried for implication with the Tweed Ring but acquitted, and Bok must have believed him innocent or he would not have risked smirching the purity of the Journal.

By 1898 Bok's editing had more than doubled the circulation of the Ladies' Home Journal. It stood at an unbelievable 850,000. It was going to 59 of the 65 civilized countries of the world. It was replete with advertising, every issue containing at least as much lucrative advertising as editorial matter. Books, food, clothes, household appliances, department stores, dress patterns, and always corsets were advertised. Corsets seemed to predominate and when blown up to page size they were fearsome and formidable engines.

Curtis never made any secret of the advertising intent of his magazines. He obtained and ran as many advertisements as he could get, but from the beginning he screened them carefully. In the Journal's second year he wrote, June, 1884, "Every advertiser in this paper is believed to do a square, honest business. Great pains are taken to know if each one intends and is able to do the right thing and treat our readers honestly. Thousands of dollars worth of advertising is rejected from parties whose responsibility is in doubt. Hence, if you want anything advertised, do not fear to buy it."

Bok was as conscious of advertising as his employer who, with his marriage to Mary Louise Curtis, October 22, 1896, became his father-in-law as well. Advertising paid his salary. It paid for the high-priced authors he was able to obtain. It brought in the Curtis profits. In its 15th years of publication he wrote proudly that the Ladies' Home Journal went wherever the mail went, crossing every sea and ocean. In the same editorial he wrote:

> The fact must never be forgotten that no magazine published in the United States could give what it is giving to the reader each month if it were not for the revenue which the advertiser brings the magazine. It is the growth of advertising in this country which . . . has brought the American magazine to its present enviable position in points of literary, illustrative, and mechanical excellence. The American advertiser has made the superior American magazine of today possible.

Bok's Journal was not only the lexicon of female deportment and the dictator of genteel domesticity, but also part of the gayety of two centuries. Charades were part of a merry turn-of-the-century party in South Brooklyn on the night of December 31, 1899, and the morning of January 1, 1900. In one a pretty young woman in Gibson Girl costume with a Madame Pompadour hairdo attacked a frightened young man with a "tomahawk." The intent was really not lethal and the violence was sanctioned, almost sanctified. An explanatory copy of the Ladies' Home Journal, its black and white cover showing a covered wagon under Indian attack, was propped up between assailant and assailed when they strained to hold still for a flash-powder time-exposure which recorded this one New Year's Eve in a hundred for all posterity.

By 1902 the Ladies' Home Journal had covers in color on heavier than body stock. It had more and more illustrations. In April there was a full page of dog pictures. These were not show animals but the pets of readers who had been encouraged to send in snapshots of Fido or Rover just as they might show them to friends. The pictures were displayed right after the opening article, "The President's Daughter." It began, "Alice Roosevelt is the typical American girl in the best sense of the word; modest, self-reliant, democratic . . ."

Bok always published as many pieces as he could get from his admired and admiring friend Rudyard Kipling. "My Personal Experience with a Lion" and "The Butterfly that Stamped" were both in the Journal in 1902. In April there were pages of the new styles, plans for a surburban mansion which could be built for $6,000, puzzles, "Fun with Silhouettes," and the corset advertisements were supplemented by the "Literary Talks" of Hamilton Mabie. In May, Bok reached farther for masculine readership when he established an outdoor and camping department, "Ernest Thompson Seton's Boys," but the intimacy with women readers was never relaxed. Again and again Bok urged, "Suppose we ask the Lady from Philadelphia what is best to be done." Always there was the reiterated promise that no secret would be divulged. Margaret E. Sangster edited a department called "Girls' Problems." In October, 1902, she wrote, "I wish to repeat something I have said before because some of you are anxious about it. You need not fear that I shall betray any confidence, nor answer in these columns any personal letter which requires an individual reply by mail." The Journal boasted that it attended to as many as 10,000 letters a day and that it took ten or 12 people all day long just to open the letters it received.

The Ladies' Home Journal comforted, caressed, and instructed. It told women how to dress, cook, build and furnish their homes, how to act. It brought them kings and Presidents, novels, biography, and autobiography. Implicitly, explicitly, unremittingly, it told the wonder of being a woman. All through 1902 it ran "Helen Keller's Own Story of Her Life, Written Entirely by the Wonderful Girl Herself."

Bok seemed inspired. He was moving at high speed. In 1904 he proved that, beyond cavil, he was a great editor. The circulation of the Ladies' Home Journal reached 1,000,000, a feat never before accomplished by any other magazine. The population of the entire United States was only a little over 76,000,000.

By 1905, cover price raised from 10 to 15 cents for its big, packed issues, the Ladies' Home Journal was going in strongly for culture and had begun to crusade for reforms. There were pages of music by Grieg, Paderewski, Richard and Edward Strauss, Chaminade, Moskowski. The young Josef Hofmann, a Bok intimate, was teaching piano to Journal readers. Kipling, Kate Douglass Wiggin, Elizabeth Stuart Phelps, and Gene Stratton-Porter were all in the book, but so were Jane Addams with the story of her work in Hill House in the Chicago slums and F. Hopkinson Smith with a vigorous exposé, "The Patent Medicine Curse." The Journal had stopped accepting patent medicine advertising in 1892, but many magazines, including the literary and cultural, were crammed with it. Bok began an all-out fight on the entire patent medicine industry.

Bok exposed its false claims. He reproduced the American and the contrasting English label used on one nostrum to quiet infants. The English label warned that the potion contained morphine and was thus designated "poison." The Journal followed this by publishing a list of 22 advertised patent medicines and telling what ingredients each contained. Collier's joined with the Journal in the fight, and the two magazines were largely instrumental in obtaining passage of the Food and Drug Act of 1906.

Bok had tasted victory, and he liked the taste. With the foreknowledge of the furor he would provoke, he decided on a far more dangerous campaign. It took courage on his part and on that of Cyrus Curtis who told him to go ahead if he thought he was right. In 1906 Bok began open discussion of venereal disease in the Ladies' Home Journal. This violation of a long-standing taboo shocked the public and horrified many Journal readers. Some 75,000 cancelled their subscriptions. Advertisers cancelled their schedules. Bok and the Ladies' Home Journal were castigated for their immorality. Bok insisted that the time had come when women should know these things and that, insofar as he could, he intended to see that they did know.

He pressed his attack in article after article. Outraged readers refused to allow copies of the magazine in their homes.

Some of Bok's friends tore out the offending pages before allowing the issues to be seen by their families. Risking their reputations and positions, Jane Addams, Cardinal James Gibbons, the Bishop of London, President Charles W. Eliot of Harvard, and the Rev. Henry Van Dyke of Princeton rallied to Bok's support in Journal pages.

Bok won. He did not eradicate venereal disease but he made discussion and measures to combat it possible. He had struck and struck hard but, as he had always done, he courted too. Howard Chandler Christy was in the Journal now with "Striking New Drawings of the American Girl." The President, Theodore Roosevelt himself, was talking to Journal readers in interviews he granted "A Writer Intimately Acquainted and in Close Touch with Him" while he was shaving. Bok had persuaded Roosevelt to give him this only free time he had during his strenuous days.

A magazine is only as good as its latest issue. Bok went all out for Christmas, 1907, in a thick Ladies' Home Journal which, except for being three inches taller, as it was in those years, looked much like the Journal of a half century later. It was Christmas all over the place in the Ladies' Home Journal for December, 1907, such a Christmas as never was until the Journal came along.

The issue opened with "My Grandfather at Christmas" by the grandson of Charles Dickens. Laura Spencer Fort had a story, "The Christmas Angels." S. Weir Mitchell, Philadelphia neurologist as well as novelist, told of Washington and the Continental Army at Valley Forge in "A Christmas Venture." Pictured riding in her coach in Concord, New Hampshire, Mary Baker Eddy told "What Christmas Means to Me." Hamilton Mabie wrote "Christmas in Shakespeare's Time." Sent there by Bok, Henry Van Dyke reported on "Out-of-Doors in the Holy Land." There was a "Mother Goose Christmas," even a "Christmas Two-Step for Christmas Night." The December, 1907, Ladies' Home Journal almost put Christmas out of business.

For months Edward Bok had been promising the best issue yet—"of glorious color on the outside; of beauty and interest within." He kept his promise with a spectacular for November, 1908. There was no illustration on the rich crimson cover. In white reverse lettering there was just the legend in large type: "The 300th Ladies' Home Journal. In celebration of the 25th Anniversary of the Magazine."

Inside there were 102 pages of text and advertising. The issue opened with a handsome photograph of the trimly bearded Cyrus H. K. Curtis and the story of the founding of the Ladies' Home Journal. Bok was photographed making "Our Birthday Bow." In his editorial he took a long and detailed look backward.

He produced a proud list of great writers and Presidents who had written for the Ladies' Home Journal. He talked of the magazine's contributions of art, music, literature, women's interests, children's interests, and of the contributions on moral and ethical subjects by the Rev. Lyman Abbott, Cardinal Gibbons, and Rabbi Emile Hirsch. Jacob Riis, Sir Henry Irving, President Eliot, Commander Perry, Mrs. Humphrey Ward, and William Jennings Bryan had writen of contemporary events and ideas.

Bok disclosed that as high as $300,000 a year was spent to advertise the Ladies' Home Journal. He assumed—it was not an unrealistic assumption in 1908—that business and business success were as important to his women readers, their husbands, and their sons as it was to him and his employer. He closed his rhapsodic editorial with "Mr. Curtis's policy for business success."

First of all: Make the very best article at the lowest possible price, and then
Second: Let the public know about it; in other words, advertise what you have to sell.

This was a sparkling, an exuberant issue of the Ladies' Home Journal. It contained, but unsigned and not acknowledged as personal experience, what later became a chapter in *The Americanization of Edward Bok.* In it Bok told how his older son, Curtis, recovering from a heart ailment, chose meeting Theodore Roosevelt as his birthday present. "The President and the Boy" described the meeting. It was a sentimental but a moving piece. It must have touched Journal readers in 1908, and many read it. The November, 1908, Ladies' Home Journal attained a fantastic circulation of 1,150,000. Assuming four readers to each copy, a conservative estimate, it reached 6,600,000 people. No magazine ever before had so many readers, and when one had more, it would be the Ladies' Home Journal.

Mrs. Humphrey Ward did not believe in woman suffrage. Neither did Edward Bok and the Ladies' Home Journal. They considered it unwomanly and said so in this 25th anniversary issue. Bok could be wrong, but he was more often right. Bok spoke of the past in November, 1908, but also of the future.

An architect's drawing showed the massive new Curtis Building which The Curtis Publishing Company planned to erect on Independence Square facing Independence Hall and the Liberty Bell and abutting Washington Park. It spoke eloquently of present accomplishment and future promise. Bok described the planned new building. He sounded almost awed as he looked back then forward from where he bowed on the editorial page.

So, on our twenty-fifth birthday, we hope that the unstinted confidence and success meted out to us by the public have made us humble and grateful rather than boastful and forgetful. If anything were needed to keep us from being boastful it is in the incontrovertible fact, incessantly faced each day, that it is so much easier to make a success than to hold it.

Either as a prophecy or foreboding, Bok's comment was astute.

Chapter 4

Purchase of The Saturday Evening Post

In 1908 Cyrus Curtis was publishing not one but two magazines, and to the dismay of Edward Bok, who never ceased to be irritated by the competition and the danger it threatened to his preeminence, the second was threatening to become as successful as the first.

As its masthead proudly announced, The Saturday Evening Post had been founded in 1821. It had been published successively as The Saturday Evening Post; the Daily Chronicle and Saturday Evening Post; The Saturday Evening Post; Atkinson's Saturday Evening Post; Atkinson's Saturday Evening Post and Philadelphia News; finally as just The Saturday Evening Post again.

Devoted to "Morality, Pure Literature, Foreign and Domestic News, Agriculture, Science, Art and Amusement," The Saturday Evening Post called itself at various times in the 19th century "A Mammoth Paper," "The Very Pearl of Literary Weeklies," and "The Great Family Paper of America." Before the Civil War there was some basis for any claim it cared to make. It was widely read and it published good popular writers. Bayard Taylor, Nathaniel Hawthorne, T. S. Arthur, Grace Greenwood, and Ned Buntline wrote for it in the 1840's. Dickens (his work probably pirated) appeared in it. Edgar Allan Poe, who wrote for most of the Philadelphia magazines and held editorial posts on several, contributed his famous "The Black Cat" to The Saturday Evening Post in 1843, verse at various times, and even conducted a code and cipher department in the magazine for a short period.

James Fenimore Cooper, Nathaniel Parker Willis, James Parton, and Harriet Beecher Stowe all appeared in The Saturday Evening Post, though some of their work was probably picked up from exchanges—common practice of the time—and not written originally for the Post.

Four pages, 22 × 30", the Post was a combination weekly newspaper and magazine, national in coverage, published by Samuel D. Patterson and Company at 98 Chestnut Street, Philadelphia, at $2 a year if paid in advance, $3 if patrons had to be billed later. Often the front page was solely fiction and poetry. Inside there were more poems, patent medicine advertisements, "Selected Articles," Postscripts (shipping news then, not humor as Post Scripts was in the later Post); Letters from New York; Congressional; "Fun and Frolic"; advertisements for *Godey's Lady's Book* or the Post itself; marriage, death, fashion, and financial notes.

A box in 1848 read: "The Proprietors of The Saturday Evening Post return their thanks to the friends of morality and pure literature for their liberal support during 1847." In another issue the same proprietors said defensively, "The Post is no second-hand edition of a Daily Paper. All matter is prepared especially for it, and it alone." At the same time the Post bristled with lively clippings from *Living Age*, the *Literary World*, and other contemporary periodicals. It ran a whole serial, *Coincidence, A Tale of Fact*, scissored from *Fraser's Magazine*, then a biography of John C. Calhoun lifted from *The Rough and Ready Almanac*, and "A Tale of the Mexican War" pasted up from *Noah's Messenger*.

Lydia Sigourney appeared often. So did Grace Greenwood. In signed advertisements, Louis A. Godey was one of the Post's chattiest authors. An example:

To the Ladies of the United States. It now being conceded that
Godey's Lady's Book
Stands at the head of American magazines, it now becomes the duty of the publisher to show what amount of reading, and how many embellish-

ments she will receive for $3. . . . the coloring of our Fashion Plates—
we say nothing of the Flowers and Cottages—costs us over
$2,000 in one year.
To omit this is certainly a savings, but is it just to subscribers? Is it
honorable? We cannot practice such a deception.

Most papers of the time were plagued by the disinclination
of their subscribers to pay for what they received. By varied
pleas the Post was usually trying to collect overdue subscription payments. Its readers got their money's worth. The
"Canterbury Pilgrims" by Nathaniel Hawthorne took up most
of the front page. A new T. S. Arthur serial, "Seed Time and
Harvest," started. The Post denied that students at the newly
founded Girard College in Philadelphia had to wear uniforms.
The Post said that Mr. Girard had expressly provided against
this in his will and added breezily, "We give the old millionaire credit." All this, and agricultural notes clipped from
The Albany Cultivator, the *Prairie Farmer,* and the *Pharma-
ceutical Times.*

The Saturday Evening Post reached for the whole man, in
fact, for the whole family. It said often: "The Post is a family
paper—*no articles not calculated to enter the family circle can
be admitted to its columns.*" It could hardly pretend to spot
coverage of the news, but it did not do badly for a weekly when
John Quincy Adams died at his desk in Congress a few minutes after seven o'clock on the evening of February 23, 1848.
Under reproductions of the Great Seal of the United States and
a draped flag the Post carried a two-column editorial which
contained the proclamation of President James K. Polk. It
read much like any comparable proclamation today. Polk said
in part: "The nation mourns; and as a further testimony of
respect for his memory, I direct that all the executive offices
at Washington are placed in mourning, and that all business
be suspended during this day and tomorrow."

On newsprint, eight pages now, The Saturday Evening Post
had varied, informative, and sometimes entertaining comment
in the 1860's, but it was a weaker magazine, more literary, less
vigorous. There was an essay on "Gifts" by Ralph Waldo

Emerson in one issue, but what predominated were stories by unknown female authors. The Post had more dignity but greater dullness. There was usually one solid page of small-space advertisements for patent medicines, Estey's Cottage Organ, books, magazines, watches, banks, photographers, as well as one more prominent. This was the advertising of Jay Cooke, 114 South Third Street, Philadelphia, for the Civil War Loans. He pushed the U.S. 7-30's hard.

The Saturday Evening Post for April 22, 1865, had for lead story "Assassination of the President, Probable Murder of Mr. Seward." The account admitted that "J. Wilkes Booth, the alleged murderer of the President, has thus far succeeded in eluding pursuit." Pages two and three of this issue were bordered in heavy black. The serial was "A Woman's Vow."

Soon afterward The Saturday Evening Post began a marked and long decline. By the 1890's it had given up all pretence to covering the news and carried little of the morality, art, science, commerce et al of which it had boasted. It was almost a penny dreadful in newsprint form. Most of each issue was compact of subliterate serial fiction. After "Davy Crockett on the Track; or, The Cave of the Counterfeiters" came "Claudia's Triumph." The Post reached somewhat higher with Mrs. Henry Wood's "East Lynne; or, The Elopement" which began in February, 1874.

In 1895 the Post switched to a 24-page format with pages of smaller size but soon returned to the larger sized 16 pages. It was faltering badly and seemed near extinction. Each issue, unillustrated now, as engraving cost money, was a blood and thunder or a lavender and old lace serial with the rest of the editorial material clipped from exchanges and usually one column of small-space advertisements. Circulation was under 2,000. The paper was edited by a reporter on the *Philadelphia Times* as a side job for which he received $10 a week.

The Saturday Evening Post was owned at this time by Albert Smythe, a friend of Cyrus Curtis's, and the two men used to talk about the periodical, for Smythe was proud of its past. When Smythe left Philadelphia to try to make his fortune in Chicago in gas he left the sheet he cherished as an antique in charge of a friend named Brady.

The August 21, 1897, issue of The Saturday Evening Post was late. When it appeared, it carried this notice.

The sudden death of Mr. A. E. Smythe, late publisher of the Post, and the legal formalities consequent on the settlement of his estate constitute the cause of, and our apology for, the delay in issue of the paper. We ask your indulgence for a few days as we expect to be regularly on time commencing with the issue of the 28th.

The "legal formalities" could have been stated more simply. The fact was that The Saturday Evening Post was completely out of funds. Brady went to see Cyrus Curtis, told him that Smythe's only sister and heir would not put up the money to get out the next issue, and asked for help.

Curtis, who had already checked carefully, gave Brady a simple answer. He told him he had nothing to sell. Like previous owners, Smythe had not copyrighted the name of The Saturday Evening Post. If the Post missed a single issue, the name was public property. Smythe's lawyer, who was with Brady, nodded agreement. Then Curtis, who had planned for some time to publish a weekly magazine to match his monthly Ladies' Home Journal, made his offer. In lieu of better it was quickly accepted. He paid $1,000 for the full rights to The Saturday Evening Post, $100 down. He sent a man with a wagon to bring the Post's well worn type to the Curtis plant and had a stop-gap issue thrown together to preserve the Post name under the imprint of The Curtis Publishing Company.

Curtis knew what he wanted to do. He wanted to publish a weekly magazine for men, a magazine for businessmen, a national magazine of information and entertainment, and to sell it in direct competition with the newspapers at five cents a copy. Announcement of his plan promptly drew the ridicule the press felt it deserved. The idea was absurd. It was an economic impossibility, and no one wanted such a magazine anyway. Then and for long years afterward the bible of the advertising trade, *Printers' Ink* prophesied early and complete failure of the venture.

Curtis made William Starr Jordan, an assistant editor of the Ladies' Home Journal, editor of the Post and let him alone. Jordan tried to imitate some of the Journal's sprightliness, otherwise he kept the Post much as it had been. Even the few changes he made displeased those who had been used to the magazine under Smythe and discontinued their subscriptions. Curtis discharged Jordan early in 1899 and announced that he was going to Europe to find an editor for The Saturday Evening Post.

He wanted to get Arthur Sherburne Hardy, editor of *Cosmopolitan Magazine*, 1893–1895, who was then acting as United States minister to Persia. They arranged to meet in Paris where Hardy was to be on leave, but Hardy was transferred to Athens at this point, and the meeting did not take place. Curtis had known before he left that he really did not need to go to Paris. Perhaps he had already found his man.

Cyrus Curtis had already done two things concerning The Saturday Evening Post.

He decided that the Post was really the *Pennsylvania Gazette* which Philadelphia's most famous Bostonian had founded in Philadelphia in 1729 after planning it a year earlier. Philadelphia is permeated with Franklin legends, and Curtis was in the midst of the printing district where stories of B. Franklin, Printer are endlessly repeated. Daily, Curtis must have seen tourists tossing pennies on the grave of Poor Richard who had counseled insistently that a penny saved is a penny earned. It must have seemed to him the most natural and fortunate circumstance that Franklin had originated what through magic and a simple name change became The Saturday Evening Post and was thus its veritable founder.

When Cyrus Curtis bought The Saturday Evening Post its heading was emblazoned with: "The Great Pioneer Family Paper of America—Founded A.D., 1821." The claim was killed. Overnight the Post aged 97 years. The volume number was changed from 77 to 170. A new line read: "The

Saturday Evening Post—Founded A.D., 1728." In 1898 this was expanded to read: "An Illustrated Weekly Magazine Founded A.D., 1728 by Ben. Franklin." Soon this was simplified. It became: "The Saturday Evening Post Founded in 1728 by Benj. Franklin." Together with a cut of a small bust of Franklin and his facsimile signature this appeared first on the cover, then on the first editorial page of The Saturday Evening Post forever afterwards.

Curtis had done this other thing. Soon after he paid the remaining $900 and got clear title to The Saturday Evening Post he went to Boston and hired a "literary editor" for the magazine.

Chapter 5

George Horace Lorimer

Cyrus Curtis was a Maine Yankee. Edward Bok was an immigrant child. George Horace Lorimer was a second-generation Scot. He was the son of an actor who became an evangelist and achieved international fame as a spellbinding money raiser. The father was famous, widely publicized, and sought after when the son was born.

Born in Edinburgh in 1838, George Claude Lorimer was the stepson of a theatrical manager, W. H. Joseph. Growing up in the theatrical atmosphere, the boy began early to play female Shakesperian roles, graduated into male parts, and at 17 came to the United States. He was lean and long with compelling eyes, stage-trained, articulate, and eloquent. When the troupe was playing in Louisville, Kentucky, he was persuaded to attend a revival meeting. Here was a kind of passionate drama, a rampant emotionalism he had not dreamed of. The impressionable and romantic looking hero was converted. Instead of returning with the company, he went to Georgetown College in Kentucky and was ordained a Baptist minister in 1859. After preaching for a time in Paducah, he went back to Louisville and the pastorate of the Walnut Street Baptist Church.

Edward Bok was Americanized in New York by Western Union, Jay Gould, Henry Ward Beecher, and his own ambition. George Claude Lorimer was Americanized in the Ken-

40

tucky of the Civil War years. There is a difference, and the contrasting times and environments had different material to work on. George Claude Lorimer was early the eloquent and popular preacher. Convinced, intense, he could and did sway huge congregations with his commanding presence, his ready wit, and he drew dollars as well as converts. Seemingly he had only to ask and money for the building and rebuilding of churches was literally showered upon him as he stood not in the pulpit but, with his eye for drama, among the humble of his congregation.

The Rev. George Claude Lorimer was still preaching in Louisville when his son, George Horace Lorimer, was born October 6, 1867. Lorimer was a Kentuckian by birth, but, as his father moved up in the Baptist hierarchy he was brought up in Albany, Boston, and Chicago. The elder Lorimer was called to a church in Albany, New York, in 1870. In 1870 he moved over to the famed Tremont Temple in Boston where, the first time, he stayed for six years. As a small Bostonian, George Horace Lorimer grew up in the attention and adulation accorded his famous father. He lived in the electric atmosphere of passionate emotion, utter conviction, dramatic appeals, and unmitigated success—and the blood of the renowned father was in the son.

In 1879 the Lorimers went to Chicago where the father was first pastor of the First Baptist Church, which he freed of heavy debt, then of the Immanuel Baptist Church, whose membership he brought from less than 200 to more than 1,100. When he returned to Boston's Tremont Temple after a disastrous fire in 1891, he rebuilt it by raising more than a half million dollars in the United States and abroad. During the summers he preached to great crowds in London. Widely read, George Claude Lorimer could memorize his sermons at a single reading, then deliver them quietly but with extreme effectiveness as if they were extemporaneous. He was never the ranting demagogue but the regally assured actor who could control crowds of worshippers and work skillfully on their emotions.

George Horace Lorimer, who inherited some of this power and control, breathed in all the rest from childhood. He read widely—and rapidly—the books that were always at hand in the minister's library. The books were religious, biographical, and historical. Lorimer was not permited to read fiction until he was 16.

During the years in Chicago, the Rev. George Lorimer worked to raise money for the new University of Chicago, originally a Baptist institution. In Boston in 1900 he delivered the Lowell Lectures, a literary distinction. In 1901 he was offered the presidency of Columbian College which became George Washington University. Instead he went to the Madison Avenue Baptist Church in New York, a distinguished pastorate. The older Lorimer's books dealt mostly with Christianity as it related to social conditions and what was then modern thought. Best known were *Isms Old and New*, 1881; *Jesus the World's Savior*, 1883; *Christianity and the Social State*, 1898; and *Christianity in the Nineteenth Century*, 1900.

There were always wealthy and influential men in his father's congregation. One of them in the Immanuel Church in Chicago was the meat packer P. D. Armour. George Horace Lorimer met him on the street one day in the summer of 1885. Armour asked what he was doing. Young Lorimer told him he was about to return for his second year at Yale. Brusquely, Armour advised the youth to give up such nonsense and to come to work for him. He told Lorimer he would make him a millionaire.

Business and money-making appealed. His father told him he would have to make up his own mind. The son chose the Chicago stockyards over New Haven, and Armour put him to work at the mail desk in his office at $10 a week. The day began at six o'clock in the morning and lasted long enough so that the new clerk usually collected 25 cents for supper money so that he could work overtime.

Lorimer liked business, meat packing, and the old packer whom later he turned into a legend in his *Letters of a Self-Made Merchant to His Son* and *Old Gorgon Graham*. He worked hard. Promotions came rapidly. Within two years he was assistant manager of Armour's canning department. He spent half the year on the road as a drummer in ham, bacon, sausage, and he thrilled to the South and West. He met businessmen of Armour's type and some of his stature, and he saw them as romantic heroes. In his eyes these were the men who had made and were making the United States. He saw that business built the United States and made it what it was. He never changed his mind about what he had seen, believed, and played a minor role in.

Obviously he was one of Armour's favorites. At 22 he was made head of the canning department at what was then the munificent salary of $5,000 a year. June 6, 1892, George Horace Lorimer married Alma V. Ennis, a red-haired beauty who was the daughter of a Chicago judge. Three years later, ambition fired anew, he left Armour, went into wholesale groceries, and failed.

Despite his predilection for business, Lorimer was drawn to journalism. His family was in Boston again. Lorimer and his wife traveled east and, evidently through his father's influence, George Horace Lorimer became a reporter on the Boston *Standard*. It ceased publication within a few months. At his father's urging, Lorimer entered Colby College in Waterville, Maine, to study English and history, act as a stringer for Boston and Maine newspapers, and write his first novel. Publisher after publisher rejected *The Search for Simpkins*, and Lorimer learned first-hand the discouragement and despair he would later have to inflict wholesale on aspiring but inexperienced writers.

Lorimer was depressed enough when after a year at Colby his father got him a job on the Boston *Post*. Again Lorimer worked hard. He became a good reporter, covered his assignments well, and drank hard with his fellows. He decided he was worth $20 a week instead of the $18 he was getting, demanded it, and did not get it. He was 30 years old and had still not conquered the world, and he did not like it. He left the *Post* for the *Herald* but did not stay long. One night a story came in over the press wire that Cyrus H. K. Curtis had bought The Saturday Evening Post and was looking for an editor. Immediately, Lorimer wired for an interview. The two men met briefly in the lobby of Boston's Hotel Touraine, and Curtis hired the hard-jawed, blue-eyed reporter, a big man but not as tall as his father, not as editor but as literary editor of his new magazine.

Seen in retrospect and as he appeared frock-coated and handsomely posed, Cyrus H. K. Curtis too often seems the epitome of the proper and conservative businessman of his time, replete with fame and charitable deeds. He was, but the little man—he believed he never grew to his full height because of overwork and little sleep in boyhood—had initiative and daring that were close to recklessness. Unlike the timid who succeeded him a generation later, he took chances. He threw good money after hard-earned money, played long shots, risked heavy loss for the possibility of heavy gain. He won because he was a shrewd gambler and shrewd in his choice of men.

Lorimer had had no magazine experience, but he had moved in the tough world of big business, and Curtis liked that. Lorimer had been in almost every state in the Union and several times in England with his family. Curtis liked that. Lorimer had had a few years of big city newspaper experience that might stand him in good stead. Curtis knew whose son he talked to. He might have some of the evangelical fervor of his father. Obviously the young man was not an editor yet, but he might become one. Probably Curtis invented the post of "literary editor" on the spot. The Saturday Evening Post had not had one and would not have one again. Cyrus Curtis took another chance.

Lorimer left Boston for Philadelphia and $35 a week on the Post in 1897. He did not leap quickly into the editorship of the magazine he created or, harder yet, re-created. The first Curtis issue of The Saturday Evening Post was October 9, 1897. The new Post format was adopted January 29, 1898. For more than a year and a half Lorimer worked under William Starr Jordan. When he left for Europe expecting to meet Hardy in Paris, Curtis placed the magazine temporarily under the direction of the 31-year old literary editor whose work he had observed approvingly. The first issue of The Saturday Evening Post edited by George Horace Lorimer was that for March 17, 1899.

When Curtis returned he looked at the four issues Lorimer had done during his absence and liked them. He asked Lorimer what his salary was. Lorimer told him $40 a week. Curtis told him that from then on it would be $250 and that he was the editor of The Saturday Evening Post.

Curtis knew exactly what he wanted in the Post. He wanted a magazine for men which would reflect their business interests, give them articles and stories about business which they would recognize as authentic, accurate comment on the political and economic news, and entertainment they would appreciate. He wanted stories like those of Richard Kimball which had delighted him as a youth in Portland. Curtis felt and thought that other men felt the romance in business and would respond to it in a magazine.

Lorimer saw eye to eye with his employer. With Curtis he believed, as Calvin Coolidge phrased it years later, that the business of America was business. He had experienced the romance in it with Armour. He knew businessmen and their tastes. He had tried to write and knew good writing from bad. He had heard words rhythmically and eloquently spoken from childhood. Man and job fitted, and, as he had done with Bok, Curtis gave him a free hand. "Get the right editor and you'll have the right magazine. Then it's only a selling proposition," Curtis said.

Lorimer sought stories of men of action, success stories, competent reporting of national affairs, sharp humor, even bits of verse. Like Bok before him, he sought well-known authors and got them to write for The Saturday Evening Post. Often in the late afternoon he took the train up to New York to visit literary agents and talk matters over with his father, who was now at the Madison Avenue Baptist and writing one of his own books.

The recognizable Saturday Evening Post was well under way by early fall. The "Fall Fiction Number" had 32 pages and 32 columns of paid advertising. It had the Post's first color cover. The lead story was "The Sergeant's Private Madhouse" by Stephen Crane. Bret Harte followed with "Under the Eaves." There was "Blaine's Life Tragedy" and an article on Portus B. Weare, a pioneer trader, in the "Men of Action" series. Named after a colonial newspaper published in Boston in the late 17th century, the Post's current events department, as it would long continue, was "Publick Occurrences." The editorial by George Horace Lorimer, "A Retrospect and a Prospect," was a statement of policy and a promise.

With this issue, The Saturday Evening Post is permanently enlarged from sixteen to twenty-four pages, with monthly special numbers of thirty-two pages. As soon as the necessary machinery can be installed— and work upon it is being pushed with all possible speed—The Saturday Evening Post will contain thirty-two pages every week.

Whether he believed it or not, Lorimer accepted the Franklin legend. He said that the Post had been read for 171 years. During the 19th century it had published more of the great work of American authors than any other periodical and in less than a year under Curtis ownership it had achieved the substance of success. Then he said:

There is nothing worthy or permanent in life that is not clean, and in its plans and purposes the new Saturday Evening Post preaches and practices the gospel of cleanliness. It appeals to the great mass of intelligent people who make homes and love them, who choose good lives and live them, who seek friends and cherish them, who select the best recreations and enjoy them.

That fall Lorimer published the first of the Post's business serials, "The Market Place" by Harold Frederick. He serialized an important novel of business, "The Pit; A Story of Chicago," by Frank Norris. In the same vein he ran later another serial by the best author he could find to do the kind of piece he wanted. In 1901 and 1902 The Saturday Evening Post published, unsigned, "Letters from a Self-Made Merchant to His Son."

There were 20 letters in the series which Lorimer based on his experiences with Armour. All of them were addressed by John Graham, head of Graham & Co., Union Stockyards, Chicago, to his son Pierrepont. Pierrepont was a Harvard freshman when the letters, all dated 189-, began. The letters continued while he was in college then, sent from the branch offices which his father was touring, while he worked at the Graham billing desk, then graduated into sales, as Lorimer had done. The letters followed him to New Albany, Indiana; Spring Lake, Michigan, and all the stops between. The letters came from Europe when the older Graham was traveling abroad to the younger, who had advanced to become assistant manager of the lard department.

Pithy, aphoristic, hard with common sense, Lorimer's Graham letters were as quotable as Poor Richard.

> Real buyers ain't interested in much besides your goods and prices. Never run down a competitor's brand to them, and never let them run down yours. Don't get on your knees for business, but don't hold your nose so high in the air that an order can travel under it without your seeing it. You'll meet a good many people on the road that you won't like, but the house needs their business. . . .
>
> You've got to believe in yourself and make your buyers take stock in you at par and accrued interest. You've got to have the scent of a bloodhound for an order, and the grip of a bulldog on your customer. You've got to feel the same solicitude over a bill of goods that strays off to a competitor as a parson over a backslider, and hold special services to bring it back into the fold. You've got to get up every morning with determination if you're going to go to bed with satisfaction. You've got to eat hog, think hog, dream hog—in short, go the whole hog if you're going to win out in the pork-packing business.[1]

Post readers loved the Merchant letters. They were funny and they were sound. John Graham was a man after their own hearts and none of your high-faluting college graduates.

---

[1] Lorimer, George Horace, *Letters from a Self-Made Merchant to His Son* (Boston: Small, Maynard & Co., 1902).

When the letters were published as a book, Lorimer dedicated it to Cyrus H. K. Curtis, "a self-made man." It is impossible to suspect Lorimer of sycophancy. He admired Curtis. He admired the self-made man. So did almost everybody else in the early 20th-century United States. The self-made man—if he were successful—stood high among all the gods in the social pantheon.

Lorimer was building his magazine with every issue. He got Harry Leon Wilson, Wallace Irwin, Jack London, Zona Gale, and Ring Lardner all into the Post. In 1905 he got Booth Tarkington.

Already famous for *The Gentleman from Indiana*, 1899, and *Monsieur Beaucaire*, 1900, Tarkington was a *McClure's* author. Lorimer wanted him and, influenced by his close friend Harry Leon Wilson, Tarkington was willing. In 1905 the Periodical Publishers Association held its annual meeting in Lakewood, New Jersey. Important authors were always invited, and Tarkington shared a hotel suite with Wilson, Lorimer, and David Graham Phillips.

Late at night, Lorimer, Tarkington, the editor of The *Smart Set* and the drama critic of the New York *Sun* were in the suite drinking generously and talking loudly. They were having a wonderful time when a man across the hall poked his head out of his room and indignantly demanded quiet. After placing his shoes in the hall to be polished, Cyrus Curtis had been trying to sleep.

The revelers were affronted by this unfeeling interruption. To show how deeply injured they felt the *Sun* man, with the others looking on approvingly, filled Curtis's shoes with champagne, and the happy trio returned to their glasses and their hilarious talk.

The Saturday Evening Post was catching on with readers, but advertisers remained unconvinced. They were used to the *Century, Scribner's, Harper's, The North American Review,* the *Atlantic* and on down the line to *Leslie's, and Harper's Weekly.* They felt they knew what they were getting for their money in these magazines and were unsure of the new weekly at the ridiculous five-cent price.

The Saturday Evening Post was losing so much money that Bok, jealous of Lorimer, argued before the Curtis board of directors that it should be dropped. Good money made by the Ladies' Home Journal was being sluiced down the drain. The Curtis treasurer was equally perturbed.

Cyrus Curtis spent one-quarter million dollars advertising The Saturday Evening Post with no perceptible result. He spent another quarter million, and the Post showed an $800,000 loss. When the company treasurer complained, Curtis comforted him by saying that they still had another $200,000 to go before the loss totaled $1,000,000, and that he liked round figures. He started a new advertising campaign. Post circulation rose from under 200,000 in 1899 to a half million, but at the end of five years The Saturday Evening Post had lost $1,350,000—all out of Ladies' Home Journal profits.

Then the Post took hold. It grabbed. Its authors appealed to the male readers the Post was reaching in increasing numbers, and Post policy appealed to authors. The Post paid not on publication, like many magazines, but on acceptance. It accepted or rejected submitted manuscripts within 72, often within 48, hours, and, if it was an acceptance, the check went out the following Tuesday. The Post soon commanded the strongest authors, and it became the ambition of new writers "to make the Post."

Advertisers saw all this. They saw the mass audience the Post was reaching. One after another they came in. They all came in, especially the big ones. The Post went solvent. Then it skyrocketed.

By 1908, as Curtis had determined it would be, The Curtis Publishing Company was Big Business.

Though it had the equivalent of 23 city lots of floor space in Arch Street, it had overflowed into larger quarters on Cherry Street and in its Appletree Street plant had 47 rotary presses working day and night and rows of folding, gathering, and binding machines. The company, which said proudly that its mail was delivered twice a day by wagon, was receiving more than 1,500,000 letters a year, as high as 24,000 in a single day. One day alone 44,750 new subscriptions poured in.

The circulation of the Ladies' Home Journal was over 1,250,000; that of The Saturday Evening Post nearing 1,000,-000. In its promotion the Journal made a daring, if involved, claim. "If the number of copies issued each month were compared with the number of words contained in the Bible, it would be found that we print a copy of the Journal each month for every word in the Bible, and more than 50,000 besides." Together the Ladies' Home Journal and The Saturday Evening Post were printing nearly 50,000,000 magazines a year. It took 50 mail cars to move one issue of the Journal alone, and the magazine was paying the Post Office $180,000 a year besides using more than 10,000,000 postage stamps.

Curtis believed that an editor should have business judgment as well as editorial ability. Both Bok and Lorimer wrote the advertising promotion for their magazines. Curtis said that no one else could know as well what they were trying to do or describe the results better. Bok said he preferred writing an advertisement to writing an editorial. Lorimer was so convincing a copywriter that, not knowing who wrote them, a New York advertising agent sent a man to Philadelphia to hire the Post's man away from Curtis. The emissary failed in his mission.

The Curtis magazines were hailed now as unique and uniquely successful. They were distinctive, handsomely designed, and superbly printed. Every 15th woman in the United States subscribed to the Ladies' Home Journal, and seemingly most of the other 14 read it too. The Saturday Evening Post was the businessman's own. It gave him the yarns he liked and supported the ethics to which he subscribed. The Post knew who counted in the good old U.S.A.

Profitable Advertising, October, 1908, paid tribute to Cyrus H. K. Curtis and his achievement over the previous 25 years. It commented that both the Journal and the Post reflected their editors. Both thought in terms of their readers, but there was a difference. Mr. Bok "has made the Ladies' Home Journal an interpreter. Mr. Lorimer has made The Saturday Evening Post an expression. The Journal is an outlet for its readers, the Post for its editor." This was a cogent observation, but it was just as shrewd and accurate if reversed: Bok expressed himself in the Journal, and Lorimer interpreted the business scene and the American businessman. Whichever, the magic worked.

It was Curtis's way to propose an idea, leave its execution to others, and turn his attention elsewhere. He would say what he had to say, look at his watch, and the interview was over. In the office he never seemed to have much to do.

Bok and Lorimer were dictators, and their powers were absolute. Bok commanded and was obeyed. Lorimer said yes or no, never maybe. They were monarchs of all they purveyed. Bok did not deign to explain. Lorimer stated it flatly.

> The conduct of a magazine should be business-like. I never could quite understand why a man should permit the offspring of his brain to be treated as friendless orphans. All writing, up to a certain point, is an artistic matter. But when the manuscript is finished, it becomes, so far as the writer is concerned, a commercial matter, too. . . .
>
> I believe in the one-man power on a magazine or a newspaper. Delano of the London *Times* had the right idea when he said that "Whatever appears in the Times should proceed from the initiative of whoever holds my place." That sounds like conceit, but it is common sense. Editors and crowned heads are the only people in the world—bar a certain historical exception—with the right to say we. Editors should be the only despots.[2]

Lorimer exercised his absolute powers shrewdly. When he got ex-President Grover Cleveland to write for The Saturday Evening Post, he established a precedent which continued through Dwight D. Eisenhower. He ran article after article by Albert J. Beveridge, Senator from Indiana, pieces by Speaker Tom Reed of Maine, and then by Speaker Champ Clark of Missouri. Public men used the Post to reach solid businessmen—who were also voters.

[2] Quoted in *Profitable Advertising*, October, 1908.

Biographies, political pieces, success stories, and general articles were solid fare in the Post, but Lorimer was a fiction editor. He liked stories well told, and he made his Saturday Evening Post a magazine in which good fiction predominated. It was seldom, critically "serious" fiction. It was stories and serials of action, character, sentiment, and humor.

Jack London's "Call of the Wild" ran in the Post in 1903. Owen Wister came in with "Lady Baltimore" a few years later. The "Potash and Perlmutter" stories of Montagu Glass began their long run in 1909. George Fitch brought his football stories of Good Old Siwash to the Post. A regular contributor along with Stewart Edward White, Cora Harris, and Rex Beach, James Branch Cabell described The Saturday Evening Post as the great American weekly which printed fiction among its advertisements.

Circulation and advertising were growing rapidly, and there was every indication that they would continue to grow. The Ladies' Home Journal and The Saturday Evening Post were bursting out of their expanded and scattered quarters. Cyrus Curtis had foreseen the growth and made his plans.

Chapter 6

The New Curtis Building
and a New Magazine

Curtis chose one of the most famous addresses in the United States and one of the most coveted sites in Philadelphia for a new building that would be both physically adequate to the needs of The Curtis Publishing Company and a nationally promotable asset.

By 1908 he had purchased 36 estates at a cost of more than $1,175,000 on Independence Square. The planned Curtis Building would take in all the area between Sixth and Seventh Streets and between Walnut and Sansom. It would cover more than an entire city block, for it obliterated one small street of 18th and early 19th century brick houses and shops with their steeply sloping roofs and smoking chimney pots.

F. C. Roberts and Company and Edgar V. Seeler were chosen as the architects and engineers. Their drawings showed a ten-story building of brick with tall, wide windows and marble columns, 36½ feet high, facing Independence Hall. The whole Walnut Street length of the massive structure faced Washington Park where veterans of the American Revolution lay buried. Ten granite steps, 55 feet wide, led to huge bronze doors embossed with colonial designs at the main entrance on Sixth Street, and these doors led into a spacious white marble lobby 18 feet high. All of the Curtis editorial, advertising, and circulation offices would be in the front of the building facing Independence Square. Presses, composing rooms, foundry, binderies, and shipping occupied all the back of the building toward Seventh Street.

In September, 1910, the Ladies' Home Journal underwent parturition. From 12 monthly issues it went into 24 fat, oversized issues a year, and it was down to 10 cents a copy again or $1.50 for a year's subscription. Most of the new semimonthly issues were special numbers: Needle Number, Spring Romance Number, Summer Porch Number, American Fashion Number. All were heavy with the advertising of those products which fitted the season.

Bok was fighting Paris now. He was trying to persuade American women to buy American designed and produced clothing. Issue after issue he pushed his campaign; and issue after issue American woman paid no attention. They loved the Journal and they loved Edward Bok, but the Lady from Philadelphia could not compete with the sirens of Paris. The rest of the Journal they devoured. It had never been brighter or more varied.

"Mother Carey's Chickens" by Kate Douglas Wiggin, Letitia Lane cut-out dolls in color for the children, Flossie Fisher's Funnies—stories, sermons, music, art—and Bon Ami, Kellogg's Toasted Cornflakes, Gold Dust, and Diamond Dyes in full color on the back covers. The book bulged with advertising, that of Curtis among them. Curtis advertised for boy salesmen for both the Ladies' Home Journal and The Saturday Evening Post. The copy was persuasive, moral, and thrifty: "They get a lot of fun out of it, earn their own spending money, and get moral and business training of inestimable value.

Many men who later attained distinction—Norman Rockwell was one on the upper West Side in Manhattan, and there were authors, jurists, teachers, admirals and generals, scientists —were Post boys. They bought their copies from distributors at three cents each and delivered them to their customers for five. Boys were proud to be seen wearing their white canvas bags with "The Saturday Evening Post" in masthead lettering on one side, "Ladies Home Journal" on the other. They did earn their own money, and this was considered admirable then. As if to reinforce the lesson, Bok warned at length in one of his 1910 editorials against giving money to child beggars on the streets. "The child takes the money home to his lazy and drunken parents." As well as money, ambitious Curtis boy salesmen competed for all kinds of prizes which the company posted as incentives to increased sales—baseball gloves, compasses, watches, ponchos, camping equipment. The most ambitious aspired to the top award, a pony, and a few won. One executive in the Curtis Circulation Company had first achieved renown as a pony winner.

At least one boy salesman used a horse and buggy to deliver his Curtis magazines. Dr. D. Norman Craig, electrochemist of the National Bureau of Standards and, until his recent retirement, guardian of the standard storage battery cell, had more than one hundred customers in Chicopee, Massachusetts. In 1911, replete with buggy, horse, Post bag, and an even smaller boy assistant, he posed for a picture which was reproduced in one of the Curtis circulation promotion magazines.

The twice-a-month Ladies' Home Journal lasted less than a year, the magazine returning to monthly publication in June, 1911. Edward Bok could use a blunt honesty when it suited him. In the June issue he said, "We have found that our readers do not like it and do not want it. They thought they did, and they asked for it. We thought they did, and we gave it." Probably there had been circulation problems. Undoubtedly advertisers had rebelled. Increased editorial, manufacturing, and shipping costs had been heavy. Issues of the Ladies' Home Journal were now so thick and heavy that it was no longer possible to staple the pages. They had to be pasted and bound like a book.

The first issue of the Ladies' Home Journal dated from Independence Square was November, 1911. It celebrated "The Most Beautiful Dining Room in America." This was the girls' dining room on the ninth floor of the magnificent new Curtis Building.

There were high arched windows in the most beautiful dining room in America. Between them, all around the walls of the room, were panels painted by Maxfield Parrish. Each of the sixteen panels was ten and a half feet high, and anywhere from three to five and a half feet wide. They showed youths and maidens of the golden age laughing and happy as they wended their way to a fête, and the fête itself was a gracefully riotous ten and a half by seventeen foot panel at the end of the room. This dining room could serve 650 Curtis women employees at one sitting. On the same floor was another dining room for Curtis editors and executives.

Edward Bok had been telling the women of America how to build and decorate their homes. Cyrus Curtis turned his son-in-law loose on the decor of the new building, and the decorator indulged his fancy to the full. In the lobby was a wall space of over 1,000 square feet in which Bok wished a striking mural. He commissioned one from Edwin Abbey, leaving choice of subject to the delighted artist. Abbey chose the Grove of Academe and promised Bok "the best Abbey in the world." Just after stretching his huge canvas in Sargent's studio in London, Abbey died. Bok decided to get Howard Pyle, but Pyle died too. Then Bok remembered a glass stage curtain done by Louis C. Tiffany of New York for the Municipal Theatre of Mexico City.

Bok brought Tiffany and Maxfield Parrish together. Parrish had long wanted to depict and later build a dream garden. He made a number of sketches which Tiffany translated into a huge glass mosaic. More than 7,000 people came to view the 15′ × 29′, 4,000 pound mosaic when it was finally completed and exhibited in New York. Cut into 20 sections, each imbedded in concrete, it was shipped to Philadelphia in two freight cars. Four men worked six months to remove the wooden frames and piece the sections together. Installation of the giant mosaic in 260 different color tones in favrile was not complete until 1916.

Cyrus Curtis had his high-ceilinged walnut paneled offices on the fourth floor of the Sixth and Walnut corner of the new building. A $10,000 antique Cabistan lay on the floor. There was a great fireplace in one wall. Oil paintings hung in heavy gilt frames. The little man who had become a very big pub-

lisher sat quietly at a large ornately carved desk when he sat
there at all, for he traveled widely.

George Horace Lorimer had his light and spacious quarters
on the sixth floor directly over Curtis. The big man in tailored
double-breasted suits worked there with his chief aides. He
was formal and courteous but tense as he worked. He kept
his nerves quiet with cigarettes, which he smoked one after
the other, and his body out of the way with a supply of Wil-
bur's chocolate buds which he kept in his desk.

Walnut-paneled like those of Curtis and Lorimer, the Bok
office on the seventh floor corner had a larger fireplace and the
only one that really worked. A Chinese court rug in buff and
Peking blue covered the floor. An entire wall was covered
with a reproduction in oil of Rembrandt's Dutch Masters, a
fitting picture for the little Dutch boy who had made good in
the United States. Hair parted boyishly in the middle, white
handkerchief protruding from his breast pocket, stickpin in
the cravat tied with something of a flourish, Edward Bok
worked at a graceful desk with delicately carved legs.

The new Curtis Building would become a Philadelphia
landmark almost as familiar as Independence Hall itself. In
marble and steel solidity it said big business success and stability. It proclaimed publishing genius, editorial acumen, the
power of the mass magazine, and the power of mass advertising—and it did not lie.

Curtis owned the women's interest field with the Ladies'
Home Journal and the businessman's with The Saturday Evening Post. He wanted to reach every important segment of
American society. More than half of the total American population lived on farms or in rural places in 1911, nearly half the
total U.S. population of 91,972,000 in places of under 1,000
people. Farming was the principal American occupation. The
family farm was the traditional American home and place of
business. Curtis had started in Philadelphia with a farm magazine. There were scores of farm magazines and regional and
state farm papers, but no farm periodical dominated. With
his new plant Curtis had the press time and facilities to pro-

The Curtis Building—Independence Square, Philadelphia.

duce another magazine and the editorial and advertising experience to make it match his other publications.

Curtis talked to Harry N. McKinney of N. W. Ayer, and McKinney advised his buying a farm paper of established repute. He suggested Country Gentleman which was published in Albany, New York, by Gilbert Tucker. Curtis went to Albany, but Tucker was not anxious to sell. His family had published Country Gentleman for 80 years, and he was proud of its standing. There was no plant. Printing was contracted, and the magazine returned a small but consistent profit. The two men agreed to meet again in an Albany hotel. On this second visit Curtis saw Herbert Myrick, publisher of a number of farm papers in Springfield, Massachusetts, in the lobby and assumed that he was there on the same errand. When Tucker appeared, Curtis urged him to the elevator away from Myrick. Curtis bought Country Gentleman that day, and the legal papers were drawn up the next. Only then did he discover that Myrick had been in Albany on some other errand.

Country Gentleman was a consolidation of the *Genesee Farmer* (1831–1839) and *The Cultivator* (1834–1865). As the property of Luther Tucker and Son it was billed as "The Oldest Agricultural Paper in the World," and it was a good one. In an early issue Luther Tucker said, "That agriculture should be taught both as a science and an art to farmers' sons I strenuously contend. If taught, however, so as to do any permanent good, it must be taught practically, and not by books alone. It should be by the management of a farm—in connection with a truly agricultural college." This was 30 years before the passage of the Land Grant College Act under which such colleges were established. Country Gentleman had a sound history.

Country Gentleman for June 29, 1911, was 20 pages on high-grade newsprint. The entire front page and the three pages following were solid small-space advertisements for livestock, farm implements and services, Ayreshires, White Leghorns, Guernseys, Jerseys, Holsteins, a Morgan colt, swine, and animal remedies. W. F. Young of Springfield, Massachusetts, advertised Absorbine (there was as yet no Absorbine, Jr.) as a cure for "puffy ankles, Poll Evil, fistula, sores, boils, wire cuts, bruises, swelling, and lameness." There were a few pictures, one of them of Holstein Cow Annie de Kol Butter Girl looking dejected. There was also a farewell editorial.

This issue of Country Gentleman is the last that will appear under the present management. From the date of the establishment of the Journal,

January 1, 1831, to the present time, eighty years and more, no one number has failed to appear on its appointed date, and there has been until now no change in ownership except from one generation to the next.

Gilbert Tucker's goodbye was both proud and sad.

The first Country Gentleman published by The Curtis Publishing Company was July 6, 1911. Issued from 425 Arch Street, it looked rather like The Saturday Evening Post in logotype and format. The slick cover in black and white was a photograph of "A Pleasant Farmhouse with Well-Kept Grounds." Beneath it in heavy black lettering was the legend: "The Oldest Agricultural Journal in the World." Inside the issue of 24 pages excluding covers were articles on "The Farming Fever," "Stump-Burning," "Success with Turnips," "Good Farmers and Their Ways," and "Midsummer in the Orchard." The agricultural advice and comment in Tucker's paper had been unsigned. All of these were acknowledged and were well displayed with illustrative photographs. The statement of the new publisher was this.

A new era in agriculture is just beginning. . . . Pioneer farming required industry and perseverance but the present demands breadth of view and intelligent management. . . . The building of permanent rural institutions requires discussion from the national viewpoint.

The implication, of course, was that The Curtis Publishing Company would supply it. The declaration was that Country Gentleman would be a national farm magazine providing a medium through which the national manufacturer of farm implements and other necessities could reach a national market.

The inside front cover of this first Curtis issue was a full-page advertisement for *The Christian Herald*. The Gent, as it was called at Curtis, also advertised itself. The per issue price was the same as for The Saturday Evening Post, five cents. A year's subscription was $1.50. Advertising rates were almost as modest: $80 for a full page, $40 a half page, $20 a quarter page. The fourth or back cover was $100 in black and white or $150 in two colors.

Publication was shifted to the new Curtis building with the issue for August 24, 1911, but there was no editorial mention of the move. Farm families might be suspicious of such citified pretentiousness. The cover showed Red Oak, a proud Morgan stallion, but inside there was an advertisement for the Hudson Motor Car and another for Cozy Cabs, a storm-proof buggy.

The first color cover on Country Gentleman came December 8, 1911. It was a photograph of a handsome sheep dog colored in brown and white. The Christmas cover was a real painting. Robert Robinson depicted an elderly farmer, snow on his cap, beard, and mackinaw, axe on his shoulder, carrying home a freshly cut Christmas tree.

J. Clyde Marquis was listed as managing editor of Country Gentleman in 1911. When Marquis left for Washington, Curtis got Harry C. Thompson as editor. Associate editors were Barton W. Currie and Loring A. Schuler. Both would become first Gent then Journal editors.

Anxious to get his new magazine off to a quick start, Cyrus Curtis poured money into advertising and promotion. Fortunately the Ladies' Home Journal and The Saturday Evening Post gave him plenty to pour. Before he was through he spent more in establishing the Gent than he had in establishing the Post—over $2,000,000 before it began to show a profit —and the results would never be anywhere nearly as gratifying.

Chapter 7

Advertising—Commercial Research

Cyrus H. K. Curtis may have originated the mass magazine without really intending to, but his creation of mass national advertising was conscious, his effort deliberate, intense, and unrelenting.

Curtis did not receive the gold medal for distinguished service to advertising, top prize in Harvard's annual Advertising Awards, until 1930. This was because the awards were not established until 1926, and as they had been created by Edward W. Bok, it would not have been seemly to bestow the first first prize on his father-in-law. Curtis had been preceded by Elmo Calkins, Orlando C. Harn, James H. McGraw, and Rene Clark. When it came, the accolade to Cyrus Curtis was "because of strict adherence throughout his distinguished career as publisher to the requirement, which he pioneered, of high standards of reliability in advertising; because of the effort and encouragement he has given to secure better typography and reproduction in magazines; and because of the example of wholesome journalism he has furnished."

The citation was as accurate as it was fulsome.

Curtis was elected to the Advertising Hall of Fame in 1954, the year in which this promotion of the Advertising Federation of America was instituted. Then he went in as one of the first ten men selected. Among the others were John Wanamaker and Theodore F. McManus.

Long before this the position of Cyrus Curtis in advertising had been recognized. Ernest Elmo Calkins, copywriter and agency man invented "Sunny Jim" for Force Cereal and "Phoebe Snow" for the Lackawanna Railroad. In 1915 he wrote *The Business of Advertising,* something of a classic in its field, and dedicated it

To Cyrus H. K. Curtis, The Man Who Has Done the Most to Put the Modern Conduct of Advertising on the Right Basis, This Book is Affectionately Dedicated by the Author.

Curtis was never primarily a journalist, an editor or even, for most of his active career, a publisher. As soon as he could, he delegated most of these responsibilities to concentrate on advertising. Through his magazines his influence was inestimable, but he was not Pulitzer or Hearst. He was not even S. S. McClure or Frank Munsey. He was Andrew Carnegie, Edward Harriman, and John D. Rockefeller. What they did with steel, railroads, and oil he did with magazines. He did not control business and industry, but he shared largely in the distribution of what they produced. Through his editors he influenced the tastes and ideas of the American public. Through the advertising in his magazines he was a moving force in the acceptance and then the sale and use of manufactured products and services. In a phrase that the Curtis Advertising Department liked to use, he "manufactured customers."

He had sold advertising space in Boston. He had scrounged for advertising for his *People's Ledger,* packed the Philadelphia *Press* with it, got it into his *Tribune and Farmer.* Then he built it into the Ladies' Home Journal and The Saturday Evening Post not as addenda or penalty, as it became in radio and television, but as essential part of their periodical offering. Advertising made his magazines profitable. Advertising produced his wealth and made the fortunes of his editors. It meant more than that to Curtis. It was the magic of business, and he loved it.

Curtis did more than sell advertising space. He sold the idea of advertising. Conservative businessmen of the late 19th and early 20th centuries had looked on it with suspicion. It meant patent medicines to them, deceit, fraud. Curtis persuaded them that advertising was not only an economic necessity in a free-enterprise laissez-faire economy, but that it was also ethical and dignified. Honest men proud of what they made and willing to stand behind their handiwork could take an equally honest pride in presenting it honestly to consumers. Only the sly and predatory who were afraid to brand their shoddy merchandise could not afford to advertise, for advertising would only direct attention to their underhand methods and their worthless products.

Curtis used the advertising of his magazines as an example of what advertising could do for sound products. He also acted to establish the advertising practices which he advocated. When actually in need of money he refused patent medicine advertising and the advertising for other questionable products. He banned all cosmetic advertising in the Journal, for he did not believe in powder and rouge. Before Bok and the Curtis treasurer got over this blow, he refused all financial advertising. He said that some offers were undoubtedly reputable but that the Ladies' Home Journal had many widows among its subscribers who lived on small legacies or insurance polices. The Journal could not afford the responsibility. Curtis wanted all the advertising he could get for all his magazines, but only if it was honest and readers were assured of value at least equal to claims made.

There was some altruism in these decisions, for Cyrus Curtis was a man of conscience and honor. There was more sound business judgment. The repute of his magazines depended upon the soundness of their content, advertising as well as editorial. It was to the advantage of The Curtis Publishing Company that all advertising—under concerted attack in the first decade of the 20th century—be trustworthy.

In 1910 Curtis issued "The Curtis Advertising Code." It was printed in a pocket-sized book bound in red leather. The paper was gilt-edged and rounded at the corners. In black type with red headings in wide margins and intricate initial letters, the little book looked like a product of the Roycrofters. It looked Scriptural. In advertising circles it was. Forty years later copies still stood on the desks of Curtis executives and on desks in advertising agencies and the offices of company advertising managers. When it was issued and for years afterward The Curtis Code was regarded as the bible in magazine advertising.

The brief foreword said: "These requirements are not intended to be arbitrary or dictatorial. They make our columns more profitable for our clients, and are based on the mutual interests of our readers, our advertisers, and ourselves." The Code itself said: "Our first consideration is the protection and welfare of our readers, and our second consideration is so to conduct our advertising columns as to command the confidence of our readers and lead them to greater dependence upon the printed message."

The Code then laid down these 21 rules:

1. Exclusion of all advertising intended to defraud
2. Exclusion of all extravagantly worded advertisements
3. Exclusion of all knocking copy
4. No medical or curative advertisements
5. No advertisements for alcoholic liquors
6. No general mail-order merchandising
7. Scrutiny of all installment advertisements
8. No immoral or suggestive advertisements
9. No cheap or vulgar advertisements
10. No blind advertisements
11. No answers to advertisements to be sent to publisher
12. No quotes from the editorial matter in Curtis magazines to be used in any advertising copy
13. No advertisements for boys or girls to work as agents
14. "Free" to be used only if an advertising offer is actually free
15. Prize competition terms to be submitted in advance for inspection by the publisher
16. No illustrations of stamps or coins
17. No use of copyrighted material unless permission obtained in advance
18. No speculative real estate advertisements
19. No use of the name of The Curtis Publishing Company as a responsible reference

20. No use of the names of Curtis publications as endorsements
21. No insertion of foreign matter between the pages of any
    Curtis magazines

In addition The Curtis Code laid special strictures. There would be no advertising of tobacco, alcohol, playing cards, or financial offers in the Ladies' Home Journal. There would be no cigarette advertising in The Saturday Evening Post or in Country Gentleman. Only financial advertising for bonds or stock in high standing would be accepted by the Post or the Gent.

Curtis went further to underwrite the reliability of advertising. In 1910 it issued its first advertising agency contract. This bound Curtis to pay the agency a 10 per cent commission on the cost of all space sold in Curtis magazines and an additional five per cent discount for cash payment. Under the terms of this contract the agency guaranteed that it would charge its clients full card rates for space in the Ladies' Home Journal, The Saturday Evening Post, and Country Gentleman. There could be no rebates to advertisers.

Curtis's intent was to abolish space price-cutting, unfair competition between advertising agencies in soliciting business —also to make it worthwhile for advertising agencies to sell space in his magazines to new clients and more and larger space to advertisers already using his periodicals. Nine years later Curtis raised the agency commission to a full 15 per cent rate which became standard and still prevails. The Curtis Publishing Company was in a strong position when it published its Code and made its agency contracts, and that position was strengthened as a result. Advertisers and agencies believed in the responsibility of Curtis, and Curtis, which accepted advertising only from agencies and only from agencies on its accredited list, got their business.

"Do you know why we publish the Ladies' Home Journal?" Curtis asked an audience of advertisers in the early days of that magazine. "The editor thinks it is for the benefit of American women. That is an illusion, but a very proper one for him to have. But I will tell you the real reason, the publisher's reason, is to give you people who manufacture things that American women want and buy a chance to tell them about your products."

Curtis was honest. That *was* the reason he published the Journal, the Post, and the Gent. To him the Ladies' Home Journal was not, as it was called, "The Bible of the American Home," and the Post was no literary or journalistic venture. His magazines were means of reaching huge national markets. What authors and illustrators Lorimer and Bok used as barkers, what short stories, articles, serials, poems, and assorted features, were details after the fact. These were the enticements. They got people into the tent to look at the prizes and to leave loaded down with their purchases.

Cyrus Curtis handled his own advertising himself. Joseph M. Hopkins, an advertising space salesman for *Printers' Ink*, which Curtis read and used regularly to promote the Post and the Journal, called on him in 1906. He suggested that Curtis appoint someone with whom he could talk as he knew the publisher's time was valuable. Curtis swung around in his chair and said, "Young man, I can hire men to conduct the editorial affairs of my magazines and to look after the circulation satisfactorily, but the *promotion* of the business is a matter I feel it is my duty to attend to myself."

Albert D. Lasker of Lord and Thomas in Chicago was traveling by train to Philadelphia in 1908. In the club car he met Cyrus Curtis.[1] Curtis was reading *Life* (the old magazine of humor) and smoking one of the long black cigars for which he paid a dollar apiece. He published no liquor advertising in his magazines. He seldom drank, but he told the younger man, "Lasker, I am just about to order a bottle of Schlitz beer as a result of an advertisement that I have read, and you ought to go and get the man who wrote the advertisement."

Lasker did. Claude C. Hopkins had already succeeded

---

[1] John Gunther, who tells this story in his biography of Lasker, *Taken at the Flood* (New York: Harper & Row, Inc., 1960) called Curtis even then "incomparably the most important magazine publisher in America."

with advertising copy for patent medicines, Bissell sweepers, and meats for Swift. He was rich and famous. Lasker got him by giving his wife an electric automobile and Hopkins $185,000 plus commissions to start. They went on to fabulous feats for Lord and Thomas.

Cyrus Curtis said that advertising was the essence of public contact, and he meant it. When The Saturday Evening Post showed that it was finally under way, he took his wife for an Italian tour. They did Naples, Venice, Rome, and Florence. Curtis was bored with the churches, paintings, and ruins. He could not keep himself supplied with the kind of cigars he favored. The only thing that made life supportable was a weekly cable from George Horace Lorimer telling him how many lines of advertising the current Post had closed with.[2]

In Philadelphia, Curtis could see for himself how the Journal and the Post were doing, and they were doing fabulously. The Journal was fat with lucrative advertising for almost everything material that any woman could wish. Bok saw to it that editorial and advertising pages complemented each other perfectly. The Post was doing even better and doing it every week instead of once a month, making the returns four times more profitable than those from the Journal.

Post advertising had been practically nil in 1897. Expensive promotion moved it up only to $2,000 the first year. More strenuous promotional effort got it up to $59,388 in 1899. A big jump took it over $159,572 for 1900. Saturday Evening Post advertising revenue was over $1,000,000 in 1905, over $3,000,000 by 1909, over $5,000,000 in 1910. These were fantastic gross advertising figures at that time, and when they were made commonplace, it was the Post that made them so. After 1910 Post advertising revenue increased by at least

---

[2] Curtis made many trips abroad, but one other shows more of his attitude toward Europe. As the ship neared Southampton, Curtis made no move to go ashore. An acquaintance warned him that they were approaching land. Curtis reassured him. "No, I'm not going ashore. I came over for a rest and am going back with the vessel." George P. Rowell tells this story in *Forty Years An Advertising Agent* (Palisade, N.J.: Franklin Publishing Co., 1926).

$1,000,000 a year, and often the gain was from $3,000,000 to $5,000,000.

Edward W. Hazen was the advertising director of The Curtis Publishing Company in 1914. William Boyd, who would assume the post later, was manager in the Chicago office. Stanley Latshaw was in the Boston office. Often in Boston on visits to the city or to his native Maine, Curtis was in that office frequently. He seldom said much. He did not need to. He knew his stature in advertising, and it was considerably higher than his five feet four inches. Once in Boston, though, he commented quietly to a companion on the clipped advertisements which the Boston manager had proudly tacked up on the bulletin board as having been obtained by his office. "It seems to me," Curtis said, "I would put up the ads I had *not* succeeded in getting into the Post."

All of the big advertisers were in. If they were not in The Saturday Evening Post, they were not big. General Mills, Hartford Fire, Colgate, Gruen, Westinghouse, American Tobacco, Heinz, Lorillard, and Union Carbide were all in very early. One of the first was the Prudential Insurance Company of America, which took 112 lines February 25, 1899. The Hoover Suction Sweeper Company of Canton, Ohio, began its long history of successful advertising in The Saturday Evening Post, December 5, 1908. The Post's first two-color back cover went to Quaker Oats, September 30, 1899. Foods, automobiles, insurance, gasoline, component parts—Timken Roller Bearings came in in 1912 and stayed in forever after—industrial products were all in the Post frequently and continuously.

The first automobile advertisement in The Saturday Evening Post was a one-inch, single column in the issue for March 31, 1900. It was for W. E. Roach of 821 Arch Street Philadelphia who described his as "The automobile that gives satisfaction; highest award at the National Export Exposition in Philadelphia, Pa., in 1899." Willys-Overland came into the Post later this same year. Oldsmobile came in two years later. Packard, Cadillac, and Ford made the Post in 1903; Studebaker and Hudson in 1909. Buick appeared in 1911.

As they were developed almost all of the hundreds of makes of automobile were advertised in The Saturday Evening Post. The Automobile Show was held in New York every year, but the real national new car show was always in the spring issues of The Saturday Evening Post. For a nickel, wherever you lived and whether you had another nickel or not, you could drool over the Saxon, the Cole Eight, the Hudson SuperSix, the Marmon, Stutz, Lozier, Rambler, Star, Locomobile, Eagle, Baker Electric . . .

It is useless to list the advertisers in the Post. They were all there. There was really no other place to schedule effective national advertising. Once they could afford the Post, manufacturers and distributors came in and stayed in. Eastman Kodak, General Foods (then the Postum Company), Swift, Armour, General Electric, Minneapolis-Honeywell, Libby, McNeil & Libby, the New York Central, National Biscuit, Hires, Wurlitzer, and Edison were all in by 1899. Socony Vacuum, Cluett, Peabody, Underwood, Pittsburgh Plate Glass, Penn Mutual Life Insurance Co., Spalding, Bausch and Lomb, Glidden, Columbia Records, Marlin, and Savage joined by 1900.

The Saturday Evening Post was salesman to the nation. It got goods distributed. It made fortunes for company after company. It underwrote the employment of those who worked for those companies. It improved "the American Standard of Living." Make any one of the familiar claims and you are safe. The Post did it. The Campbell Soup Kids, Phoebe Snow, Sunny Jim, the Arrow Collar Man, the Corticelli Silk Kittens, the Dutch Boy, the yawning Time-to-Retire Fisk boy were all in the Post. So were "The Ham What Am," "His Master's Voice," "The Flavor Lasts," and all the rest.

Directly and indirectly The Saturday Evening Post helped provide the industrial capacity and the tax money which helped the United States fight its wars and survive the periods between. Undoubtedly it was crass materialism, but money the Post helped to make still supports proliferating government and even charitable foundations. Idealism has not yet learned how to do without money, and the Post earned it for itself and an appreciable section of the economy.

Office buildings have changed from steel and stone to glass, aluminum, and concrete, but the men in them have not changed that much. In some offices in many large companies you will still find a framed copy of "The Penalty of Leadership." It ranks as literature with Kipling's "If" and as inspiration with Edgar Guest. "The Penalty of Leadership" begins, "In every field of human endeavor, he that is first must perpetually live in the white light of publicity." It ends, "That which deserves to live—lives."

The chastely printed and unillustrated copy did not mention the product. The name "Cadillac" appeared only in the modest trademark superimposed on the classic border surrounding the print and "Cadillac Motor Car Co., Detroit, Mich." centered in the bottom of the border. "The Penalty of Leadership" was written by Theodore McManus, Detroit copywriter who handled the Pope-Toledo, Pope-Waverly, American Underslung, Detroit Electric, Apperson, Elsmore, Cadillac, Willys-Overland, Hupmobile, Dodge, and later the Chrysler accounts—a busy and successful man. Millions of copies of "The Penalty of Leadership" were requested and distributed by Cadillac, but the black and white advertisement appeared only once. It was in The Saturday Evening Post for January 2, 1915, which passed the 2,000,000 mark in circulation in that year.

Oldsmobile was the first automotive advertiser to buy the back cover of the Post in color. That was May 2, 1903. The Franklin took the first inside page in full four colors, but not until January 9, 1926. Lorimer believed in print, in black and white. He fought color as long as he could. Studebaker, November 16, 1912, took the first multi-space unit with five pages, but the Cole Motor Company outdid it with six, July 26, 1913. If the automobile swept the country, Cyrus Curtis and The Saturday Evening Post helped with the sweeping.

Curtis was consistent in preachment and practice. One story became folklore in Philadelphia. The superintendent of the new Curtis Building supplied the washrooms with cakes of soap on which he had embossed, "Stolen from The Curtis Publishing Company." Immoral Curtis employees had been filching the soap and taking it home. Hoping for the approbation of his employer, the superintendent placed a cake in Curtis's washroom. The soap disappeared. He replaced it. As often as he put a new cake in the publisher's privy it vanished. This kind of thing can be very disconcerting to a conscientious building superintendent, and his perturbation increased when an unused cake of soap was found in Washington Park and brought in by an honest subordinate.

The cake in his hand, the badgered superintendent went to Curtis and explained that soap had been disappearing every night from his washroom. Curtis told him why. "Yes, I know. I threw them out of the window. They weren't *advertised*."

Curtis contended that in advertising you had to start with the fact that no one was interested in your business or what you had to say about it. To sell a man your goods you had to put yourself in his position of complete disinterest. He believed that the best way to advertise was to say little, say it in a striking way, and to display the copy prominently with plenty of white space around it.

Bok asked his father-in-law what one factor had brought him to the top. Curtis was then employing 5,000 people, using 2,000,000 pounds of paper a year to print 27,000,000,000 magazine pages, and printing over 100,000,000 newspaper pages yearly. Curtis mentioned none of this, but he had a ready answer to Bok's question.

"Advertising," he said flatly.

"Advertising?"

"Sure. That's what made me whatever I am."

In 1910, the 36th year of their marriage, Louisa Knapp Curtis died. She had been the first editor of the Ladies' Home Journal, responsible for its early success, responsible really for The Curtis Publishing Company. The only child of Cyrus and Louisa Curtis was married to Edward Bok and living in her own seven-bathroom mansion in Merion, first stop on the fashionable Main Line of the Pennsylvania Railroad out of Philadelphia. Rudyard Kipling had named the Bok home "Swastika" and from Capetown sent a door knocker for it marked with the mystic sign.

Except for the servants, Curtis was alone in his country home, Lyndon. His triumphs had lost some of their savor. Even his new building on Independence Square and the acquisition of Country Gentleman stirred him little. He derived what solace he could from the organ he had had built into his mansion. Curtis could not read music, but he loved it and could play his organ in a way which suited him.

He was not enthusiastic when Stanley Latshaw broached a new idea. Latshaw believed that Curtis space salesmen needed more business facts. Business knew little of itself. He had talked with the chief of the Bureau of the Census. Masses of statistics were available, but they had to be analyzed and interpreted. More facts had to be uncovered. Curtis salesmen should know all about the business of a client or prospect and more than he knew himself about his markets, how large they were, where they were, the kinds of people who composed them. Latshaw believed that he not only knew what was needed, but that he also knew just the man to amass the data, study it, and put it into usable form. The man had been his high school principal in a small city in Wisconsin.

Curtis was unimpressed, but he had long ago established his operating principle. If an idea showed any promise, try it. If it worked, good; if it did not, discard it and forget it. If a man seemed to have ability, give him a chance to show it. If he failed, supplant him or abolish the job. On these terms he agreed and hired Charles Coolidge Parlin to do what he could in the Advertising Department.

No taller than Curtis himself, Parlin was far less prepossessing. He looked rather gnomelike, but he was quick, curious, alive with ideas, and he knew his way around. Summers he had escorted parties of school teachers about Europe. He had handled hundreds of inquiring students. He was given an office and a desk in Philadelphia, but he refused a secretary and a telephone as he could think of no use for them. Neither Curtis, Latshaw, nor he knew exactly what he was supposed to do or even what it was called. He decided it was "Commercial Research" and cast about for a start. Curtis had recently purchased Country Gentleman, and no one on the business side of the organization really knew how to start selling space in it. As no one asked him to do anything else, Parlin started to study the manufacture and sale of farm implements.

He wrote the manufacturers of farm machinery and tools for catalogues. They poured into his small office so he got some filing cabinets and filed them alphabetically. He studied them, then he started out on the road. Like most Curtis editors and executives, Parlin was a great traveler. Curtis believed in it and was continually urging his men to get out, see and talk to people, know Curtis readers and advertisers. Parlin liked to move about. He liked to ask questions, and he loved to talk. He quizzed farm implement manufacturers about their production and sales methods. He studied the wholesaling and retailing of agricultural implements.

Six months later he produced a formidable report. A typescript of 460 pages with 19 charts and an index, it pointed out that the smaller manufacturers were failing or consolidating with larger companies. According to Parlin, this made sense because "the man who restricts his sales to a narrow territory is apt to be ruined by any disaster to the crops of that locality, while the manufacturer with his world-wide interests offsets failure in one section with prosperity in another. The probabilities are that the smaller manufacturer of the staple lines will continue, but their number is likely to grow continually smaller, for some will fail and new ones are not likely to arise to take their place."

This was not as familiar a circumstance in business in 1911 as it became later. Parlin's conclusions and his foresight often proved correct. His conclusion here, of course was just what The Curtis Publishing Company wanted. Large manufacturers controlling an industry looking for national markets should advertise in a national farm magazine, i.e., Country Gentleman. Parlin gave Curtis salesmen something to talk about besides the virtues of their magazines. In this instance, they could call on a manufacturer of farm implements or his advertising agency thoroughly versed in his business. They were not just space salesmen, they were consultants, and they had just the remedy he needed for his sales problems.

Parlin left the farm and went to town. His Commercial Research was gathering momentum. He hired assistants to help him ask questions. Parlin visited every one of the 100 largest cities in the United States and got an estimate of the volume of business done annually in every department store, dry goods store, and principal merchant tailoring shop. He and his men traveled 37,000 miles. They held 1,121 interviews in stores throughout the country. Parlin quadrupled his output this time. "Department Store Lines" was typed in four large volumes. Bound in heavy leather, copies were distributed to all the Curtis advertising sales offices. Some were retained in Philadelphia, and others given important clients.

"Department Store Lines" bristled with statistics. Any department store could compare or contrast its volume and profits with competitors in other cities. There was a plentitude of facts, but there were also conclusions. Parlin was observant and imaginative. He wrote clearly, if with occasional flourishes of rhetoric. He drew clear distinctions. He opened "Department Store Lines" with these shrewd declarations.

Woman is a shopper. Out of that fact has come the modern department store. Partly by nature and partly by education, woman is a comparer of values. In the management of the household there are two economic functions: the earning of the money and the spending of the money, the former usually the duty of the husband, the latter often the privilege of the wife. . . .

A woman's purchase may be divided into three groups: convenience goods, emergency goods, and shopping lines.

Convenience goods are articles of daily purchase, such as groceries, aprons, children's stockings, and in general those purchases which are insignificant in value or are needed for immediate use. These goods are, to a considerable extent, bought at the most convenient place without a comparison of values, and the fact that they are bought as a matter of convenience . . . makes possible the suburban dry goods store, grocery store, and the crossroads store.

Shopping goods include all those purchases which require thought and will permit delay, such as suits, dress goods, high grade underwear, in fact high grade goods of all kinds. Values are compared and a serious effort is made to secure the best value for the money.

Because in buying shopping lines goods women wished to compare values, a shopping center—and Parlin used the term now current—had to have at least three stores.

Now Curtis space salesmen had something to show in selling the Ladies' Home Journal. Women compared goods and products. The best way was to presell them through national advertising so that when they entered a department store they were already predisposed in favor of a given brand. It was the same way with convenience goods. Make sure through advertising in the Ladies' Home Journal that women asked not just for a spool of white thread but for Smith's or Jones's —or Clark's.

In "Department Store Lines" Parlin made one other notable and often quoted comment. "The consumer is King. His preference is law and his whim makes and unmakes merchants, jobbers, and manufacturers. Whoever wins his confidence controls the mercantile situation; whoever loses it is lost."

What Parlin advocated was to court the king. Make a good product then, as Curtis so often said, let the public know about it. Pay homage to his majesty the consumer and win his—usually it was her—royal favor.

Parlin set his sights higher. He undertook what was, in effect, the first census of distribution ever attempted. He analyzed all U.S. cities above 40,000 in population and 35 smaller cities to determine the size of their trading populations. Estimates were made for other cities. Then he and his staff calculated the volume of business in each place for department stores, dry goods stores, and women's ready-to-wear shops. The Commercial Research Division of the Curtis Advertising Department then sent letters to the clerks of 1,132 towns and the city clerks in places of from 5,000 to 53,000 population for substantiating data on population divisions, predominating industries and nationalities, and the names of leading stores. The result was the "Encyclopedia of Cities" in 1913.

Parlin seemed inspired. He sought new worlds to subdue through his pioneer marketing research. Automobile advertising was becoming more and more important to The Saturday Evening Post. There were hundreds of makes of cars put out on assembly lines like Ford's, handcrafted for the carriage trade or stuck together in backyards by ambitious ex-bicycle mechanics. To Parlin it looked as if the automotive industry was in the United States to stay—but not as it then existed.

Commercial Research traveled 43,000 miles this time. It held 881 interviews in 118 cities, 24 states, and two Canadian provinces. "Automobiles" appeared in 1914 in five bulky typed volumes. They were fact-packed, complete, and accurately prophetic. "Automobiles" covered manufacture, consumer buying, the branch house of the car manufacturer *v.* the general distributor, causes of manufacturing failure, the possibility of monopoly, costs, profits, makes of cars in the various price ranges, the influence of woman in the buying of cars, the farmer and the automobile—and Parlin said this. "It seems probable from a manufacturing standpoint that there will remain five or six distinct grades [of automobiles], and in each grade there will be from five to eight companies." He warned that there really was not room for more than 20 to 30 companies to succeed, and even then some one company could reach a place at the top. The best sales possibilities, he felt, lay in what was then the $750 class of pleasure car.

Long since canonized as the patron saint and the "father of marketing research"—the Philadelphia chapter of the American Marketing Association holding an annual dinner to bestow the Parlin Award which is coveted in marketing circles—Parlin wrote in 1914:

The automobile industry from the start to the present day has been an industry of extravagance. . . . It is an industry of extravagance from the standpoint of the consumer. Comparatively few people who buy an automobile can afford one. . . . It has been an extravagance from the standpoint of the retailer. He has rented a fine location on a fine street, has put up a building with an imposing front, has employed salesmen at high salaries, has advertised with a lavish hand, and has furnished gratuitous services he could ill afford. . . . Manufacturing has also been characterized by extravagance.

Parlin then warned that strong dealers wanted popular cars and that all manufacturers wanted strong dealers. The strongest dealers could practically pick what makes they would stock and sell, but ". . . a good car, national exploitation and strong dealer—all pull together to swell the business of the popular car, and against this powerful combination the weaker companies with less national advertising and weaker dealers are playing a losing game."

Parlin's findings and conclusions coincided with experience in the automotive industry. Makers and dealers were convinced that national advertising was the way to reach, if not monopolize, the lead position. They bought space in The Saturday Evening Post.

Curtis research became well and favorably known. It provided service that advertisers and agencies could not then get elsewhere. No other magazines supplied it. You could not get business facts like these from *Munsey's, McClure's, Harper's Weekly* (which still had two years to go in 1914), *Collier's* or even the strong *Literary Digest;* and none of them, of course, had anything like the circulations of the Curtis magazines. Everybody read them, and everybody was your customer for dry goods, automobiles, foods, clothing, building materials, hardware, household appliances and furnishings, oleomargarine, and what else. Parlin went on to study them all and then, as techniques developed and the demands of clients dictated, to make more complicated marketing studies of many kinds.

The Advertising Department made good use of all this Curtis Commercial Research. Advertisers were impressed and many of them were convinced. One of Parlin's assistants had his doubts.

Like the others in Commercial Research, Robert Benchley knocked on doors, asked questions, and solemnly recorded the answers. Back in the office he soberly tabulated the answers and analyzed the results. It all got to be too much for him. He concocted a survey report on "The Woolen Mitten Situation."

Benchley went all through the question and answer routine. His careful analysis showed that in view of the indisputable findings it was best to advertise in the Curtis magazines, but he had had one difficulty in doing the research which he was afraid was reflected in the results. Despite his careful explanation, many times repeated, that he was making an intense and completely disinterested study of the woolen mitten situation, people kept thinking he was talking of woolly kittens and insisted that they had drowned them. When Cyrus Curtis heard "The Woolen Mitten Situation" as a skit at a Curtis Advertising dinner, he was not perceptively amused, and before long Robert Benchley took his unappreciated talents elsewhere.

Charles Coolidge Parlin became one of the legendary figures of The Curtis Publishing Company. Short, heavy, pockets stuffed with papers, he made a lasting impression through his influence on what became the standard Curtis method of basing advertising presentations on research findings. Commercial Research conducted increasingly large and complex surveys using questionnaire and sampling methods which it developed and numbers of small-scale surveys made at the behest of advertisers. In addition it developed a series of marketing tools which the Advertising Department endeavored to get accepted as standard indices to sales potentials and the setting of sales quotas by manufacturers and distributors. In general, these consisted of population counts and geographic and sociometric breakdowns of the circulations of the Curtis magazines showing that advertising in them reached the profitable segments of the market.

Sales Opportunities, beginning in 1919 and published periodically, gave Post and Journal circulations for every state, county, and city of over 25,000 population. The "little red book" was widely used by salesmen. *Markets and Quotas* gave marketing data for counties and urban places over 10,000 together with the combined circulations of the Curtis magazines. Developed later, *City Markets* divided urban areas into red, yellow, green, and blue areas by residence from the highest to the lowest incomes and showed that the Ladies' Home Journal and The Saturday Evening Post circulated primarily in the red and yellow areas where people had the education and intelligence to read and the money to buy.

Curtis space salesmen had plenty of ammunition to back up their arguments, and The Post and Journal grew thicker and thicker with advertising. Under William Boyd the Advertising Department performed nobly. Parlin and his staff helped. One of his Wisconsin students, Ellen Jones, joined him after her Vassar graduation and was for many years his enthusiastic and indefatigable interviewer. On the same day in 1923 Fred Bremier, who had been assistant dean of the Wharton School of Finance of the University of Pennsylvania, and Donald M. Hobart, an Ohioan and a Wharton School graduate who taught merchandising there, joined Parlin.

Aided at Curtis by Research, Advertising brought in the orders, but the best space salesman on any mass magazine is always the editor. He creates the magazine, draws the readers, builds the circulation, and establishes the repute of his periodical. Essentially he provides everything that the publisher has to sell.

Edward Bok and George Horace Lorimer were doing all this and more.

Chapter 8

The Curtis Magazines and World War I

Edward Bok had planned to retire at 50, but the outbreak of World War I in Europe made him change his mind. He felt that the Ladies' Home Journal needed him and that the world needed his continuing editorship.

There was no mention of the war in the Journal until November, 1914. The three months closing date of the magazine made earlier recognition impossible. From that point on the Journal showed full awareness of the first world conflict of the 20th century. In this November, 1914, issue Bok pointed out that the United States was now isolated. Some 2,000,000 men were out of work as the great ports of Europe were closed and imports of materials for which the United States was still dependent upon other lands ceased. Bok saw this as opportunity. "America's isolation," he wrote, "means America's chance."

He returned to a favorite crusade and made it a matter of patriotism now. For seven years, he said, the Ladies' Home Journal, alone and unaided, had fought for American fashions for American women. "It is the time for every woman to be an American. The great question is—will she be?"

In the Ladies' Home Journal for December, 1914, Bok was shocked, unhappy, but comforting.

. . . six great nations of the world, the very custodians of Christianity, are facing each other with hatred in their souls, the most fiendish contrivances for the destruction of human life in their hands, and literally slaughtering each other by the tens of thousands.

82 THE CURTIS MAGAZINES

NEVERTHELESS

One fact remains incontrovertible and indisputable:

"God's in his Heaven:
All's right with the world."

Bok's contention, after Browning, did not seem very convincing then or for another five years.

Two years after this optimistic editorial the war seemed remote from the Journal. In 1916 Grace S. Richmond was in with a new "Red Pepper Burns" romance. Pavlova was teaching dance steps to Journal readers. There was a new feature, "My Government and I," designed to tell women all they needed to know about who ruled them and how, but the striking feature throughout the year was a series of colored reproductions from private art collections. Woodrow Wilson wrote in October on "The Mexican Question." In December Andrew Carnegie wrote "A Millionaire's Money." The subtitle asked, "What should be done with it?" Carnegie really seemed to be in a better position to answer than most Journal readers.

When the United States entered the war in 1917, Bok, who had been prepared for the contingency, made the Ladies' Home Journal a patriotic—World War I was a patriotic war—organ to enlist the support of American women in all kinds of wartime activity. Bok adjured them that it was their greatest chance for service. Christopher Morley wrote on Woodrow Wilson. Wilson's wartime messages were publicized. William Howard Taft wrote on the work of the Red Cross. Pages of advice from Food Administrator Herbert Hoover were a monthly feature. The Journal covered wardogs, the work of the Y.M.C.A. and the K. of C. with the fighting forces, and gave detailed instructions for knitting khaki sweaters, mufflers, helmets, and socks. John Philip Sousa, Lieutenant U.S.N.R.F. wrote on "Playing the Star-Spangled Banner 'Round the World.'" From somewhere in France where he went on a tour with other editors Bok wrote rhapsodically:

During the past days I have seen thousands of our boys, and have sat beside British and French officers as they have viewed with undisguised admiration these young giants of physical fitness, well fed, well clothed, every one of them holding an attitude of thought and action toward morality that is absolutely austere, every eye alert, clear and dancing with merriment, each heart overflowing with a buoyant merriment that has made the conservative Englishman, for the first time in his life, use superlatives when he speaks of the American army, while the faces of the French officer and poilu positively radiate their delight.

This was the stuff to feed the troops, at least their mothers, wives, and sweethearts, but working members of the A.E.F. could hardly have recognized themselves from Bok's description.

Bok stayed on for the duration and a little longer. The circulation of the Ladies' Home Journal was over 2,000,000. It had just concluded the autobiography of Buffalo Bill's widow. The issue for November, 1919, had 224 pages of packed editorial and advertising. Bok's name as editor appeared for the last time in December. He relinquished his title and his $100,000 a year salary at the end of the year, but his farewell editorial appeared in January, 1920.

Under a picture of himself at his desk in his regal office and over his facsimile signature Edward Bok said goodbye. Properly he thanked his associates, his assistants, and his readers for "their almost superhuman forbearance with my shortcomings and mistakes." Cyrus Curtis assured the world that the retiring editor would remain on the Curtis board of directors, and Edward Bok said emotionally, "What I am you have made me. What I have you have given me. Whatever I may accomplish in the years before me will be because of you."

Many thought that the Ladies' Home Journal would never be the same again. They were right. It never was.

Edward Bok was the formative editor of the magazine. Assured, didactic, masterful, even belligerent sometimes, he was certain that he was right, and for the Ladies' Home Journal he was. Though to protect his masculinity he denied it, he understood women. He knew what they wanted in his magazine, and if they did not know, he told them. He was undeterred by subtleties for he had none. He told his readers how to dress, mend their manners, decorate their homes. He flattered them, ordered them about, gave them all his attention, and made his convictions stick.

After he retired he gave himself over to good works and civic endeavors. Having got them, he looked with misgivings on those who were still pursuing fame and fortune and urged other successful businessmen to retire. He was all for service now. He said he was no longer Edward Bok the editor but Edward W. Bok, the man, the full man.[1] In *Dollars Only,* 1926, he listed all of his accomplishments during the first six years of his retirement. It was a long list in which Bok proudly included his retirement, his fund raising for the Philadelphia Orchestra, publication of his *Americanization,* the Pulitzer Prize awarded him for the book, honorary degrees from Tufts and Rutgers, and his establishment of the Bok Peace Award of $100,000.

Much of what Bok inserted in his books he had first written in the Ladies' Home Journal. He was still for business. It inculcated all the Christian virtues. Yet he deplored the fact that money was king and business the god of Americans. There was a new ebullience about Bok after 1920. He closed *Twice Thirty* with an advertisement: "By the same author; to be published in 1954: THRICE THIRTY."

Bok was busy but, as Curtis had promised, he remained active in The Curtis Publishing Company. His tailored English jackets were much in evidence about Independence Square. His voice was loud and clear at the head table in the executive dining room. It was authoritative on the Curtis board. He was active in choosing a successor to himself as editor of the Ladies' Home Journal. His first choice and that of Cyrus Curtis was Mary Roberts Rinehart.

Born in Pittsburgh in 1876, Mary Roberts Rinehart was a trained nurse who married a doctor. She established herself as a leading author of mystery stories with *The Circular Stair-*

[1] Yet he was careful not to deride. In *Twice Thirty* (New York: Scribner's, 1926) he wrote, "It must not be construed for a single moment that I belittle the wonderfully constructive piece of work carried out by Edward Bok during his editorship of the Ladies' Home Journal. The record of that achievement speaks too loudly to minimize its influence and potentiality."

case, 1908, and *The Man in Lower Ten,* 1909. She became a
regular contributor to both the Ladies' Home Journal and The
Saturday Evening Post, where she was a Lorimer favorite,
particularly with her "Tish" (Laetitia Carberry) stories about
that eccentric and delightful spinster. Mrs. Rinehart was tall
and handsome, always beautifully dressed, a sound reporter
and an accomplished popular writer. She was covering Paris
for the Post when she received a cable from Curtis offering
her the Journal editorship. After an inconclusive interview
with him in Philadelphia she suggested that she work part-
time, editing the magazine from Pittsburgh, spending only
three days a week in Philadelphia.

To complete the Curtis persuasion, Edward Bok took Rinehart to dinner and while they were still at table—perhaps to
indicate the wealth in store for her as Journal editor—took a
handful of unset gems from his pocket and trickled them
through his fingers. He said casually that he always carried
them around as he liked to look at them. Rinehart was re-
pelled by the gesture.

She went to Lorimer for advice. He laughed at her and
told her that instead of spending three days a week on the
job she would spend seven days and seven nights. "How
do you know you're an editor anyway? You're doing all right
as you are. Why change?" [2] After two days of indecision
Rinehart lunched with Curtis at the Bellevue-Stratford and,
much to his annoyance, declined with thanks.

More urban in appearance, typographically resembling The
Saturday Evening Post, Country Gentleman was running less
practical advice on farm matters, more fiction, and more articles on controversial farm legislation. It had a rotogravure
section. It ran cartoons. The Gent was trying to be entertaining as well as informative, more a general magazine than
an agricultural bulletin.

An editorial in the March 10, 1917, issue began trenchantly,
"One conspicuous fact about Kansas is that most folks who

[2] Rinehart, Mary Roberts, *My Story* (New York: Holt, Rinehart & Co., Inc.,
1948).

live there seem glad of it." Another editorial quoted a prophecy of John D. Rockefeller, Jr. "I believe that the personal
relation in industry will eventually be regarded as an important part of those college courses which aim to fit men for
business life."

Such frivolous comment went quickly by the board when
the United States entered World War I. A soldier and a sailor
stood at strict attention on the cover of May 19, 1917. Between them was a large-type announcement of a new series
of articles, "Feeding the World." The blurb said sternly, "It
is up to the American farmer to stave off a greater calamity
than any that has so far attended the World War." From
that point until the Armistice, lauding farmerettes as well as
farmers, Country Gentleman turned the United States into
one giant Victory Garden.

The Gent was willing to admit the Curtis Building now.
Proudly it admitted that it was the most magnificent building
of its kind in the world. Its 120 giant presses printed 13,000,-
000 magazines a month, using 43,000 tons of paper every year
and 750,000 pounds of ink. With over 3,000 employees in this
one building, Curtis was a town which dwarfed in size many
of the villages in which Country Gentleman readers lived.
Bigness was no longer suspect. The country expected big
things of everybody during World War I.

By 1920, when it lost its editor to the Ladies' Home Journal,
Country Gentleman was running to nearly 100 pages every
issue. In covers, layout, fiction, and articles it looked more
and more like The Saturday Evening Post. It carried advertising for automobiles and tractors, even for Sunday suits for
dirt farmers, but increasingly it was directed to the entire farm
family.

The Saturday Evening Post was the most powerful magazine in the country during World War I. Sans the talkies,
sans radio, sans television, the Post led and other magazines
imitated. People turned to the Post and the Literary Digest
for war news and comment beyond what they could obtain
from their newspapers. The Post had the money to send its

own correspondents to the front, and it had the circulation and influence which made it the target of all the propaganda and publicity-demanding agencies born of the war.

Lorimer sent some of his best reporters to France: George Pattullo, Will Irwin, Mary Roberts Rinehart, Richard Harding Davis, Irvin Cobb, Isaac Marcosson. He had the formidable Sam Blythe covering Washington from the inside. Men in uniform, Red Cross girls, airplanes in dogfights, aviators, and all the rest appeared on Post covers. Lorimer published biographies of the war leaders, Wilson and members of his cabinet, Bernard Baruch and other members of the Advisory Committee on national defense. With the other magazines the Post backed the Liberty Loan campaigns, the Food Administration, the Fuel Administration. As always, it backed business and advertising. January 18, 1918, Isaac Marcosson told how Sir Hedley le Bas, head of Britain's Caxton Publishing Company, used advertising for recruiting, placing women on farms, and raising millions of pounds in the British war loans.

The Post's advertisers did as much to publicize the war as the Post itself, and their attitude was more belligerent. Kodak took full pages in color in the Post urging people to cheer up the boys in camp by sending them snapshots, then cameras so that they could take snapshots to send home. "Ask Your Soldier Boy or Sailor Boy to Send Pictures to You!"

Ambulances equipped with U. S. Tires were pictured on No Man's Land with shells bursting around them. Everyone was Stepping On to Victory on Cat's Paw Cushion Rubber Heels. The U. S. Army used more dust-proof, chainless Packard trucks than any other make. The War Department had requisitioned the entire output of Bull Durham Tobacco for the armed forces. The American Tobacco Company was sorry, but " 'Bull' will come back with ribbons of honor. Have no fear."

Happy soldiers cried "Aunt Jemima Rings the bell with me!" then gathered around their camp fires to hear kindly Velvet Joe sing the praises of Velvet Tobacco or to fill their pipes with Prince Albert, "The National Joy Smoke." How did it feel to bayonet your first Hun? The battle-grimed doughboy under his combat helmet, a White Owl stuck in the side of his mouth, said it didn't feel. It was kill or be killed. "We smash 'em hard!" he assured the home front, and the General Cigar Company assured everyone that White Owls at seven cents each and plain Owls at six were as dependable as the troops.

Happy smooth-shaven soldiers and sailors announced that the Army and Navy had declared for Ever-Ready Razors, but there was one forbidding indication of things to come. The Strengthen America Campaign of the Federal Council of Churches of Christ in America took a full page in The Saturday Evening Post in 1918 urging everyone to "join hands and to destroy the Liquor Traffic forever."

People wanted war news but Lorimer knew that they also wanted relief and diversion. He gave them the best escape fiction in America and kept the Post in balance. Conservative and the complete isolationist, Lorimer had backed Woodrow Wilson for the Presidency in 1916 when the Democratic slogan was "He Kept Us Out of War." When, despite promises which events would not let him keep, Wilson took the country into World War I Lorimer was angered and withdrew the Post's support. Yet Wilson wrote, April 8, 1918, to thank him for ". . . the admirable way in which you have been filling The Saturday Evening Post with matter which interprets and emphasizes the meaning of the great struggle we are engaged in. The method you have adopted is all the more admirable because it is not carried in headlines but runs like an essence through the whole contents of the weekly. Will you not accept my sincere expression of admiration."

When Lorimer saw the end of World War I approaching, he shifted quickly to postwar subjects and lighter material in the Post. He had had enough of the war and so had most other people. The United States raced into its excited postwar spree of relief and self-congratulation. The country had proved itself a world power. It happily embraced Harding's "return to normalcy." Came Texas Guinan, companionate marriage, boot-legging, and Freud while George Horace Lorimer took The Saturday Evening Post to the heights.

Chapter 9

The Saturday Evening Post of the 1920's

In 1916, greatly daring, a slight youth of 22 traveled from New Rochelle, just outside the City of New York, to Philadelphia with a huge case covered with black oilcloth which he had had a harness maker build for him. It was almost as large as he, so large that he was not allowed to take it on the subway with him. It is unlikely he could have gotten it through any of the car doors anyway.

Norman Rockwell, who had been a choir boy in the Cathedral of St. John the Divine as well as a Post boy when he lived on West 103 Street, had been doing illustrations for children's books, pictures for the *Youth's Companion*, advertising art, and covers for *Leslie's* and the old *Life* and *Judge*. A cartoonist friend, an older man named Clyde Forsythe, suggested his trying The Saturday Evening Post. John T. McCutcheon and N. C. Wyeth did Post covers. Its most characteristic covers, vivid, boldly finished, often humorous, were done by J. C. Leyendecker, creator of that beau ideal of masculine American beauty, the Arrow Collar man. Rockwell was abashed at the idea of attempting the biggest and to his mind the greatest of all the magazines, but he decided to try.

At Curtis, Rockwell was taken to Walter H. Dower, then art editor of both The Saturday Evening Post and the Ladies' Home Journal. Face expressionless, Dower looked at the work Rockwell submitted. He then took it in to show to George Horace Lorimer. Dower came back all smiles. Lorimer had directed him to purchase both the finished cover paintings Rockwell submitted. He gave the delighted youth a check for $100, $50 each for them. He also told him to go ahead with the finish of a sketch he had shown Lorimer and said that the Post would buy three more covers.

Sam Blythe and Irvin S. Cobb had been in with Lorimer. They came out and saw Rockwell's enormous black case. They frowned. They walked around and around it as if they could not believe what they saw. As Rockwell was leaving with his first Post check and stunned disbelief in his good fortune, Cobb pointed at the case.

"Young man, is that a coffin?"

Rockwell denied it.

"That's good. We were afraid you had a body in it."

Rockwell's first Post cover appeared May 20, 1916. It showed a boy dressed in his Sunday best—derby, stiff collar, flower in his buttonhole, and a nippled bottle in his breast pocket—pushing a baby carriage. Two other boys in baseball uniforms mocked him as they hurried the other way. Between 1916 and 1969 Norman Rockwell painted more than 360 covers for The Saturday Evening Post and did innumerable illustrations for it. Rockwell covers became as familiar as the Post itself. They said the Post, and they said America. Humorous, narrative, sentimental, they glamorized the homely and familiar with a photographic realism that caught every detail of a scene, a face, a costume—which, to a large extent, is just what the Post did.

Walter Dower and the various art editors who succeeded him carried Rockwell's paintings in to Lorimer who, as he did with manuscripts, made the actual buying decisions. Often he dealt directly with Rockwell. Over more than a half century, Rockwell worked with Dower, W. Thornton Martin, Wesley Stout, Adelaide Neall, Ben Hibbs, Robert Fuoss, Kenneth Stuart, and many more Post editors and art editors. A few of the latter, to show their expertness, made it a point to suggest changes in details of his paintings. Overhearing, Lorimer would overrule them. "Norman, I like it just as it is." Lorimer called him "Norman." He called Lorimer, "Mr. Lorimer." It was that way with all but the closest friends and associates of "The Boss."

Two or three times a year Rockwell, whose price for a cover went from $50 to $2,500, then to $5,000 for originals that now command perhaps ten times that amount, would travel from his home in Arlington, Vermont, to Philadelphia with his finished work and act out his ideas for new covers which he had sketched. None of his covers was ever rejected. These were happy occasions. One was happier than he might have wished.

On a generous expense account one of the Post's art editors took him to dinner and the theatre in New York. At dinner the art editor insisted on drinking absinthe. They were at the theatre before it began to show its disastrous effects. The editor became so uproarious that the slight but wiry Rockwell tried to haul him to the men's room. On the way the editor got into a fight of such proportions that the play had to be stopped and the police called in. Reluctantly they agreed to let the man go if only Rockwell would get him out of there.

All Rockwell could think of was to get him to the nearest Child's restaurant and try to get some black coffee into him. As so often, the strategy was sound but execution proved difficult. The art editor got stuck in the restaurant's revolving door. No one could get in or out. As he did not know which he wanted to do and could do neither, the art editor just stayed where he was. At this point Norman Rockwell gave up and fled. As far as he knows the absinthe with the art editor wrapped around it and the revolving door wrapped around him are still where he left them.

There were other men and other incidents. Rockwell remembers many of them, but always he reverts to Lorimer. Granite-faced, autocratic, George Horace Lorimer towered over all the others. At one point Norman Rockwell studied the modern artists in Paris and bought a Picasso to inspire him. He essayed a new style in his Post covers. Lorimer put them aside and suggested mildly that Rockwell be himself.

On such direct order from The Boss, Rockwell never again dared try to be anybody else.

When it was getting under way *Liberty* tried to raid Post authors and illustrators. Its publisher sent a man to Rockwell's studio, then still in New Rochelle, with instructions not to leave until he had signed Rockwell on. *Liberty* would double the prices paid him by the Post. The man stayed all day as Rockwell worked. The painter did not know what to do. Finally he excused himself to go to the bathroom, escaped from the house, and took a night train for Philadelphia. He told his story to Lorimer the next morning.

"Well, Norman, what are you going to do?"

"Mr. Lorimer, I'm going to stay with you."

"All right. I'll double your payments."

Lorimer recognized no real competitor to The Saturday Evening Post. Other magazines were imitators or also-rans. He would not be held up, but after Rockwell had made his decision he met the terms. Rockwell looked at George Horace Lorimer with a painter's eye and an artist's perception and made his sure judgment. "Lorimer was a King!"

On The Saturday Evening Post, Lorimer *was* king, and he lived and worked like one. His home, like that of Cyrus Curtis, was in Wyncote. A few miles away he had his large farm, King's Oak. He traveled abroad to rest, find new writers, and strengthen his perspective on the United States. He traveled west as often as he could. An ardent conservationist, he promoted the national parks continually in The Saturday Evening Post. The Grand Canyon was a special favorite. It was in 1909 at the El Tovar Inn on the south rim that he met Adelaide Neall, a recent Bryn Mawr graduate from Philadelphia, and hired her as his assistant. Listed on the Post masthead as A. W. Neall to disguise her sex on a man's magazine, she was Lorimer's trusted lieutenant during all the rest of his career. Lorimer traveled, ate well, smoked incessantly, drank deeply, but mostly he worked.

At the office he read manuscripts, and his decision on those that got that far was unqualified and irrevocable. In soft

George Horace Lorimer. Reprinted by special permission. Copyright 1937 The Curtis Publishing Company.

black pencil he marked them OK/GHL or NO/GHL. That was that, and he wanted no discussion later. He took authors to lunch in the executive dining room or the Bellevue-Stratford. He checked proofs and made it a point to see callers who had legitimate claims on his attention. His letters were short, his interviews brief. His manner was formal. At home he took a short nap before dinner, then six nights a week read manuscripts. He read fast, able to get the substance of a type page almost at a glance. Unlike Bok, he sought privacy. He and Curtis shared a dislike of ostentation and a reserve that kept even their intimates at a distance. Lorimer's work was his life. He could never have really relaxed. As near as he came to it was planting trees. Lorimer loved trees and planted them everywhere about his estates.

His wife's chauffeur wore the gold-braided uniform of an honorary Philadelphia police captain. According to Isaac Marcosson, Lorimer's salary as editor of The Saturday Evening Post before the Depression when all Curtis executives took percentage cuts, was $225,000 a year.[1] Cyrus Curtis knew he was worth it. He liked to say that he could explain the success of The Saturday Evening Post in three words—George Horace Lorimer. Curtis never interfered, never suggested an article. Once when a powerful group pressed for a Post article on labor and management, Curtis said, "You will have to see Mr. Lorimer, the editor. I am merely the proprietor."

Lorimer was a writer. He had proved that with *The Letters of a Self-Made Merchant to His Son, Old Gorgon Graham,* and *Jack Spurlock.* He understood writers. He knew how they thought and worked and, more important, how they felt. He was an editor. He had proved that since 1899. He favored fiction and felt closest to the novelists and short story writers he used most, but he knew what he wanted in articles too. He could lay out a series with accuracy and despatch even when he seemed to be amusing himself with a group of writers on the Curtis yacht, the *Lyndonia,* or on one of his beloved motor trips in search of antiques. He hunted them down in friendly and usually triumphant rivalry with Kenneth Roberts, Edwin Lefevre, and Joseph Hergesheimer. He could buy what pleased his expert fancy. He had the money. The only difficulty was smuggling new purchases into the already crowded house without arousing the suspicions of his rather imperious wife.

Once when Lorimer was making one of his periodic trips to England and wanted ready cash Kenneth Roberts and another of the inner group of Lorimer writers spent the whole

---

[1] Marcosson, Isaac, *Before I Forget* (New York: Dodd, Mead & Co., 1959).

morning at Lorimer's safe deposit box in one of the banks near the Curtis Building clipping coupons. "I knew The Boss was rich," Roberts said, "but I didn't know he was *that* rich." Lorimer's Curtis stock and his other investments must have provided income equal to his Post salary.

Kenneth Roberts seldom qualified what he spoke or wrote. Irreverent, impatient, a hard-working writer of firm accomplishment, Roberts was intolerant of many things and most people. He knew exactly what he thought of George Horace Lorimer. "In stature, in perception, he surpassed any statesman, any ruler, any prime minister, any leader of his generation. . . . To me Lorimer is still alive; I can see him and hear him." [2]

Born in Kennebunk, Maine, of seafaring ancestry, Kenneth Roberts joined the *Boston Post*, Lorimer's old paper, after his graduation from Cornell where he had edited the *Widow*. Through a New York agent he sold his first story, "Good Will and Almond Shells" to The Saturday Evening Post in 1917, then another, "With Neatness and Despatch," in 1918. A big, powerful man, Roberts wangled a commission in Military Intelligence in World War I and was sent on the American expedition into Siberia. Before he left Washington, Roberts wired a query to George Horace Lorimer, whom he had never met. Would the Post be interested in articles about Siberia? A reply waited him in San Francisco. The Post would be interested in articles on the social, political, and economic situation in Siberia. It was Lorimer's way of fobbing off presumptuous inquiries. He gave Roberts plenty of rope to hang himself. Roberts did not.

When he got back to the United States, Roberts went immediately to Philadelphia with a 22,000-word piece on the Svetlanskaya Front. Lorimer said it was far too long—and bought it for $1,000. He advised Roberts not to try to tell everything he knew in one piece, told him he would probably still be on the *Boston Post* himself had it met his demand for

[2] Roberts, Kenneth, *I Wanted to Write* (New York: Doubleday & Co., Inc., 1949).

a raise to $20 a week, took him to lunch, and when they returned to his office gave him a handful of chocolate buds from the supply in his desk. Roberts and Lorimer hit it off from the first.

Roberts returned to Kennebunkport—where he began his long friendship with Booth Tarkington, a summer resident—and went to work. "The Random Notes of an Americansky" appeared in The Saturday Evening Post of May 17, 1919. Lorimer bought more Roberts articles and a play he had coauthored. It appeared when the Post was serializing Sinclair Lewis's "Free Air," his story of crossing the country in a flivver in August, 1919.

The Post paid Roberts $500 an article at first, raised him to $900, to $1,100, to $1,500, to $1,750. Lorimer called him to Philadelphia and gave the ex-reporter a reporter's dream assignment. With a $2,500 expense check to start he sent him off to England, Ireland, Scotland, France, Germany, Czechoslovakia, Poland, Austria, Greece, and Turkey. What Lorimer wanted was a series of articles as background for a planned series on immigration. Lorimer was against the unrestricted immigration which he saw as placing the American workmen in unfair competition with cheap foreign labor. Then and always, George Horace Lorimer believed in America for Americans.

Kenneth Roberts became and remained throughout the Post's golden decade its international reporter. He sent back trenchant, hard-hitting—sometimes brash—articles from many parts of the world. In 1921 Lorimer brought him back for a time to replace Sam Blythe, who was retiring, as the Post's Washington correspondent, and Roberts covered the national scene from the capital which he came to detest.

Between 1917 and 1948 Kenneth Lewis Roberts wrote prolifically for The Saturday Evening Post on anything and everything—tonsils, astrology, exercise, the American universities, women in knickerbockers, Benedict Arnold, hurricanes, antique hunting, house building, the Florida real estate boom. . . . He derided Oxford, politicians, diets, and the Pulitzer Prizes and those who made them. Including his historical novels which the Post serialized in shortened form, Kenneth Roberts wrote some 225 pieces for The Saturday Evening Post, all but two of them for George Horace Lorimer.

Companion in Maine of Tarkington, who was his generous literary mentor, and of Hugh McNair Kahler, Post perennial who bogged down on his 100th short story for the magazine and later became strong fiction editor of the Ladies' Home Journal, Roberts was both one of the most characteristic writers of The Saturday Evening Post of the 1920's and one of Lorimer's chosen.

Once a coldness threatened when Roberts wrote Lorimer from Maine instead of appearing in Philadelphia as The Boss had suggested. When he realized what had happened, Roberts hurried to Philadelphia and waited two hours in the white marble lobby before he could see Lorimer. He would have waited all day. Lorimer, who said he had not known he was there, received him as of old, and Robert's world was all right again.

Badgered by a world of damned fools, Kenneth Roberts despised self-conscious intellectuals and sweated over his work when he became a hard-hitting, no-nonsense historical novelist. He was not a scholar. He had too many *a priori* convictions for that, and he pled for lost causes—Benedict Arnold, the Tories in the American Revolution. He knew he saw the truth about the Revolution, Maine, water dowsing, food, hot buttered rum, education, and a dozen other subjects. Anyone who did not agree with him was a fool and being a fool on purpose to annoy him, but he worshipped George Horace Lorimer. To Roberts, Lorimer was a great editor but, above all, a man.

One night after dinner at Rocky Pasture, his stone house above the sea in Kennebunkport, and hours of talk over his favorite Irish whiskey, Roberts paid a younger writer the highest compliment he could pay a man. He could not tell him directly. The words would have been too emotional. He told the man's wife, "It's too bad he did not know Lorimer. The Boss would have loved him!"

Mary Roberts Rinehart was another Lorimer favorite, and with good reason. Rinehart did her first "Tish" story for *Harper's*, which had asked her to write for it. When it came back with a mere rejection slip, she sent it to the Post which, mecca of all writers then, she had been afraid to tackle. It was accepted with a request for more, and "Tish" belonged to the Post forever after.

Lorimer sent Rinehart to cover what she could of the European War before the entry of the United States. She sailed on the *Franconia* just after Christmas, 1914, taking with her a large and fashionable wardrobe, a military cape, and high boots and an umbrella to wear in the trenches. Before she left London and wangled her way into Allied Headquarters in France, she took out a 2,000-pound war protection policy from Lloyd's and bought a light, warm fur coat, both of which she charged to her expense account. It was approved. She said later, "I rather imagine that I am the only woman in the world for whom The Curtis Publishing Company, as an organization, ever purchased a fur coat." [3]

In New York the literary agent Paul Reynolds, Sr. was signing up well-known popular authors to high-paying exclusive contracts with other magazines, and some deserted The Saturday Evening Post for what seemed quick and easy money. Along with others Rinehart was approached by Ray Long of *Cosmopolitan* who offered $5,000 each for a story a month. She refused and stayed with Lorimer—who would make no long-term contracts with authors and who paid his Curtis associates less than the going rate. He would not buy loyalty. He felt it was honor enough to work or write for The Saturday Evening Post.

Lorimer could be ruthless. Rinehart once saw him turn down some stories by Rudyard Kipling with the simple com-

3 Rinehart, *op. cit.*

ment, "Not good enough." Yet Lorimer gave the writers he trusted the same free hand that Curtis gave him. He never suggested or advised about a piece. If he liked it, he took it and paid for it immediately; if he did not like it, he did not take it.

Lorimer was jealous of his writers. He had made most of them, and he felt the creator's proprietary interest in his creations. When Rinehart, because she considered it a woman's success story which fitted a women's magazine, gave her autobiography to *Good Housekeeping* Lorimer was annoyed. He had thought the Post was to have it. Rinehart explained that she did not think it was his kind of thing. "I wish you'd let me edit the Post," Lorimer complained.

Tarkington was not one of the inner group to which Roberts and Rinehart felt they belonged. Already distinguished before the bibulous meeting with Lorimer in 1905, he became the Post's highest paid author, but his relationship with the magazine was always touched with courteous formality. Tarkington was the product of Meridian Avenue affluence, social position, and literary culture in Indianapolis. After Shortridge High School, art study at Purdue, then Ivy and the Triangle Club at Princeton, he eschewed salaried employment and went home to write. It was an indomitable sister who brought his work forcefully to the attention of S. S. McClure, and *McClure's* serialized his first successful books.

Harper's asked Tarkington for *His Own People,* then was fearful of some satirical scenes in it and when Tarkington refused to delete them turned it down. Lorimer took it and published it in the Post with no omissions or revisions. That was the beginning. Lorimer took "Mary Smith" in 1912, then Tarkington's first Post serial, "The Flirt," in 1912. Tarkington wrote his "Little Orvie" stories for the Post. He wrote many Post stories, then began his long series of "Mr. Rumbin" stories for Lorimer in 1936. They were written with Lorimer's understanding connivance.

In the 1920's Tarkington suffered from both cataracts and a detached retina and underwent many operations at the Wilmer Institute of Johns Hopkins. For three years he was almost blind; for five months he was totally blind. He wrote his letters to Lorimer and then to Adelaide Neall with a soft pencil on large sheets of lightweight yellow cardboard so that he could make out what he was writing.

Tarkington collected paintings on a large scale. Their bright colors gave the nearly blind writer so much pleasure that his wife encouraged his purchases, many of them made through Abris and David Silberman, New York art dealers. It was to help pay for his pictures, notably an expensive Velasquez, that Tarkington, using the Silberman brothers as models, wrote his stories of the art dealer, Mr. Rumbin.

Tarkington's work for The Saturday Evening Post continued to within three years of his death in 1946. His autobiography down to 1899, "As I Seem to Me," began July 5 and ended August 23, 1941. In 1943 Tarkington wrote the brief text to accompany "Freedom of Speech," one of the "Four Freedoms" which Norman Rockwell painted for the Post in that year.

Tarkington, Rinehart, and dozens of others in the Post of the 1920's wrote stories that people read for pleasure. They used plot, suspense, characterization, sentiment, and humor. They wrote seriously but they wrote for readers to enjoy what they read. There was no psychoanalysis, no biological sex, no stream-of-consciousness introspection in Post fiction. Lorimer did not look for studies of sexual deviation, social righteousness, laboratory findings or statistics from his imaginative writers. He wanted stories that were stories, and he got them.

He liked Arthur Train's "Tutt and Mr. Tutt" stories. The shrewd old lawyer was a favorite with Post readers. He did not particularly like Joseph Hergesheimer's romances, all lavender and old lace and an aesthetic style, but the Philadelphia bookseller's tales had charm for many Post readers who enthused over "Java Head" in 1918, "Balisand" in 1924, and Hergesheimer's many other Post stories. Hergesheimer became one of Lorimer's friends.

Now the worshipped of a cult who see in the pathos of his life and the romanticism of his novels ineffable qualities which they cannot quite describe, F. Scott Fitzgerald was a prolific short story writer for The Saturday Evening Post all through the 1920's and into the 1930's. He was as typical in its pages as Clarence Budington Kelland and as intent on the money to be made from the Post. Though Fitzgerald made his mystical reputation with *This Side of Paradise,* his jazz-age story of Princeton undergraduate life published when he was only 24, and later with *The Great Gatsby* and *Tender Is the Night,* he was a professional Post writer and in bulk and quality his writing for it has to be considered as much a part of the man and his work as his novels. To discount them is to say that Fitzgerald spent much of his time writing contrived and insincere fiction.

In his Post stories as in his novels, Francis Scott Key Fitzgerald worked and reworked the incidents and emotions of his life and the people he knew. His alcoholic and marital miseries are the lyric in them as in his books. Lorimer was never queasy, and the Post with other magazines of the post-World War I world was looking for the new glamor. Here it was in the college-life, college-prom, cocktail world of the boy from St. Paul who was himself beglamorized by Princeton, New York, and the new sophistication.

Beginning with 1927 Fitzgerald wrote 55 stories for The Saturday Evening Post, creating different heroes for different aspects of his own character. He knew very well what he was doing. Lorimer often published bits of authors' autobiographies. Writers interested him and as an editor he felt that their lives interested his readers. He ran "One Hundred False Starts" by F. Scott Fitzgerald in 1932. In it Fitzgerald said that all professional writers repeated themselves. They drew on the moving experiences of their past. He admitted that all his stories resembled each other. He could not help it. Whether it had happened 20 years before or only the day before, the author of *The Beautiful and the Damned* and *All the Sad Young Men* had to start with an emotion he had felt and understood and write from there.

The financial crash of 1929 and the long Depression which followed changed people's tastes. Flappers, adolescents, and the emotions of the very young became old hat. The Post published "Babylon Revisited" but Lorimer's aides began to send back Fitzgerald's stories with requests for improvements, and F. Scott Fitzgerald faded out of the Post.

Another Lorimer regular lasted a far longer time. He began earlier and stayed later. Born in Louisville, Kentucky, Isaac F. Marcosson, who had only a few months of high schooling, became a reporter on the *Louisville Times*, owned then by Henry Watterson's *Courier-Journal*. Marcosson got his magazine education when he went to New York to work for Walter Hines Page on the *World's Work*. A ready writer on almost any subject, he left after a difference of opinion with Page and began as a staff contributor on the Post. He became one of Lorimer's star reporters, his by-line one of the most familiar in the Post for 31 years.

At a time when Marcosson had no savings and had never seen a bond or a stock certificate Lorimer put him to work on a weekly article title "Your Savings." He told Marcosson that, learning as he went along, he would write so simply that the average man or woman would be able to understand what he wrote. These articles ran for five years. Then Marcosson began to write the business articles that Lorimer wanted for his businessman readers. He served as a Post war correspondent. He became the Post's best-known interviewer. He wrote about George L. Whelan who ran a small store in Syracuse into the United Cigars Stores chain all over the country.[4] Marcosson wrote on the use of the Ford car on the farm and on the business methods of the National Cash Register Company. He dubbed Ivan Kreuger "The Match King" in a piece that was in press when Kreuger, a swindler on a gigantic scale, shot himself in Paris, March 4, 1932. The presses were stopped and Marcosson's piece was retitled, "A Last Talk with

---

[4] The result of Whelan's venture would turn up again in a very different way in The Curtis Publishing Company many years later.

Ivan Kreuger." The Post was praised for its timeliness—though castigated by some for giving space to a crook—when the article was published.

Lorimer did not go in for muckraking, but he had his own crusades—against over-taxation, against unrestricted immigration, against despoilers of the nation's natural resources, against forgiveness of the war debts. He fought these enemies of business, but he kept his business articles expository, not critical.

In the early years of his editorship Lorimer watched the newspapers closely, then asked the writers of signed articles he liked to get in touch with him. He got Sam Blythe, David Graham Phillips, and Will Payne this way. Charles Van Loan called his attention to Ring Lardner, then a sports writer and columnist in Chicago and later in New York. Lardner's short stories made his lasting reputation when they appeared in The Saturday Evening Post. Octavus Roy Cohen, a Birmingham, Alabama, reporter submitted 25 pieces to the Post before his first was accepted and his humor became a Post feature. After he had written many serials and stories for the Post, Emerson Hough began to slip. It was Lorimer who suggested to him the epic story which Hough turned into "The Covered Wagon" for the Post.

Ike Marcosson brought in Irvin Shrewsbury Cobb when the New York columnist asked him to take a story down to Philadelphia and submit it to Lorimer. Thus Cobb brought his native Paducah, his operations, and his stories of Old Judge Priest to millions of enthusiastic readers in The Saturday Evening Post. Cobb admired the Post, and he knew why. "The uncanny soundness of its literary judgment is demonstrated firstly by the fact that more people on this planet read the magazine and like it than any other magazine. And secondly by the fact that it buys nearly everything I write." He knew what he thought of George Horace Lorimer too. He called him "one of the big outstanding human nouns of his day and time" and said he was closer to the popular conception of the typical American, in the best sense, than any man he had ever known.

Lorimer liked Cobb, liked his humor and the response it provoked in Post readers. Then something happened which he did not like. Cobb capitulated to the siren call and went to *Cosmopolitan* under a three-year contract to write exclusively for it. When the contract terminated, it was not renewed, and Cobb could not get back into The Saturday Evening Post. Lorimer could neither forget nor forgive what he considered apostasy. In a bulletin from Post editors to the Curtis Circulation and Advertising Departments in 1923 was this passage.

There is, today, a group of magazines which shop around almost exclusively for well-known names, and either bid for them competitively or contract for all the work of these men over a period of one, two or three years. . . . The Saturday Evening Post never makes contracts with authors, never buys stories that have not been read by its editors before acceptance, and never buys stories on "name" only. . . .

With very few exceptions, every writer who has left The Saturday Evening Post to sell his output under the contract system to another magazine, has given us the first opportunity at his work before tying up elsewhere, and almost invariably at the conclusion of his contract, he wants to come back to the Post again. But an author who was slipping a little when he left us has usually slipped a long way at the end of three years of contract work.

The Curtis Publishing Company had thousands of manufacturing and clerical employees in Philadelphia, but the editorial staffs of its magazines were small. The Saturday Evening Post with its more than 2,000,000 circulation, its issues running over 200 pages often, sometimes to 244, even to 260, listed only seven editors, six men and one woman. Associate editors under Lorimer were Churchill Williams, F. S. Bigelow, Adelaide Neall, Arthur McKeogh, T. B. Costain, and Thomas L. Masson. This was the staff that in 1922 put out 52 issues containing 272 short stories, 269 articles, 20 serials, and seven two-part stories.

Every week for a nickel the reader could buy the equivalent of a full hard cover book containing, generally, six stories, six articles, and two serials along with the Post's regular departments such as "Short Turns and Encores," the precursor of Post Scripts. He got Marcosson, Roberts, Tarkington, Clarence Budington Kelland, and almost always Garet Garrett.

Garrett, who had been executive editor of the New York *Tribune*, joined the Post after World War I and became a steady contributor of political and economic articles. His pieces were too long, often prosy, often dull, but they were thorough and they carried conviction—Lorimer's convictions which were also Garrett's. In a sense, week after week, Garrett was the editorial voice of Post policy. Garrett, like Lorimer, was an isolationist angered at the neglect or refusal of European countries to pay their war debts to the United States.

One of the Post's 1922 serials, "The Driver," was by Garrett. Others were by Henry M. Rideout, Harry Leon Wilson (it was "Merton of the Movies" that year), Emerson Hough ("The Covered Wagon"), Julian Street, John Taintor Foote, Roland Pertwee, Frances Noyes Hart, Nina Wilcox Putnam, George Kibbe Turner, Hal G. Evarts, and Kelland. One of the two-part stories was "Popular Girl" by F. Scott Fitzgerald; another, "The Road to Casualty" by Ben Ames Williams.

Lorimer might not buy "names," but he had them all. These were the popular writers, and, issue after issue, they were Post writers. You could depend on The Saturday Evening Post. You got "Tol'able David" by Joseph Hergesheimer, "The Reminiscences of a Stock Operator" by Edwin Lefevre, "The Young Man in Journalism" by Chester S. Lord, "The Beggar of Berlin" by Philip Gibbs. The Saturday Evening Post was complete and sound, and it was there. Just as the sun rose every morning, the Post came out every Thursday. Thursday was "Saturday Evening Post Day" in the post offices of the United States and everywhere else. As The Curtis Publishing Company proudly claimed, The Saturday Evening Post was an American publication for American readers. Lorimer agreed, only he thought it *the* American publication for all decent Americans.

When unfriendly critics attacked, Lorimer knew why. They were un-American. Probably they were disappointed would-be contributors. Lorimer was suspicious of "pinks and professors." He was suspicious of Europe and felt that his suspicions were justified when country after country defaulted on its war debts. That was not honest business.

In his editorials in the 1920's Lorimer pointed to the weakness of the Treaty of Paris which, he warned, carried in it the seed of future wars. He supported disarmament. He condemned excessive taxation, unrestrained government spending, and the growth of a federal bureaucracy. Socialism was always a Lorimer bogeyman. He had the strong man's contempt for the weak. A man, as he had done, did his work and lived his life through his own efforts. He did not look to society for support. "The simple and amply proven fact is that government ownership does not make men, and rarely money. It makes weaklings, dependents, grafters, bureaucrats, autocrats, and deficits. It is the first lesson in Socialism."

Lorimer and the Post supported Harding, Coolidge, and Hoover. Lorimer disliked Harding, but he stood for the right party and the right understanding of America. He liked Calvin Coolidge and associated with him. He assigned Garrett to write about him. After Coolidge left office, he paid him $10,000 for an article, "Party Loyalty and the Presidency."

Lorimer was not producing a magazine for the critics, the literati or the intelligentsia. He did not know what they were and would not have cared had he known. He was editing for corporation heads, salesmen, accountants, foremen, entrepreneurs, and even office boys. They were the men of intelligence, the men who did things. The effeminate fringe of the masculine elect were no concern of his. He gave sensible men and women the best reporting on national and international affairs by the best reporters he could find and the best fiction by the best novelists and short story writers the country could produce.

Who read The Saturday Evening Post? Everybody. That was the estimate of Leon Whipple in 1928. He described the Post as a miracle of technical publishing, a supersalesman through advertising, a purveyor of entertainment through its articles and fiction, and "an engine for the propaganda in favor of American nationalism and the present economic system." [5] Whipple wrote:

> This is a magic mirror; it not only reflects, it creates us. What the SatEvePost is we are. Its advertising helps standardize our physical life; its text stencils patterns on our minds . . . it molds our ideas on Russia, oil, preparedness, immigration, the World Court. Finally it does queer things to our psychology by printing tales that deceive us with a surface realism but are too often a tissue of illusions. . . . This bulky nickel's worth of print and pictures is a kind of social and emotional common denominator of American life.
>
> Who reads the Post? Who looks in the mirror? Everybody—highbrow, low-brow, and mezzanine; the hard-boiled business man and the soft-boiled leisure woman; the intelligentzia, often as a secret vice . . . You read it—and I. . . .

Whipple might have qualified his judgment on Post fiction. It was a commonplace of the time to castigate the "slick" fiction in the magazines, but the short stories and serials in The Saturday Evening Post were in general superior to those in the other mass magazines and far superior to those in the women's books. Lorimer knew he had plenty of readers who liked stirring yarns about men who were men, women who were women, and horses that were horses, and he liked some of them himself. Kelland, William Hazlitt Upson, Norman Reilly Raine, Charles Francis Coe, and a dozen others gave them such yarns by the gross. Lorimer also ran more substantial fiction and lots of it.

J. P. Marquand could write to entertain or he could write to say something. He did both for Lorimer. In the ten years between 1921 and 1932 he contributed 59 short stories and five serials to The Saturday Evening Post, the Post paying him up to $3,000 for a short story and up to $40,000 for a serial. When the death of Earl Derr Biggers ended Charlie Chan's long career in The Saturday Evening Post, Lorimer sent Marquand to the Far East, and in Tokyo, Marquand discovered another oriental detective, Mr. Moto.

Marquand wrote five "Mr. Moto" serials for the Post, but the Post also ran parts of The Late George Apley in 1936, the

[5] "SatEvePost, Mirror of These States," Survey, March 1, 1928.

same year in which it published "Thank You, Mr. Moto" and "Think Fast, Mr. Moto." The Saturday Evening Post serialized *Wickford Point* in 1939 and ran the final "Last Laugh, Mr. Moto" in 1942.

Booth Tarkington's serious fiction appeared in Lorimer's Post. Kenneth Roberts' novels were realistic enough for anyone. Before he created Yoknapatawpha County, William Faulkner was a frequent short story writer for The Saturday Evening Post. Between 1930 and 1943 Faulkner contributed 17 stories.

For the rest, Whipple was accurate. The United States had the sun, moon, and stars, the capitol dome, the Washington Monument, Independence Hall, and The Saturday Evening Post. The heavenly bodies were undependable, and Independence Hall was in constant need of repair, but the Post was sure. It was Cyrus H. K. Curtis, George Horace Lorimer, the American people, and a fact of nature. Only quibblers tried to make petty distinctions among them.

In later life Kenneth Roberts wore a silver identification bracelet. It bore the small gold and enamel insignia of the Order of the Cincinnati of which he was an honorary member. Flanking it were replicas of the Phi Beta Kappa key awarded him by the Dartmouth chapter in 1932 and the nearly identical Kappa Beta Phi key he had earned while an undergraduate as president of the honorary drinking society's chapter at Cornell. That bracelet said Kenneth Roberts in the very elements he shared with George Horace Lorimer and the tight inner circle on The Saturday Evening Post of the 1920's— hard-thinking, hard-drinking, rock-bed conservatism and a sense of republican aristocracy.

As Norman Rockwell saw, George Horace Lorimer was a king, just, convinced, firm, a little unbending even when he unbent. The Saturday Evening Post with its hold on the interests, beliefs, and prejudices of the ordinary intelligent man was his kingdom, and he knew it.

Chapter 10

The Curtis Stronghold

If Lorimer was a king, William Boyd, Director of Advertising of The Curtis Publishing Company, was a despot who ruled in his own realm with arbitrary authority. Heavy, arthritic, a zealous Methodist in his Germantown church, Boyd was dictator in the Advertising Department and almost a dictator in advertising.

Boyd did not drink, smoke, or swear. Lorimer, who did all three and perhaps had experienced religiosity enough in his youth, twitted him about it in public. There was that thorn in Boyd's side, for Lorimer was his Curtis superior, but he knew few other discomforts in office. He interpreted Curtis advertising policy, announced his decisions, and enforced them with energy and confidence.

He could because Curtis was Curtis. In advertising it stood supreme and alone. Cyrus Curtis had sold the idea of advertising then created the media to carry it. His magazines had the circulations and the hold on the public that guaranteed the advertiser the attention he wanted for his wares. If you wanted to advertise nationally and effectively, you had your choice. Depending on your product and the market you strove to reach, you could use The Saturday Evening Post or the Ladies' Home Journal.

The Post was without peer. The *Literary Digest* was the nearest thing to strong competitor. *Collier's* came in a poor third. Everybody who was anybody in big business was in the Post. The Post was the stronghold of American business just as The Curtis Publishing Company was the stronghold of magazine publishing and of Philadelphia. That was the place for any aspiring advertiser—if he could get in.

You did not just go out and buy space in The Saturday Evening Post in the 1920's. You could get in only through a recognized advertising agency, and the agency could not always make it. The Curtis Advertising Department decided whether or not your product or service could be mentioned in Post advertising pages. It decided on what schedule of frequency and continuity you might be admitted. It was ridiculous to try to buy one insertion. It was unlikely you would even get a hearing. You had to pass examinations for admission to the Post. Sometimes you had to come hat in hand as a supplicant and even then the door might be closed.

For years one unhappy Philadelphia advertising agent told a story he could not forget. For months he worked on a client, persuading him finally to a large appropriation to be spent in the Post. Gleefully he took order and schedule and hurried down to the Curtis Building. He was told to wait in an outer advertising office. He waited two hours at the end of which he was told that advertising rates had been advanced again while he sat there and that his order could be considered only on the basis of the new rates. The client refused to spend the extra money, and the agent's hard work, hopes, and 15 per cent commission went down the drain.

Both in editorial and in advertising the Ladies' Home Journal was slipping under the editors who succeeded Edward Bok. It would slip until it slumped in the next decade. The Journal had sharp competition from Good Housekeeping, The Delineator, Woman's Home Companion, Pictorial Review, and McCall's, but the advertising was coming in.

It was never as easy with Country Gentleman. Despite hard circulation effort and advertising solicitation it was difficult to make the farm magazine pay for itself. The number of farms was dwindling. Farm youth sought and found city employment. When drastic change was indicated, Cyrus Curtis changed it from a weekly to a monthly and dropped the subscription price to $1 a year.

The first monthly Country Gentleman, January, 1925, was a huge issue featuring name contributors. The opening dog story by Albert Payson Terhune was followed by "Being Vice President" by Thomas W. Marshall and other articles by Andrew W. Mellon, Secretary of the Treasury, Vilhjalmur Stefansson, and Paul de Kruif. These with ex-Governor Frank Lowder of Illinois and the popular novelist Mary Heaton Vorse were all in the book.

A year later Country Gentleman, Loring A. Schuler its editor, ran to 154 pages, had a circulation of over 1,000,000, and was an even greater bargain. In a new effort to get the farm circulation its advertisers demanded, Curtis lowered the subscription price—the magazine was not sold on the newsstands —to three years for $1.

Albert Payson Terhune was back in with his collies in 1926. Walter Pritchard Eaton, Konrad Bercovici, and Jeffery Farnol were in the book. There were departments on gardens, crops, dairy, livestock, orchards, poultry, beekeeping, and even one on radio—a word forbidden in The Saturday Evening Post. The presumption was that farm families listened on lonely nights.

The Gent was manifestly trying to cover the national farm front with informative and entertaining material that would appeal equally to the Connecticut Valley tobacco grower, the New Jersey truck farmer, the corn and wheat farmers of the Middle West, and the cotton growers of the South, but Country Gentleman was becoming less an agricultural and more simply a rural publication. The common denominator among its readers was farm life and farm living. A major department was "The Country Gentlewoman." This was a touch of the Ladies' Home Journal in a magazine that had more than a touch of The Saturday Evening Post.

When Philip Rose, an agricultural engineer, was made editor in 1926, Country Gentleman began to look more and more like a rural Saturday Evening Post. Characteristic Post regu-

lars dominated its pages: Clarence Budington Kelland, Court-
ney Riley Cooper, Hugh McNair Kahler. This was partly
design, partly unavoidable. Lorimer often gave the Gent and
saw that it used manuscripts which he had bought for the
Post then decided were not good enough for it but were quite
good enough for Country Gentleman. The trouble was that
rural families who wanted to read the Post were reading The
Saturday Evening Post itself.

Evidently, Philip Rose liked to see his name in print. It
appeared in large type on the masthead and again in large
type and alone at the top of the editorial page under a silhou-
etted bust of George Washington. Curtis tried to identify the
Gent with Washington as it had identified the Post with
Franklin. Rose inserted departments called "The Outdoor
Boy" and "Girls' Life" for youth appeal and featured Paul
de Kruif, the burly Michigander biologist, early associate of
Sinclair Lewis. Rose ran de Kruif's crusading medical pieces
as often as he could get them.

Country Gentleman was a sound and lively magazine, but
farm publications did not have either the audience or the
appeal they had enjoyed for so many years. Cyrus Curtis
wanted a farm magazine, but he had to pay for the privilege.
He could afford it.

The Saturday Evening Post brought in its golden harvest
every week. Once a month the Journal dumped its harvest
into the Curtis bins. The Curtis horn of plenty was filled and
flowing over and it had not even been tipped. No one at
Curtis saw any reason why the golden flow should ever stop.
It would be hard to stop it, and no one wanted to.

There was some upstart competition. Bruce Haddon and
Henry Luce came out with *Time* in 1923, but there was little
reason to take it seriously as a competitor for advertising.
People could read the newspapers for themselves. They did
not need two Yale boys to rearrange and explain the news
to them every week. *The New Yorker* came along in 1925,
but it was only an offspring of the A.E.F.'S *Stars and Stripes*,
one more of the college humor magazines then popular and

written and edited only for New York sophisticates. There was another small magazine, but it was hardly real.

DeWitt Wallace put together a sample *Reader's Digest* in St. Paul in 1920 and had several hundred copies printed so that he could submit his magazine idea to publishers for possible adoption. At that time he wrote the editors of the established magazines asking permission to select, condense, and reprint articles which they had already published. Sensing valuable publicity through this additional circulation of credited material they had already used, all of the editors readily granted the Wallace request, but George Horace Lorimer had a long established rule limiting quotation from The Saturday Evening Post to 400 words.

Fortunately for Wallace, magazine publishers unanimously rejected his digest idea so he was forced to risk publication himself. The first *Reader's Digest,* small, unillustrated, no advertising, appeared in February, 1922. It contained a condensation of an article from the Ladies' Home Journal but none from The Saturday Evening Post. In subsequent issues the Post appeared frequently, but for about two years only in the brief passages permitted under the Lorimer stricture. Wallace chafed under the restriction.

He took the train from New York to Philadelphia and with some trepidation asked to see the most powerful magazine editor in the country. Lorimer, he remembers, received him with complete graciousness in his big sixth floor office. He got interested as Wallace explained and made his first exception to the limits on quotation which he had imposed.

Thereafter, The Saturday Evening Post appeared more often and at greater length in *The Reader's Digest.* Lorimer was as surprised and pleased as other editors when, about 1928, Wallace voluntarily began to pay small sums for material abstracted from their magazines. He may have been a little amused. Against the tremendous income of The Saturday Evening Post at that time, the money must have seemed insignificant. He could hardly have forseen the day when far more substantial payments from the very successful *Digest* would constitute an important part of the income of many magazines and the *Digest* would be a prime competitor of the Post for advertising.

Radio was the miracle of the 1920's. It began quietly enough when Station 2ZK began to broadcast music two hours a day from New Rochelle, New York. WJZ in Newark, New Jersey, aired its first program October 5, 1921. WBZ in Springfield got the first broadcasting license, and the American Telephone and Telegraph Company opened WEAF in New York, July 25, 1922. At first no advertising at all was permitted, and the programs were mostly music. Then WEAF began to permit "indirect" advertising. Companies sponsoring programs could announce their names: thus the Gold Dust Twins, the A&P Gypsies, the Ipana Troubadors, the Happiness Boys. Then the Radio Corporation of America established the National Broadcasting Company in 1926 and Columbia Phonograph the Columbia Network in 1927. All rules abolished, advertising came in with a rush. There were 7,000,000 radio sets in use by 1926, and advertisers spent more than $4,000,000 for commercial radio time in 1927. The number of sets in use and the amounts of advertising rose year by year. Before 1930 more than half the homes in the United States had radios, and in 1930 advertisers spent more than $40,000,000 in radio advertising.

In the competition for the public's time and attention the big magazines had taken the bicycle, the automobile, and the movies from nickelodeon to the talkies in stride. They felt they would do the same with radio. Undoubtedly some idiots would sit up all nights with earphones clamped over their empty heads and more listen to the new plug-in sets equipped with speakers, but they were not the kind of people the Post and Journal reached or the kind advertisers would consider good, interested, able-to-buy circulation. People believed what they read in print. Radio advertising went by them like a thief on the night airways. The Curtis Publishing Company considered radio no real threat and was more annoyed than alarmed when it became an active competitor. Paper and print had ruled for centuries. They would outlast the new toy.

Yet when in 1928 Donald M. Hobart left Research in the Curtis Advertising Department in Philadelphia to become a Saturday Evening Post advertising space solicitor in Cleveland, he found radio hard to sell against. Radio was reaching vast audiences who were entranced with the music, sports, vaudeville, and soap operas. Advertisers of goods mass produced and mass distributed for mass audiences were equally entranced. Hobart's fellow salesmen in all the Curtis branch advertising offices were making the same unpleasant discovery, but it hardly mattered yet. In 1929 The Curtis Publishing Company made a net profit of $21,000,000 on a gross of $84,000,000.

Friday, April 8, 1927, more than a month before Charles A. Lindbergh landed the Spirit of St. Louis at Le Bourget in Paris only 33½ hours after takeoff from New York, *The New York Times* carried a story under a two-column head at the top of the front page. The headline and subheads read: "Far-off speakers seen as well as heard here in a test of television—like a photo come to life—Hoover's face plainly imaged as he speaks in Washington—the first time in history—pictures are flashed by wire and radio synchronizing with speaker's voice —commercial use in doubt." Secretary of Commerce Herbert C. Hoover had spoken 200 miles away. The Bell Laboratories of the American Telephone and Telegraph Company had donè the rest.

It was a portent considerably larger than a man's hand, but there is no record that Cyrus Curtis or any of his hard-headed and capable staff, most of them avid newspaper readers, was impressed. If they thought about the item at all, they could reflect comfortably that even the careful and often prescient *Times* doubted the commercial value of television.

The pleading space salesmen of other magazines crawled stooped into the offices of agency media buyers carrying a 240 or 260-page issue of The Saturday Evening Post by a baggage handle and weighed down by the load. They lifted it to the man's desk top, panted, and urged that anyone's advertising was lost in such a crowd. Advertiser and agency men smiled and remained in the Post. "As Advertised in The Saturday Evening Post" was a magic phrase for any merchandiser.

The Post was on top, but the Journal was not doing as well. It needed attention. It got it.

Commercial Research conducted an every-home survey in Canton, Ohio. Curtis hired school teachers during the summer months to knock on doors and ask about the family's reading tastes, which among the women's magazine women preferred, what they liked about them, what they did not like. The work was done in the name of an independent organization, Patterson & Andrus of New York. Results of the survey, which was repeated in the same way in Schenectady, then in several of the northern New York counties, showed that women greatly preferred the Ladies' Home Journal. This was hard and accurate research with flatly competitive findings. Curtis Publishing promoted them heavily, and the Ladies' Home Journal scored in subscriptions and in advertising.

Fred Bremier, who had had early experience in making a private railway car study for the Interstate Commerce Commission and in setting up a public utilities commission for North Dakota, had become the Curtis Advertising Department's expert in the automotive field. He spent almost as much time in Detroit as in Philadelphia. The automotive industry was glad to cooperate in Curtis research as its studies provided useful information they could not then obtain readily elsewhere. At one time and another he talked with Henry Ford in Dearborn, with Harvey Firestone, and with Edison in West Orange, New Jersey. Parlin was an enthusiastic admirer of "Boss" Kettering, and Kettering worked with Curtis.

When Edward S. Jordan designed the Jordan Playboy after the dashing custom car Flo Ziegfeld had made for Billie Burke, he broke it in The Saturday Evening Post of June 23, 1923 with the boots and saddle rhetoric that set a new mode in car advertising—"Somewhere west of Laramie there's a

118   THE CURTIS MAGAZINES

bronc-busting, steer-roping girl who . . . can tell what a sassy pony that's a cross between greased lightning and the place where it hits, can do with eleven hundred pounds of steel and action that's going high, wide and handsome. . . ."

Fast transport thrilled the 1920's. The public had been made very conscious of flying by the feats of Lindbergh, Bert Acosta, Clarance Chamberlin, Amelia Earhart, Richard E. Byrd, and the rest. Air mail was the new pony express. Passenger lines were in pioneer operation. Curtis led by many lengths in automotive advertising. Here was a new field for exploitation.

Parlin was enthusiastic. Boyd had been succeeded by Fred Healey who had been manager of the Curtis Detroit office, and Healey wanted to have a study of commercial aviation made. It was Bremier, who had been in Naval Aviation in World War I, who suggested that Curtis buy a plane to use

The Curtis tri-motored plane in California in 1929. Left to right: Charles Coolidge Parlin, Pilot Gorton, Fred Bremier, Eustace and Bailey of the San Francisco office. Courtesy of Mr. Fred Bremier.

in conducting the survey. Fairchild got wind of the decision and almost sold Curtis one of its small planes, but Ford had just placed a new schedule of a minimum of 13 Post pages annually. Curtis bought one of the new Tri-Motored Ford planes for about $75,000.

The Navy lent Curtis one of its test pilots, Jake Gorton, and Curtis took delivery of the Ford plane in Dearborn in July, 1929, and Parlin and Bremier climbed aboard. At South Bend they struck a storm with visibility near zero. As they flew by roads, railway lines, other landmarks, and had only land maps, they needed to be able to see. With some difficulty they finally landed in the mud. The next day they made South Chicago. There were few airports, and those they found were primitive. Sometimes they had to land in a field near a town and ask someone where the airport they had been unable to find was located. In this way they flew on to St. Louis and after several more jumps reached San Diego.

The research men asked questions at airports, of airline officials and mechanics. They talked to passengers. They held interviews at Douglas, Boeing, and North America. The flight brought publicity. Big advertisers asked for and got a ride in the Curtis plane. When they were released, the research findings showed that people would fly—if educational advertising in the Curtis magazines told them about the advantages of flying. A new and mammoth industry was developing. In his survey report Bremier insisted that the future of the aviation industry was not in the air but lay on the ground. Arguing from observation, question-and-answer discussions, and from uncomfortable experience during the Curtis flight, he advocated the construction of new and more adequate airports, fuel and maintenance facilities for the planes, and ground accommodations for passengers. The factories could produce the aircraft, but the industry would have to look to the supporting conveniences.

Curtis could pick and choose among its advertisers, but it made sure that there were always plenty of clients to pick and choose from. It not only sold space, but also advised with its big advertisers on how to use that space effectively. When the bearded Smith Brothers were suddenly presented clean shaven on the company's cough drop packages, sales slumped. The public was fond of the three old men. On Curtis advice, they grew their beards again. Curtis Research made production, pricing, packaging, and distribution methods a part of its study.

Parlin, who loved to make speeches, was a loud but hesitant speaker. As he wore a half to three-quarters of an inch of rubber on his shoe soles to give him height, he seemed to be on stilts as he addressed meetings of salesmen in convention. The audience always listened because Parlin had something to say. He had almost unlimited facts at his disposal, and he could be hypnotic when he talked about advertising—particularly magazine advertising—and particularly magazine advertising in The Saturday Evening Post, Ladies' Home Journal, and Country Gentleman.

Curtis advertising salesmen had all the advantages of fact-finding, the prestige of the magazines and their top circulations behind them. They worked from a position of strength and with all the confidence of unassailable success. Radio might be becoming a nuisance, but where "salesmanship in print" was concerned Curtis was incomparable. Curtis salesmen called wherever they saw a smokestack or a prosperous looking new office. When a small company reported substantial earnings, they assured its management that advertising in The Saturday Evening Post could develop the company to national importance and fabulous returns. Often they were right.

Chapter II

The Curtis Trust

When The Curtis Publishing Company was at its peak, the structure was already weakening, and the man who was weakening it was the same man who had built it. Who had a better right?

When she was ill and knew that she was dying, Louisa Knapp Curtis said that she hoped Curtis would marry a cousin, Mrs. Kate Stanwood Pillsbury of Milwaukee. Curtis did. With her the second Mrs. Curtis brought three daughters, two of them already married. The big house in Wyncote was alive again. Curtis had a full family life, his organ, his estate on Penobscot Bay in Maine. There were parties, travel, and long cruises on the *Lyndonia*.

The Curtis Publishing Company was in capable hands. Bok's voice was strong in company councils until his death in 1930—when he left an estate valued at over $16,000,000. Curtis's faith in George Horace Lorimer, the matchless editor who was also a director, vice president, and chairman of the Curtis executive committee, was boundless and well placed. P. S. Collins (always called "P. S.") was the capable business manager of the company; the austere C. H. Ludington, Jr., its secretary and treasurer. In Boyd, then in Healey, Curtis had strong advertising directors.

Cyrus Curtis had always paid little attention to operating details, and he paid less and less to The Curtis Publishing Company. The continually mounting circulation, advertising sales, and profit figures were all he really needed to know.

Cyrus Curtis had started as a boy selling newspapers in Portland. He valued the experience always, and he never got over his fascination with newspapers. He watched them sharply and purposefully. Having succeeded so magnificently with type, ink, and coated paper he had the not unnatural delusion that he could do as well, perhaps even better, with ink, type, and newsprint.

He had, too, this intent. He had created national magazines. He wanted to create a national newspaper in Philadelphia. January 1, 1913 he bought the *Philadelphia Public Ledger* from Adolph S. Ochs, owner of *The New York Times*. Ochs urged the purchase, and Curtis was easily persuaded. He wished to restore the *Ledger* to Philadelphia ownership and make it the paper of national significance he planned.

Curtis began to rebuild the *Ledger* immediately, journalistically and physically. On Sixth Street, just across alley-width Sansom Street and extending to the corner of Chestnut, he built a near replica of the adjacent Curtis Building. He brought in new editors and executives and established his step-son-in-law John C. Martin as manager of the Curtis-Martin Company which he founded to publish the *Ledger*. He began to publish an evening edition. To get a needed Associated Press franchise, Curtis bought the *Evening Telegraph* from John Wanamaker. In 1920, to get a larger supply of paper, he bought and closed out the *Philadelphia Press* for which he had once worked. Following the methods he used successfully in establishing his magazines, Curtis poured millions into his newspaper endeavors—they just happened to be a different kettle of fish. At great expense he established the *Ledger's* own foreign services, syndicating it to other newspapers.

Much as Frank A. Munsey did in New York, Cyrus H. K. Curtis bought and combined or closed out newspapers in Philadelphia, those which he thought the *Ledger* needed or which threatened competition. He bought and shut down *The Philadelphia North American* which dated back to 1838

and behind that, through the *Pennsylvania Packet* to 1771.
He shut down the tabloid *Star*. Before his newspaper de-
bauch was over, Curtis bought the New York *Evening Post*,
which had been founded in 1801 and edited 1829–1879, a half
century, by William Cullen Bryant. In 1930 Curtis bought
the Philadelphia *Inquirer*, which was merged for a time with
the *Ledger*.

Cyrus Curtis was not a newspaperman or a newspaper publisher. He proved it with the failure of his newspaper ventures and the loss of many millions of dollars. His attempt to
make a national newspaper of the *Philadelphia Public Ledger*
was fruitless. It ceased publication in 1938, though the evening edition lasted until 1942. Curtis could afford to lose the
money, continually replenished from the earnings of his magazines, but his preoccupation with his newspaper ambitions
meant that The Curtis Publishing Company lost the primary
interest and astuteness of its founder and publisher.

Curtis was 70 years old in 1920 and beginning to withdraw.
He had done his job. There was no perceptible slackening
of his energy and acuteness, but he was, in many ways, the
millionaire at play. He must have come as near exuberance
as his control and placid manner allowed when in 1925, when
he was 75, he gave seven per cent preferred stock as a bonus
to the holders of Curtis stock which was already paying large
dividends and paying them not quarterly but monthly. The
company could afford this splendid largesse. There seemed
no reason why it could not always afford it and more. The
advertising revenue of The Saturday Evening Post alone went
from over $16,000,000 in 1917 to over $28,000,000 in 1922 to
more than $53,000,000 in 1927.

Cyrus H. K. Curtis was more than a magazine publisher
now, more even than the newspaper publisher he fancied
himself. He was a civic leader, a public figure. After the
manner of the other self-made millionaires he admired he had
his estates, one of the largest yachts afloat, and his philan-
thropies. He gave away large sums of money, his generous
benefactions going to the University of Pennsylvania, Temple

University, Ursinus College, The Franklin Institute, Drexel Institute, and, through his daughter, to the founding of the Curtis Institute of Music.

In the public mind Curtis was indisputably one of the country's great men in the tradition of the poor boy who through his own efforts rose to multi-millionaire riches. The gently spoken little man was particularly venerated in that the achievements which brought him success also benefitted the rest of American humankind. "The Henry Ford of the magazine world," as the Philadelphia *Record* called him, was also the patron of the arts and the generous contributor to every worthwhile cause.

When Cyrus H. K. Curtis, 83, died at Lyndon, June 7, 1933, he was not just the chairman of the board of The Curtis Publishing Company and the president of Curtis-Martin Newspapers, Inc. The Man from Maine was the friend of Ed Howe of Kansas, who sent his tribute from Miami where he and Curtis had often met and talked, and of the boys of the Burroughs Newsboys Foundation of Boston. They sent flowers to his bedside on the day of his death and a message "to our loyal friend who is an inspiration to all newsboys." When Curtis's death was made known, Sinclair Lewis wired George Horace Lorimer, "My wife, Dorothy Thompson, and I wish to express our sadness at the death of Mr. Cyrus H. K. Curtis. Mr. Curtis and The Curtis Publishing Company gave us both our first chance."

The city of Philadelphia lowered its flags to half staff. All the usual and tactful tributes were sent, but they came from many and diverse people: Andrew Mellon, Adolph Ochs, Grover Whalen, officials of the Red Cross, the Salvation Army, the Jewish Charities, the presidents of colleges and universities and the Associated Press, the Philadelphia Business Progress Association, *The Times* of London, Bonwit Teller, Gimbel's. . . . It is always wise to stay on the good side of the press. It was particularly wise to stand well with Lorimer's Saturday Evening Post, but many who sent their condolences seemed to mean what they said.

President Franklin D. Roosevelt, who as assistant secretary of the Navy had once signed a Post article but never again had cause to be grateful for the magazine's attentions, wrote Mary Louise Curtis Bok, "In the passing of your father, America has lost a great publisher, a noted leader in the field of journalism, and a generous and kind employer. Please accept my sympathy." Herbert Hoover, whom the Post had backed and who represented all the Republicanism, conservatism, and big business economy which The Saturday Evening Post upheld, could be less guarded. He told the Associated Press, "Cyrus H. K. Curtis was a great American. The great publications which he developed, the high standards of journalism they maintained, their devotion to national interests and their consistent advancement of the sane understanding and constructive action in every avenue of American life have been for more than half a century of inestimable service to the American people."

The important newspapers of the country all had their editorials on the passing of the publisher who was "one of the gentlest and most lovable of men," as the Washington *Star* called him. Ochs's *New York Times* was effusive. "Mr. Curtis was a great publisher and a great citizen. He contributed mightily and for good to the life of America through the publications whose 'editors he edited' and whose wholesome influence he carried into its homes, its offices, its schools and even the streets of villages, towns, and cities. And there is yet 'more to it' in the standards he set during his life and the continuing of these influences even beyond his death."

The New York *Herald Tribune,* the New York *Sun,* the Cleveland *Plain Dealer,* the Detroit *Free Press* and all the rest said much the same thing. It was the achievement, The Saturday Evening Post, the cleanness, and the "Americanism" of the Curtis magazines they praised. Even in 1933 there was a lingering fondness for the individualistic self-made man on the approved American pattern.

Curtis's second wife had died in her sleep in Jefferson Hospital, where she had gone to be near her husband who was a patient there, in 1932. It was after her death that Curtis drew up his will, which was dated October 31, 1932. Three days before, at his urging, George Horace Lorimer had been made president of The Curtis Publishing Company.

Cyrus Curtis left an estate conservatively evaluated at from $18,000,000 to $20,000,000, and his chief beneficiary was his only child, Mary Louise Curtis Bok. She and Curtis's step-son-in-law John C. Martin were named executors in the detailed will. To Mrs. Bok went the Curtis estates in Wyncote and in Camden and Rockport, Maine, the *Lyndonia,* and the net income for life of her father's stock in The Curtis Publishing Company and the Curtis-Martin Newspapers. The will contained many provisions, but the one which most affected The Curtis Publishing Company was this.

Curtis established a board of seven trustees to administer the stock in his publications. These trustees were empowered to administer this controlling interest and to turn over the earnings to Mrs. Bok. The trust would continue to the death of his youngest grandson, Cary W. Bok. The seven original trustees were: Mary Louise Bok, her two sons, Curtis and Cary W. Bok, Harold C. Martin, George Horace Lorimer, Curtis vice president Walter D. Fuller, and the secretary treasurer of the Curtis-Martin Newspapers, Charles A. Tyler. The trustees were empowered to fill any vacancy which might occur among their membership, making it a self-perpetuating body. The Curtis will held these trustees to this policy.

Believing that the success of The Curtis Publishing Company will be promoted and best insurance by the continuance, as far as possible, of the present management and policy, it is my wish and I direct that during the continuance of this trust my common stock of The Curtis Publishing Company shall not be sold unless some extraordinary contingency shall arise making it desirable to sell, and then only in the event that my trustees unanimously agree.

In effect, Cyrus Curtis forbade the sale of his control of The Curtis Publishing Company. He insisted that his magazines continue the policies that he had established, and placed the power to enforce his will completely in the hands of his daughter and her sons and those top Curtis executives most interested in preserving things as they were. From this point thenceforward and forevermore The Curtis Publishing Company would be controlled by the Curtis Trust, the Bok estate, and employees who were their agents.

Seven pipe organs which Cyrus H. K. Curtis had given institutions in various parts of the country—including those at the University of Pennsylvania, Drexel Institute, and the Unitarian Church of Germantown—played selections he loved in memorial concerts as Unitarian funeral services were held for him at Lyndon. His own organ was played by the municipal organist of Portland, and four members of the Portland Men's Singing Club sang "Softly now the light of day," composed by Hermann Kotzschmar for whom Curtis had been named. The boy from Maine was buried in Philadelphia's West Laurel Hill Cemetery.

Chapter 12

The Saturday Evening Post
and the New Deal

As Edward Bok said proudly, Curtis's editors were not of
the literary kind. George Horace Lorimer had always been
businessman as well as editor. He had been on the board of
directors of The Curtis Publishing Company for 30 years,
chairman of its executive committee and first vice president
of the company since 1927. He had a strong voice in the
advertising activities of Curtis. When its space salesmen met
in their jamborees, Lorimer talked to them with the same
exhortatory authority as Boyd or Healey.

Cyrus Curtis wanted Lorimer to succeed him, and Lorimer
was willing. He knew himself the real surviving power at
Curtis, and, though he might resent not being able to give his
full time and attention to his Saturday Evening Post, knew he
was capable of running the company and liked the idea.

Lorimer was well aware of the complete insubstantiality of
the magazine business and the transiency built into any magazine or group of magazines. The publisher sells the magazines
which his editors produce. In reality, he gives them away,
for they cost more to manufacture and distribute than they
are sold for. Except as waste paper the magazines have no
physical value. Profit has to come from a parasitic byproduct,
the advertising he manages to sell in his magazines. He does
not even sell advertising, only white space for the purchaser
to use as skillfully as he can.

Editors edit to please readers, and they may succeed beyond all question. This does not necessarily produce a profit. The advertising comes in only if the advertiser and his agency are convinced that there are enough loyal readers of the right kind to constitute a market for his automobile, cleaning tissue, world cruise, encyclopedia, or bottle of pop. Magazine success depends upon whether or not the advertiser *thinks* that his message will gain more attention in the magazine than if it is shouted from billboards or trailed in smoke across the sky, whether he *thinks* that the magazine is trusted by a few million readers who will pay attention to what he has to say. That is the basic uncertainty in magazine publishing.

Lorimer knew all this. He also knew that if his magazine was not acceptable to readers, none of the advertising consummation wished for happened. It worried him to leave any part of the preparation of each week's issue of The Saturday Evening Post to the discretion of anyone else. Now he had to, and, perhaps for this reason, he enforced his will more strongly than ever on the Post.

He had made it. It was entertaining, instructive, bright. It stood for hard work, thrift, honesty, industry. It was directed to the responsible, god-fearing, scrubbed American man and woman. It carried no liquor or cigarette advertising. It was as upright as the America it reflected and sustained. No other America was good enough for The Saturday Evening Post, and no other could be admitted to its pages.

Now George Horace Lorimer was confronted by a United States at which he was aghast. Even when it ran to 240 or 260 pages, The Saturday Evening Post was essentially the small-town weekly of a small town named the United States. The town had grown larger, and to Lorimer it seemed as if its new national leaders and a deluded majority of the population had gone crazy.

The stock market crash of 1929 had come as no surprise to George Horace Lorimer. For years The Saturday Evening Post had been warning of the inevitable bursting of the speculative bubble. The unreality of paper prosperity had been apparent to Lorimer. When the crash came, he saw it not as brought about in any way by American business but by the machinations of financiers and the hysterical credulity of the mass of speculators. Financial panics were nothing new in his experience or in United States business history. Good times and bad times came in cycles or as an act of God. The man of sound common sense prepared for the bad times and rode them out until conditions improved.

When the Great Depression of the 1930's set in, Lorimer knew it to be just another period of bad times following a financial crash. The country was larger. The crash had been bigger and louder. Bad times usually meant a change in political administration. People blamed their misfortunes on the party in power when the disaster occurred, threw it out, and put in the opposition. Though the Post backed Hoover and a sound Republican business administration for re-election in 1932, he could not have been surprised when Hoover was defeated and Franklin Delano Roosevelt came to power. The Democrats never stayed long in office. They would be thrown out when business came into its own again and people returned to their senses.

What appalled George Horace Lorimer was Franklin Roosevelt, the Brain Trust, and the New Deal. He felt that Roosevelt was a traitor to his kind. The Brain Trust was composed of the pinks and professors that Lorimer had always hated and feared. The New Deal was setting up a maze of bureaucracies all of which would have to be supported by confiscatory taxation levied on corporate business and the incomes of individuals. Roosevelt was substituting a planned economy for the laissez-faire economy Lorimer understood and the Post espoused. Lorimer was an individualist, and The Saturday Evening Post was written and edited for all the stalwart individuals who had built the country and were its moral and spiritual backbone. Now "Rugged Individualism" was a term of contempt. Roosevelt curled his tongue around the epithet in what Lorimer heard as his loathsome "Fireside

Chats." Roosevelt chose this vulgar method of talking to the people rather than, as decent Presidents had done from the first Roosevelt on, addressing them in sharp black print on clean white paper through the pages of The Saturday Evening Post.

Lorimer saw treachery and disloyalty in the country's abandonment to the New Deal, and he suffered more from it than he had ever suffered from defaulting Post authors. This was not the way he had taught the country to look at things. Strong men competing with each other had developed the resources of the United States and built its industries. Now, led by a hypocritical rabble rouser surrounded by a court of ivory-tower professors, each scheming for his own ends, and bristling with a confusion of newly established agencies known by an incomprehensible jumble of initials, government was taking over what it had not even helped to create. This was not merely government intervention in business. It was government domination of the minds and honest earnings of men and women.

The Boss loathed and detested it. He determined to stamp it all out. He would fight Franklin Roosevelt and the New Deal if it was the last thing he ever did.

As editor he risked displeasing some of his readers. As Curtis president he knew he could hardly displease advertisers. Like him they were on the side of the right, but there was one trouble here. It was a sacred part of advertising gospel, promulgated by Curtis and solemnly approved in the advertising world, that in depression as in wartime advertising should continue strongly so as to take advantage of the pre-sold market when good times returned. Hurt and frightened, many advertisers forgot the gospel and others, as badly frightened and intent only on conserving what finances they had left, followed them from the fold. Business after business failed. They had nothing to advertise at all. Instead of improving, conditions worsened. Their fortunes lost, some entrepreneurs killed themselves as banks failed and bankruptcies mounted. Hundreds of thousands of men lost their jobs, their homes, and their hopes. Advertisers cut their appropriations or ceased to advertise at all.

The Saturday Evening Post cost only a nickel. Even under pressure Lorimer refused to increase the cover price. His magazine would remain the best nickel's worth in the country. Many no longer had a nickel to spend on other than food, but they managed to see the Post anyway. It was escape into the good world that had been and they hoped would return. The Saturday Evening Post represented the normal and the good; the Depression, the abnormal and certainly unpleasant. In its familiar essentials the Post did not change, but Lorimer was angry. He could not relent in his attack on what he was convinced was the falsity, the ridiculousness, and the immorality of the New Deal.

Ten years before, in 1923, Lorimer had stated his position and that of the Post in an editorial statement prepared for distribution by the Curtis Advertising Department.

Advertisers, at least the kind of advertisers that The Saturday Evening Post wants, tell the truth in their copy. They do not misrepresent their goods. They do not try to sell them by specious and misleading advertisements designed to appeal to the passions of any class.

What is sauce for the advertising department is sauce for the editorial, and an extension of that policy into the editorial pages . . . makes for more business and better business in the long run. A periodical that pretends to reflect American life must reflect American business which is so essential a part of it. . . .

Undoubtedly some employers of cheap labor are opposed to immigration restriction, but the profits that can be derived from the kind of labor that we have been importing during the past ten years are over, and in their stead we are getting strikes and revolutionary radicalism.

The same thing applies to an intelligent development and use of coal, wood, and other resources. Any man who wishes to stay in business and to declare dividends over a term of years must ultimately get behind a program for the wise conservation, development and use of these resources.[1]

That was George Horace Lorimer, conservative, conservationist, and common sense businessman. "We are not crusad-

[1] "Truth as a Business Asset" (Philadelphia: The Curtis Publishing Co., 1923).

ers or up-lifters or muckrakers in our editorial policy," he said in this same statement, "but we are trying to follow the dictates of ordinary business common sense and to work for the best interests of all America over a term of years." Lorimer could not and certainly would not change. He did not view the New Deal with alarm but with abhorrence and consternation. This was "revolutionary radicalism" at its most ridiculous and most dangerous. He attacked it in the Post and in the paid newspaper advertising of The Curtis Publishing Company. In the Post in 1934 he wrote:

> It is impossible to escape the conclusion that today we are having government by amateurs—college boys, irrespective of their age—who having drunk deep, perhaps, of the Pierian spring, have recently taken some healthy swigs of Russian vodka.

The Curtis Publishing Company did its best for its people during the Depression. Advertising was falling off in its magazines, but the company continued to show a profit each year, though not enough to continue dividends on its common stock. Curtis was solvent, and it took care of its own. Percentage salary cuts were instituted throughout the big organization, the median about ten per cent. Employees who died, retired, or went elsewhere were not replaced. The others were safe. Safety was what you had at Curtis. Except at the very top, salaries were always low, but you were sure they would be paid. Men and women spent their whole working lives at Curtis and were proud of it. Often their sons or daughters followed them and felt the same.

During the Depression an important arm of Curtis even had jobs to hand out. The Circulation Department took on good men who at the time could get no jobs of any kind elsewhere, paid them liberal commissions, and looked after them. Many of them remained with Curtis for the rest of their careers.

A 21-year-old farm boy in western Illinois, Dean S. Miller, wanted to marry Jeanette Burchell, but he had no money, no job, and no prospect of getting one. His fiancée's aunt, Mrs. Beulah Brown, and her husband, like so many others, had lost their business. They had begun subscription canvassing for Country Gentleman and were doing well at it. Mrs. Brown suggested that Miller try it, so December 29, 1930, Dean Miller started work in the newly established Rural Program of Curtis Circulation. By spring 1931 he was manager of a subscription crew of about 20 men working out of Galesburg. He and Jeanette Burchell married, then worked together canvassing from silo to silo and grain elevator to grain elevator in the Illinois farm country.

Established procedure was for the field staffs to turn in all moneys collected, then to be paid their commissions by check from Philadelphia. The checks had just gone out when the Bank Holiday of 1932 was declared. Miller promptly cashed his check at a bank, and his men cashed theirs at stores or filling stations where they were known. Without waiting to see if the checks cleared and fearing its agents might be stranded, Curtis duplicated the payment in cash, sending Miller the full payroll by registered mail. For the next eight weeks Curtis did this so that Miller and other crew managers could pay their men promptly and in full. Such measures earned the gratitude and loyalty of the men.

Sometimes during this period the canvassers were paid in cash for subscriptions to Country Gentleman. More often they were paid in chickens, corn, oats, wheat, or other farm commodities. As these were readily salable, Dean Miller did very well. Ultimately he became vice president and director of all field staffs for Curtis Circulation, directing the activities of some 4,000 subscription agents of different kinds across the country.

Lorimer, who moved up from the presidency to the board chairmanship of The Curtis Publishing Company in 1934 and almost absolute control, was a strong man and an angry man. In big Fred Healey, the advertising director, he had another strong man to help him. He and Healey respected each other and worked well together, but Lorimer was responsible, and it did not improve his temper. To the ordinary Curtis employee he became something of a fearsome figure.

One story was long current at Curtis for its principal loved to tell it. Lorimer could no longer write all of the advertising for The Saturday Evening Post himself. Part of the work was delegated to a circulation promotion copywriter. He wrote the advertising for one issue, then took it to Lorimer for approval. Lorimer frowned, took his pencil, and began to rewrite the copy. When he looked up and saw the promotion man looking dubious, he demanded to know why. Pride of creation overcame the man's caution. He explained that his copy would draw such and such a percentage response where Lorimer's changes would drop it to a much lower percentage. To prove that he was right Lorimer ordered a test made. He was not pleased when the results showed the circulation man correct.

"All right," he snapped. "Use the original copy, but if that s.o.b. ever shows his face on the sixth floor again, fire him!"

The dean of the Wharton School, who presumably knew about such things, advised a Curtis executive who was his friend to leave Curtis. He said that Lorimer was no business-man and would wreck the company. Perhaps Lorimer was not the executive he fancied himself, but he did not do badly.

On the Post he had capable editors of his own choosing in the early 1920's. Adelaide Neall was, in effect, managing editor. Thomas B. Costain, born in Brantford, Ontario, in 1885, who had come to the United States in 1920, was a smooth contact man. Lorimer used him to work with the New York literary agents. When he had to be away, Lorimer would leave Costain in charge of the Post—after giving him specific and detailed instructions. Costain was in a preferred position. He knew it and counted on the promise it implied, but his British mannerisms annoyed The Boss, who distrusted all foreigners.

Wesley Winans Stout, born in Junction City, Kansas, in 1890, had worked on small newspapers in Kansas, Missouri, and Texas before coming to Post editorial. He was the faith-ful worker who shared most of Lorimer's ideas and attitudes.

Lorimer's son Graeme was now an associate editor. He had joined Country Gentleman after his graduation from the University of Pennsylvania, spent a year on the Ladies' Home Journal, then gone to his father on the Post in 1932 when he was 29.

It was Graeme Lorimer who brought in Martin Sommers in 1936. Sommers was certainly a sport in the Post galley. Son of a Lutheran minister, he had been born in St. Louis in 1900. Once a carnival strong man, he was city editor of the Cincinnati *Commercial Tribune* when he was 21. Following a string of reporting jobs on various other papers, he became a correspondent in the Far East, then night city editor of the tabloid New York *Daily News*. Chunky, almost an albino blond, with a big head, short-sighted light blue eyes, and the rasping voice of a "Front Page" newsman, Marty Sommers was one of Lorimer's most fortunate acquisitions.

Roughly, The Saturday Evening Post was all right, but decidedly the Ladies' Home Journal was not, and Country Gentleman never was. Under Barton Currie, a few others who were briefly on the job, then Loring Schuler, the Journal had lost circulation, advertising, and reader position. New surveys showed that women readers preferred *Good Housekeeping, McCall's,* and *Woman's Home Companion.*

Myron C. Leckner, who had been a Post salesman in Boston, then manager of the Chicago office, had left Curtis to become advertising director of the *Delineator.* Healey persuaded Leckner to return to help do something to restore the Ladies' Home Journal. They agreed that one weakness was that the Journal did not offer its readers the kind of service provided by the Good Housekeeping Bureau and the Good Housekeeping Institute. At *Woman's Home Companion* crusading Gertrude Battles Lane had established a Better Babies Bureau and set up a reader service.

Reporting directly to Healey and Lorimer, Leckner investigated the possibilities and made his recommendations. His young son-in-law, Robert M. Fuoss, typed out most of them on a rickety old Corona portable—and gained an education in practical magazine editing and publishing. When his recommendations had been approved, Leckner set up the Ladies' Home Journal workshop in New York. Leckner hired the complete staff, including Ann Batchelder, for the Workshop which was laboratory, kitchen, laundry, and all the other facilities and appurtenances for testing foods, fabrics, and other household necessities. Ladies' Home Journal was back in competition again and Leckner moved on to McCann-Erickson and agency advertising.

Graeme Lorimer brought in another associate editor on The Saturday Evening Post. Out of small towns in Iowa, Charles Bruce Gould, born in 1898, and Beatrice Blackmar married in 1923 after they left the University of Iowa and went to New York to conquer the literary world. They did not. They did odd bits of journalism, had a play produced by the Theatre Guild in 1929, wrote book reviews, and pursued the successful. Early in 1934 Graeme Lorimer told Bruce Gould that the Post could not use a piece he had submitted but offered him a job on the post at $6,000 a year. Gould grabbed it.

He wrote a few Post editorials which Lorimer rewrote and did other odd jobs under Adelaide Neall but made no great mark on the Post. Beatrice Gould did better. At a party she charmed George Horace Lorimer by telling him that he had made a hero-worshipper of her husband. As a result, or as a result of both his normal susceptibility to flattery and his shrewd appraisal of the capabilities of this country-bred and self-assured man and wife in combination, Lorimer dismissed Schuler and offered the Goulds the joint editorship of the Ladies' Home Journal at $25,000 a year. It did not take the ambitious couple long to accept. From that point in 1935 for the next 27 years the Ladies' Home Journal became, for better for worse, for richer for poorer, from diet to delivery, Bruce and Beatrice Gould. They restored the Journal to dominance and ruled both in Curtis and in the malicious and temperamental milieu of the women's magazines with queenly hauteur.

Lorimer kept his eye on Country Gentleman but made no fundamental changes in the magazine. Philip Rose continued as editor, with one of his subordinates Ben Hibbs, a Kansan who had joined its staff in 1929. Hibbs did minor work for the Gent, then was trusted with larger assignments. In February, 1931, he contributed "Rolling Back the Horizon, A World Drive for Good Roads." It was featured in an issue with Hugh McNair Kahler, Clarence Budington Kelland with another of his Westerns, and even Dorothy Dix. She said that the flood of letters she received at her home in Pass Christian, Mississippi, revealed a world-wide change in women. Listerine, Chrysler, and Octavus Roy Cohen were as prominent in the issue as "Body by Fisher." With Lorimer as Curtis head, the Gent no longer merely resembled the Post. It was a monthly Saturday Evening Post for countrymen and women.

A few years later Ben Hibbs wrote a long promotion piece for Country Gentleman. Distributed by Gent promotion between hard covers, "Two Men on a Job" lauded the collaboration and soul affinity between Rose and de Kruif. This was for public consumption. Hibbs was so discouraged under the difficult Rose that at one point he told his younger friend Robert M. Fuoss, then Country Gentleman promotion manager, that he intended to quit and get a copywriter's job in one of the New York advertising agencies. Fuoss, who had been early with Batten, Barton, Durstine & Osborn, laughed at the picture of shy Hibbs on Madison Avenue. "They'd eat you up!"

In March, 1931, Country Gentleman celebrated with a 100th Anniversary Issue. E. H. Taylor reviewed the progress of agriculture during the century passed. The issue made optimistic forecasts for the future of the magazine. Hugh Kahler was in again. Kelland was back. De Kruif wrote on "The Immortals of Medicine." A biography of Cyrus Hall McCormick was the typical Curtis business success story. Country Gentleman was 186 pages and rich with advertising. It looked a handsome and prospering centenarian.

Curtis was strong but competition was mounting. *Collier's* was inferior to the Post, and Lorimer considered *Liberty* under Bernarr MacFadden cheap, which it was. *Time* had moved up as a competitor for advertising. Then in 1936 both *Life* and *Look* were founded. They were picture books. Lorimer used photographs when he had to but fought the use of color photography. He was a print man who believed magazines were meant to be read. Radio was almost universal now. During the Depression it was the cheapest entertainment available and often the only kind a family could afford. All the blue chip advertising accounts, from automobiles to salad dressing, were in radio.

With Healey—whom Fuoss later described as the nearest thing to a publisher Curtis ever had after the death of its founder—Lorimer made drastic changes in Circulation.

They removed the department head who had been cutting activities to save cost and replaced him with the vigorous Ben Allen, a Philadelphian and a Penn Charter graduate. To that time Allen had been just one of the boys in a rough and often boisterous business. Curtis Publishing went further. In 1932 it transformed its Circulation Department into a separately incorporated subsidiary with Ben Allen as president. State taxes would be less on the smaller company which sold magazines within their borders. Curtis Circulation Company had its own officers and its own board of directors made up of its top executives and officers of the parent company. This proved a wise and profitable move.

The Curtis magazines, particularly Lorimer's Saturday Evening Post, were still dominant in circulation and as advertising media, but they had an inherent weakness born of their strength. They stood for something. They had a position.

Life was all pictorial drama and melodrama. *Look* at the time was a bucolic *Life*. *The New Yorker* was sophisticated urbanity or something like that. *Time* digested the news crisply and served up its crispies with smart assurance. *The Reader's Digest*—no advertising and circulation undivulged though it was known to be enormous—was mostly eclectic. They all reflected life or chosen aspects of it, but radio and the newer magazines stood for nothing in particular. They reported, but they assumed no responsibility for what they reported. Except, perhaps, for the *Digest*, they did not attempt to influence life in any direction. This was the new attitude.

It was not Lorimer's. The Post stood for business, success, America-for-Americans Americanism, and the time-honored virtues of manliness, integrity, and decency. If the newer magazines did not take a stand, Lorimer did. He intended to fix life in the pattern The Saturday Evening Post had long upheld, and he would make no concessions to the New Deal or to any deal at all.

Chapter 13

The Second Generation

When George Horace Lorimer moved up to the Curtis board chairmanship, there were strong contenders for the company presidency. The most competent was Fred Healey. He was a power in the company, knew it thoroughly, and was eminently qualified. He wanted the job, but he did not get it.

Older son of Edward Bok, William Curtis Bok attended Williams College and took his law degree at the University of Virginia. He became judge of the Court of Common Pleas in Philadelphia and later a justice of the Pennsylvania Supreme Court. Author of several books and a member of the Curtis trust, he never went into The Curtis Publishing Company.

His younger brother, Cary William Bok, did. After graduation from Williams in 1926 and two years at Oxford, he got his indoctrination in the Curtis New York office and in the Advertising Department in Philadelphia before he became, mostly *in absentia*, treasurer, a vice president, and director. Cary Bok could not see Healey as president. Largely through Bok influence, the Curtis presidency went instead to Walter Deane Fuller at the end of 1934.

Born in Corning, Iowa, in 1882, Fuller had sold the Ladies' Home Journal as a seven-year-old schoolboy in Norwich, Connecticut. He spent four years, 1899 to 1904, as a bank clerk, then began to sell dress patterns door-to-door for the Butterick Publishing Company. He became office manager for the Crowell Publishing Company, then for S. S. McClure. In 1908 he joined The Curtis Publishing Company, again as an office manager.

Fuller came to the attention of Cyrus Curtis when, using his bookkeeping and Butterick experience, he made a cost study of the small pattern business Curtis had at the time, showed that it was unprofitable, and Curtis dropped it. Fuller advanced through the business department, becoming secretary of the company, then a vice president. He was first vice president when Cyrus Curtis died and in his will made him one of his trustees, a position which gave him the inside track with the Curtis board of directors.

Fuller's accession meant little at first for Lorimer was still very much the effective head of The Curtis Publishing Company, but late in 1936 The Boss sent for Kenneth Roberts. He told him he was resigning as head of Curtis and editor of The Saturday Evening Post. Roberts had sent him the manuscript of the first half of *Northwest Passage,* and Lorimer had wired the Post's acceptance. He wanted Roberts to meet the new editor.

George Horace Lorimer had tendered his resignation August 1. Thomas Costain, who had hoped for the editorship, resigned after a disagreement with Lorimer. Having made useful connections in the literary mart, he went to Twentieth Century-Fox as its eastern editor. He did not last long and, after another job interlude, Roberts and Booth Tarkington helped place him as an editor with Doubleday in New York. Costain went on, of course, to write his series of best-selling costume historical novels: *Black Rose, The Moneyman, The Tontine, The Conquerors,* and the others. It was Wesley Winans Stout, who had worked under him for 14 years, whom Lorimer recommended for the editorship of The Saturday Evening Post, and Stout got the job.

When Kenneth Roberts reached the Curtis Building, he found that The Boss was out ill and that Graeme Lorimer was acting in his father's stead. The son explained that the Post planned to use the first half of *Northwest Passage* in seven parts and that a little cutting was needed. Roberts went to work on the manuscript in Lorimer's empty office.

After lunch Adelaide Neall drove him to Belgraeme to see The Boss. Lorimer looked and sounded the same to Roberts, but he could sense that something was amiss. He did not know what. Lorimer told him that the Post staff had wanted him to conclude his editorship with a Kelland serial but that he had insisted on "Roger's Rangers," Post title for the first half of *Northwest Passage*. Stout could start with Kelland. The Boss ordered Roberts not to change a word of the final installment.

The next day Roberts and Lorimer lunched on cold pheasant and beer at King's Oak. Lorimer kept insisting that he was glad to be leaving the Post. He said he had been brooding over a novel for years and wanted to get at it. He protested too much to a man who knew him well. Roberts stayed the night in the home of Adelaide Neall and her sister, all of them depressed by Lorimer's imminent departure.

The Saturday Evening Post of December 26, 1936, carried the first editorial George Horace Lorimer ever signed. It was his last editorial. Lorimer wrote that he had formulated the policy, planned the issues, made the final decisions, and read and selected the material in them. He alone was responsible. By unanimous decision of the Curtis board of directors Wesley Winans Stout would succeed him as editor. The editorial was brief and business-like, but Lorimer, patriot and evangelist's son, could not resist striking one last blow at the New Deal. "Everytime we enact a panacea into law, we take something fine and sturdy from the American character, for character cannot be improved from without."

The masthead of The Saturday Evening Post for January 2, 1937, read:

Cyrus H. K. Curtis, founder and president, 1883–1932

Walter D. Fuller—President
Philip S. Collins—Vice President and Treasurer
Fred A. Healey—Vice President and Advertising Director
Allen L. Grammer—Secretary
Lewis W. Trayer—Division of Manufacturing
Benjamin Allen—Division of Circulation

The editorial staff of the Post was Wesley Winans Stout, editor, and A. W. Neall, Graeme Lorimer, E. N. Brandt, Marion V. Reinhard, Richard Thruelsen, Martin Sommers as associate editors, and W. Thornton Martin as art editor with L. B. Kritcher his associate.

Though there was color in the advertising and it was packed with automobile advertisements, the editorial matter in the issue was all black and white. The by-lines of John Gunther and Corey Ford appeared, but the chief feature was a full-page editorial, "Au Revoir, But Not Good-Bye," opposite a full-page portrait of George Horace Lorimer. Lorimer had come to The Saturday Evening Post when it had 16 pages, 1,600 subscribers, and one-eighth of a page of advertising. Post circulation was now over 3,000,000. During his 38 years as its editor "He brought the Post from the status of an inferior weekly to the greatest magazine on earth in prestige, circulation and revenue."

Had The Saturday Evening Post been sold or discontinued publication on the resignation of George Horace Lorimer— both contingencies virtually forbidden by the Curtis will—it would have gone in glory. As Curtis had known, the Post was one man's accomplishment. It would have one more twenty-year period of competent editing and publishing success, but it would never be the same again.

The public poured out its admiration and sadness when Lorimer retired. What the public did not know was that Lorimer had not retired because he wished but because he had to. He was seriously ill. He went to Palm Springs determined to renew his interest and vigor, but the West did not inspirit him this time. In Philadelphia and in Wyncote again, he pretended to himself and his intimates that he was serenely happy, at least not despondent. He planned writing projects which he never started. Doctors finally discovered that what he had was throat cancer. Lorimer suffered greatly before he died October 27, 1937.

As five years earlier when Curtis died, tributes overflowed the newspapers and the Post offices. Enemies as well as friends acknowledged his greatness, his integrity, his skill, his understanding. They had to for they were on the record in 38 years of The Saturday Evening Post. Lorimer had been a man.

His authors were grief-stricken. They were professional writers, but none of them could use their skill now. They were too deeply moved. Booth Tarkington, Kenneth Roberts, Sam Blythe, Joseph Hergesheimer, Edwin Lefevre, and Garet Garrett were among the honorary pallbearers, as were jurists, Senators, manufacturers, merchants, university presidents, and bankers.

Stout, Fuller, and Healey represented The Curtis Publishing Company at the funeral, but Roberts, Blythe, Rinehart, Neall, Lefevre, and May Wilson Preston represented themselves and the Lorimer they loved. The Post had been part of their lives, often, it seemed the most important part and the most real. They held their own services at Adelaide Neall's after the funeral. They sat drinking scotch and talking of George Horace Lorimer. They laughed until they cried as one remembered some instance involving The Boss, and another told a story of Lorimer that he knew or they all knew. Kenneth Roberts wrote, "I'll swear Lorimer was in the room with us . . ."

In the perspective provided by Lorimer's death, it was quickly evident that Cyrus H. K. Curtis, Edward W. Bok, and George Horace Lorimer were geniuses. "Genii," with its suggestion of magic seems a better plural—the word used here to mean men of energy and intelligence who were in complete accord with their time and in the right place to exercise their temperaments and their talents.

Despite his quiet self-effacement, Curtis was a gambler who took frightening chances and won against long odds. He possessed what seems to have been an innate understanding of mass magazine publishing. Bok was creative, self-confident, and just as aggressive. He dared beyond discretion and time and again proved that he was right about what women wanted in a magazine. Untroubled by nuances in his masculine field with his masculine approach, Lorimer was as convinced as Bok but under no compulsion to vocalize himself or his intent. He was strong, controlled, incisive, and decisive.

These three men complemented each other. Through their concentration and force of character they dominated The Curtis Publishing Company and the magazine world, both of which they created.

They were followed in Curtis by men of lesser stature. Some were men of marked ability and most were well meaning, but the giants were gone and in some instances were succeeded by pygmies. All of the new men were salaried employees with no major financial interest in the business. They lacked force and vision. The company was directed by and for the Curtis trustees and the Bok Estate. The second generation of Curtis editors and executives inherited the most successful magazine publishing house ever built. Their job, as they saw it, was not to continue building but to keep the structure intact and the operation running smoothly.

"It almost killed Fred Healey when Fuller was made president instead of him," one of Healey's friends says, "but he took Fuller around to all the branch advertising offices, introduced him to advertisers, taught him all he could, and did his best for him." Healey almost had to.

Like Cyrus Curtis, or Benjamin Franklin, for that matter, Walter Deane Fuller was a self-made man, more self-made than most. Short, dark, erect, brisk in speech and movement, humorless, he was celebrated for years by the International Correspondence Schools as one of its most eminent graduates. He brought a first-rate bookkeeper's mind, conscientious devotion to duty, and a complete lack of imagination to the job of running a great publishing company.

Fuller saw himself as a cost-cutting curator for the Curtis board of directors and the Curtis trustees. He viewed The Curtis Publishing Company as Big Business, and he liked that. That for continuation of its success a magazine publisher must be sensitive to changing public taste and that his response must often come as much from quickness of wit as from cost

analysis was an idea which transcended the range of his awareness. The Curtis Publishing Company manufactured magazines, just as some other company manufactured soap and
another shoelaces. Fuller was careful about editorial, i.e.,
product, costs but almost oblivious of what his editors attempted or realized in other than monetary terms.

Under Walter D. Fuller, The Curtis Publishing Company
became, as it proudly boasted, the only completely integrated
magazine publishing enterprise. It grew its own trees in its
own vast forests to make its own paper in its own mills on
which to print billions of magazines in its own printing plant.
It was a way of investing Curtis money in Curtis properties
and avoiding contact with the dangerous outside world. Unlike its competitors, most of whom bought their paper and
contracted for their printing, and some of whom owned no
physical plant or properties at all, giant Curtis proudly owned
all it used and—slowly and expensively—did all its own work.

Sitting in the walnut-paneled fourth floor office that had
been Cyrus Curtis's, Fuller loved the trappings of office, the
kudos, the board memberships in other companies. He loved
to make the pretentious speeches he gave in response to in-
vitations proffered in acknowledgment of his position. Using
always the largest figures which company statisticians could
discover or concoct for him, he made broad economic pro-
nouncements and solemn forecasts. He mingled importantly
with the heads of other corporations in meetings of the American Manufacturers Association, of which he became president
then life-time vice president. He was impressed with his
standing in the Committee for Economic Development, the
National Industrial Conference Board, the Magazine Publishers Association, and the National Association of Office
Managers.

Walter Fuller looked and acted the part of Curtis president
and public figure in business, many thought, better than he
functioned in the job, and he held that job a long time. He
remained as president of The Curtis Publishing Company
until 1950. Then as chairman of the board he was effective

company head until 1957. Even after he stepped down from the chairmanship he remained on the board and one of its executive committees. Fuller spent 56 years with The Curtis Publishing Company.

Under Fuller, Benjamin Allen built the subsidiary Curtis Circulation Company into a formidable engine and his own empire. Curtis Circulation expanded and expanded. It had branch offices in all the principal American cities. It distributed Curtis magazines single-copy to over 100,000 newsstand dealers and had thousands of part-time or full-time subscription agents. It came to have its own catalogue agencies which sold many different magazines outright or on the installment plan.

Broken into Single Copy and Subscription Divisions, with hard-nosed, hard-selling men staffing each in the home office, the Circulation Company had the United States broken down into principal districts and these into scores of sections. They all held uproarious sales meetings. Staff men spent as much time on the road as in the office. They ran competitions and gave awards for years of service—gold cuff buttons, rings, pins —and prizes for meeting sales quotas and bonuses for outdistancing them. They sang the songs of selling and salesmanship until they were hoarse. They knew that magazines were not bought. They were sold. They boasted that theirs was a nickel-and-dime business, but they brought in the nickels, dimes, quarters, and dollars in lovely profusion.

Curtis Circulation always made money. Its books were always in the blackest of black ink. They could hardly be otherwise. The sales subsidiary had no manufacturing costs. It obtained its products, the magazines, free. It had no distribution costs and no overhead for it charged all these back to The Saturday Evening Post, the Ladies' Home Journal, and Country Gentleman. Then in 1938 Curtis Circulation started a magazine of its own, the first new Curtis magazine since Cyrus Curtis started the Ladies' Home Journal in 1883.

William Rudderow was for many years manager of the important New York office of Curtis Circulation. It was he who suggested the new magazine, and the Circulation board agreed. It was still Depression. They wanted another periodical to use as incentive with the field people. It would give them an opportunity to add to their commissions, thus whip them up to greater effort. What Rudderow suggested was a magazine for children. It would not cost much to produce, and Curtis could stand the expected manufacturing and distribution loss if it meant gains in another quarter.

Daughter-in-law of the editor of Country Gentleman, Ada Campbell Rose had been born in Cincinnati in 1901, graduated from Northwestern, then spent five years on the Pueblo, Colorado, *Chieftan* and two or three years as a textbook editor in Chicago. She was hired to study the market for a children's magazine. She reported that there was one if the magazine were for younger children, and Circulation offered her the editorship of the planned periodical. As the mother of two small boys, Mrs. Rose had the maternal as well as the journalistic qualifications.

She went to work with two women assistants, determination, and an ideal. Her ideal was the well-remembered *St. Nicholas* and Mary Mapes Dodge; her determination was to edit a good children's magazine. As one of a group of schoolgirls she had been asked what she wanted to be when she grew up. Her instant reply had been, "Editor of the Ladies' Home Journal." This was not the Journal, but it was almost as good.

The first issue of Jack and Jill appeared November, 1938. It was edited not for the approval of parents and teachers but expressly for its child readers. Successive issues kept unswervingly to that policy. Ada Rose put out a good children's magazine with serials, stories, verse, pretty pictures, puzzles, riddles, cut-outs, things-to-do, and especially pages given over to drawings and letters from children. The magazine went zealously after reader rapport from the start and quickly gained—and earned—the trust of its readers. Jack and Jill was literate and it was lively. The Curtis Publishing Company took over publication of the magazine which was an almost immediate success.

Circulation went to over a half million before the magazine was very old, and contrary to the expectations of its surprised founders, it made money. It took no advertising, but it cost little to produce. Salaries of the small editorial staff were low, and there were no other departments to support. As it paid little or nothing for contributions, editorial costs were insignificant. Teachers, mothers, and grandmothers were the Jack and Jill authors. Ada Rose or her dedicated and hard-working assistant, Anne Ford, rewrote the material. Nancy Ford wrote many of the best Jack and Jill stories herself. When the magazine, its costs still absurdly low, had become established, profits ran usually from $200,000 to $250,000 annually.

It is usual to discount The Saturday Evening Post under Wesley Winans Stout as a complete failure. It was not that bad. Stout had worked so long under Lorimer that it was natural he tried to imitate him and just as natural that he could not. He had other handicaps. One of them was that, unlike Lorimer, he did not have Cyrus Curtis behind him. Radio was universal, and magazine competition was more severe. The Post was losing writers to Hollywood and the fortunes they made or expected to make there. It lost other Post regulars because Stout lacked the judgment and tact of Lorimer; also, perhaps, because he was urged to keep costs down. Like many publishers, the new Curtis management looked on writers as a necessary evil. Most of them did not have ordinary common sense, thus it was ridiculous to pay them as if they were intelligent and hard-working businessmen.

Kenneth Roberts, who had dealt only with Lorimer, went to Philadelphia in 1937 to discuss a proposed new serial with Stout. He was disconcerted when he did not see the new editor alone but was confronted with a conference composed of Stout, Neall, Erdman Brandt, and Graeme Lorimer. Stout then announced that he had decided to accept just one chapter from *Trending Into Maine* and that he would pay $1,000 for it. Roberts was astounded and outraged. Then he saw that Neall, Brandt, and Graeme Lorimer were embarrassed.

Roberts objected to the price. Stout said that $1,200 was the most he could pay. Roberts told him that if the Post was really that hard up it could have the piece for nothing. In telling the story with indignation still hot, Roberts exclaimed, "He cuts my price in half, then asks me if I'm not satisfied!" It was 11 years before Roberts, his novels best sellers and strong movies, bothered to write for The Saturday Evening Post again, and then only for a new editor when the subject was one he felt he could not neglect.

Roberts was a writer and assumed that editors ran magazines. He knew and cared little about a publication's management. In the middle 1940's he asked a minor Curtis executive who was president of the company. He did not know the name when he was told that it was Walter D. Fuller. The Curtis man described him, and a light dawned. "That must be the little guy The Boss was always kicking out of his office!"

Tarkington offered to lower his prices when he knew the Post was hard pushed during the Depression. His correspondence, chatty, friendly, making suggestions and asking advice about his Mr. Rumbin series was with Adelaide Neall, not with Stout. They had known each other many years, but he addressed her always formally as "Miss Neall." The day of instant familiarity was not yet for men like Tarkington.

Clumsy with Post authors and sometimes inept with his staff, Stout made a physical innovation in the Post. Where Lorimer, almost angrily, had eschewed color, he experimented with it timidly. Colored rules and printer's ornaments, an occasional piece printed in red or green appeared. They made the Post look shabby and a little silly.

By generally poorer writers, many of the articles in Wesley Stout's Post were Sunday newspaper features on shiny paper. There were more Westerns, more boy–girl romances. The Post let up in its attacks on the New Deal. Roosevelt was in his second term. Most of the Brain Trusters had disappeared, but planned economy and government controls were fact. The Post still stood for free enterprise and cash-on-the-barrelhead common sense, but it seemed to lack firm subject or sharp point.

Stout did run some exceptional material. Thomas Wolfe made his first sale to The Saturday Evening Post which, because it paid well and promptly and reached a huge audience, was still the goal of most authors. His story, "The Child by Tiger," appeared September 11, 1937, and Wolfe delightedly planned to write more stories for the Post. His next submission was rejected, and he had little chance to try again, for he died in 1938. Stout continued the popular Glencannon stories of Guy Kilpatric. After the death of Ed Howe he ran a piece by the Kansas "philosopher's" son titled "My Father Was the Most Wretchedly Unhappy Man I Ever Knew."

September 7, 1940, The Saturday Evening Post published "The Atom Gives Up" by William L. Laurence, science reporter for *The New York Times*. In his article, which told of the work of German and American scientists, Laurence said that one pound of U-235 would have the explosive effect of 15,000 tons of TNT. The piece was so accurate a description of the possibilities of the atom bomb that the government forbade the distribution of copies of the Post containing it or tear-sheets during World War II. The War Department asked Laurence to write the official release after the United States dropped its atom bomb on Hiroshima.

Post editor before the Depression ended, Stout also had the misfortune to run into World War II which drew people's attention to more immediate matters, left advertisers with nothing to advertise except their names, and drastically cut the supply of magazine paper. Then, like editors before him and since, Wesley Stout was victimized by his own mistaken judgment.

He ran a series of articles on the Jews. The first was "Red-White-and-Blue Herring" by Jerome Frank; the second, "Jews Are Different" by Waldo Frank. The public read and accepted these with approval or at least without protest. March

28, 1942, The Saturday Evening Post published "The Case Against the Jews" by Martin Mayer, and there was an explosion. Cries of anti-Semitism were raised. Subscriptions were cancelled. Some advertising schedules were jerked out of the magazine. Posts were torn from newsstand counters and destroyed. The article was not anti-Semitic, but the unfortunate title was a red flag to U. S. Jewry at a time when Nazi Germany was systematically exterminating Jews in a pogrom which dwarfed all previous persecution.

This 92-page issue—wartime restrictions on paper had cut down the size of all the national magazines—opened with a story by William Faulkner, its title, "2 Soldiers," featured on a pale tint block. It carried an article by Boss Kettering attacking critics of the United States war effort: "There Is Only One Mistake: To Do Nothing." One of the serials was a murder mystery by Leslie Ford. "Heroes—Wholesale" was an article by the Post's staff contributor Richard Thruelsen. Seemingly no one noticed any of them.

In "Keeping Posted" there was an item about Martin Mayer which no one seemed to notice either. It said that Mayer, 33, had distinguished himself at the University of Chicago by being placed on permanent suspension for throwing beer bottles out of his dormitory window. It also said that his "scorn for his fellow American Jews is exceeded only by his scorn for the gentiles." No one cared anything about Mayer's scorn for gentiles. Many cared a great deal that the powerful Saturday Evening Post—they insisted—had attacked the Jews.

The Post was already in trouble and Stout in disfavor. There was nothing else for it. His resignation was promptly accepted.

Chapter 14

Resurgence of the Ladies' Home Journal

In Philadelphia it was socially correct to be with The Curtis Publishing Company. It was more than a half century old by 1935. It had made money, an accomplishment always respected on Broad Street. Curtis, Bok, and Lorimer had been figures of national importance; Curtis as a donor and Bok as a fund raiser and participant had been active in civic affairs. The Saturday Evening Post was conservative, and Philadelphia was conservative.

The Curtis Publishing Company was a family business. It was almost as if it were a shoestore, selling stout boots and patent leather dress shoes of the best quality, which had been established on Market Street in 1883. It was being run now for the benefit of the original proprietor's heirs, who were certainly entitled to enjoy the rewards of parental industry. The thousands of Curtis employees were fairly treated but not spoiled. If they came to work on time in the morning, paid attention to business, and did not question the decisions or eccentricities of their betters, they could look forward to steady employment at reasonable wages for the rest of their working lives. They also got free copies of The Saturday Evening Post, the Ladies' Home Journal, and Country Gentleman.

Curtis had been in business long enough so that at the top or near it there were intermarriages and family connections. Graeme Lorimer left in 1938 to write in collaboration with his wife, Sarah Moss Lorimer, but William Boyd's son went into the Advertising Department and attained managerial status. Boyd's daughter married the son of Charles Coolidge Parlin. Crippled by arthritis, Boyd attended the farewell dinner for the odd but brilliant research man in 1937 in his wheel chair. Ada Rose came to Jack and Jill through marriage to the son of Philip Rose. The son of another Country Gentleman editor became an associate editor on the Post. Before he left to become president, then board chairman, of the Benton & Bowles advertising agency in New York, Clarence Goshorn was one of the chief figures in Curtis Circulation. His son, Robert M. Goshorn, became circulation manager of Country Gentleman, then of American Home, and finally subscription vice president of the Circulation Company. Son of Walter H. Dower, John Dower became promotion manager of the Ladies' Home Journal. There were numerous other instances of friendly nepotism.

Curtis seldom went outside to fill top management or editorial spots. It felt it did not have to. It trusted its own—just as it distrusted the speed and slickness of New York, and the personalities of the new Washington. Curtis which had expanded under Curtis and Lorimer during its peak years was contracting now. This was not a deliberate move. It was a protective shrinking to security from what was new and disturbing. It was becoming parochial and a little withdrawn, rather like the older man replete with success retreating out of competition to live on his interest and dividends.

To be part of Curtis on its higher levels conferred a sort of cachet in Philadelphia. It was never as good as Episcopal Academy, then Princeton, then private banking, and the Philadelphia Club, but it had its standing. The proper Curtis editor or executive had some inherited income, preferably from Curtis. A graduate of some college or university, often Pennsylvania, he belonged to the Downtown Club, where he lunched, and to the Haverford Cricket Club, where he relaxed with other Curtis men of his echelon and their families.

Curtis meant security and a certain pride, but it was not without its problems. The Advertising Department had long boasted the preeminence of the Ladies' Home Journal. It could claim and its space salesmen could emphasize a long list of "firsts." The Journal was the first magazine to reach a million circulation, the first to use color printing in its advertising, the first to expose patent medicine frauds, the first to present architecturally distinctive house plans, the first to give its readers reproductions of fine paintings. . . . In 1935 Curtis Advertising made the startling and unwelcome discovery that all of these achievements dated back to the editorship of Edward Bok. For 15 years the magazine had accomplished no promotable feat. A new Journal crusade was indicated.

Because of his familiarity with the automotive industry and its leaders, Fred Bremier of Commercial Research was assigned to the job under Fred Healey. Editorial cooperation was assured, and the Ladies' Home Journal began a campaign for safe driving. Big Bill Knudsen of General Motors, Roy Chapin at Hudson, and Walter Chrysler all lent their support. The tire, oil and parts companies contributed. With the National Safety Council helping, some $1,250,000 was spent in an "I Will Drive Safely" campaign. This slogan was imprinted on stickers with a white cross on a red, white, and blue background. Gasoline stations distributed them. Towns and cities strung "I Will Drive Safely" banners across their streets. The campaign broke in the Ladies' Home Journal in 1936 with a lead-off piece by Paul de Kruif.

When he assumed the Journal editorship, Bruce Gould brushed the whole thing aside. The Automobile Manufacturers Association and the National Safety Council took the campaign over as a joint promotion, pushed it and got the deserved credit, the Journal none. Gould made a tour of the Curtis branch advertising offices and was unimpressed. He thought Curtis circulation and promotion men timid and said so. He scrapped a few hundred thousand dollars worth of manuscripts and art work already purchased for the Journal.

Bruce Gould brought an assurance at least equal to that of Edward Bok to the Ladies' Home Journal. An unshakable egotism has to be part of any strong editor's equipment, and the Goulds had that too. The Goulds had a Middle Western freshness. They had another quality too, the ability to back up their pretentiousness. Tall, mustached, big teeth prominent in his smile, Bruce Gould could be charming with the women on the Journal staff. As one of them, Beatrice Gould could be more realistic. This gave them an almost unfair advantage over the help. The women could win Gould's approval but know at the same time that they were transparent to his wife. It was safest to take refuge in deference that ran all the way from envious admiration to hero and heroine worship.

The Goulds overhauled the Ladies' Home Journal from bodice to bustle. The Journal had been getting cultural. It ran the antiquarian and archeological with its household hints and shopgirl fiction. It had begun to bore its readers. The Goulds changed some of the contents of the magazine and its direction. They strove to make it contemporary and to cover the widened field of women's interests and activities. Women were in and out and around and about the world now. They were at work in what had been men's jobs. They were interested in politics, community affairs, education, business, the professions, and often active participants. The Goulds targeted their Journal at these women.

At the same time they made the Ladies' Home Journal more feminine. They told women they were different and insisted on the femaleness of the female of the species. The new editors understood the delicious seductiveness of flattery and used it lavishly. They told their readers that they were women of fashion and charm as well as women of unappreciated intelligence. They brought women all the glamor and romance of New York and Paris. The Journal created an aura of boudoir intimacy with the celebrated; it was in on the secrets of kings and queens. It partied with the aristocracy of wealth and fashion and whispered all it heard and overheard.

At the same time the Journal told realistically of American home and family life, of marriage, conception, child bearing, and divorce. Bok's more genteel approach to women was too Edwardian for the tastes of the 1930's when women as well as men had been enfranchised from their scruples and hesitancies.

In a promotion piece a few years later, Beatrice Gould phrased what she and her husband believed and attempted from the beginning: ". . . we had one major idea—that the working intelligence of the average American woman was far greater than generally believed. It was our aim to bring our readers not only the most accurate and honest information possible in the traditional areas: health, nutrition, education and the moral guidance of children; community, social and cultural activities . . . but also to widen the boundaries of what had been considered her traditional areas of interest."

Mrs. Gould said it a little more personally and a little differently in the Ladies' Home Journal in May, 1949.

As my own life developed, as I realized more and more the complexity and fascination of housekeeping and motherhood, I became intensely interested in the opportunity of women's magazines—to interpret the present world fully and richly in women's terms; to bring women the best present information on nutrition, child guidance, home care, marriage, and to bring them also stimulation through articles and fiction.

This was looking back with pardonable complacency, and the phrases were turned after success had been achieved. Bruce Gould was more colloquial in a 1943 letter to the Journal editorial staff, but his point was the same. When they were offered the Journal editorship, he and his wife knew that no national magazine which had achieved leadership under one editor had ever regained its lost supremacy under another.

"So what?" we asked each other.

So we said, "Let's have some fun,"—and took the job.

Well, it seems that tradition, at least in part, has been upset. The Goulds lived in Hopewell, New Jersey, not far from where their in-law Dr. George Gallup, also out of Iowa *via* its university, was conducting his early studies on the readership of women's magazines for a large New York advertising agency. There was useful information and advice to be got from this source, and the Goulds put it to good use. In 1938 the Ladies' Home Journal published the results of a continuous series of nationwide surveys on what American women thought about war, marriage, divorce, and morals.

As Bok had done, the Goulds exploited women celebrities. One of their first coups was to obtain, through the literary agent George Bye, the autobiography of Eleanor Roosevelt. They paid $75,000 for "This Is My Story." Great admirers of Mrs. Roosevelt, they got her later—at $2,500 a page—to do a monthly column for the Journal, "My Day."

They returned to Bok again for inspiration, shock value, and social service in 1938 when the Journal joined the war on syphilis and urged passage of anti-venereal disease legislation.

In February, 1940, the Ladies' Home Journal began a series of articles on the lives and homes of typical American families. These pieces satisfied women's curiosity about their neighbors and were beautifully promotable for circulation and advertising purposes in the communities where the exploited families lived. Planned to run for one year, "How America Lives"— title changed to "How Young America Lives" to attract the youth market—was still running 18 years later.

The Goulds brought in Chicago-born Mary Bass, publicity director of the Brooklyn department store of Abraham & Strauss, as executive editor. They refurbished and redecorated the Ladies' Home Journal Workshop atop the RKO Building at Sixth Avenue and 50th Street in New York. They had their own New York apartment there where the Journal had its kitchens, parlors, reception rooms, its recipe testing, and its fashion shows. Bok's "Lady from Philadelphia" now had her own smart salon in New York.

The new editors chose wisely when they obtained Hugh McNair Kahler as fiction editor for the Ladies' Home Journal. After his long career as short story writer for the Post and the Gent he became a Curtis employee at 60, commuting from Princeton, where he had graduated. About half way between New York and Philadelphia, he spent several days a week with literary agents in New York and was adept at spotting bestselling novels in manuscript or proof for Journal serialization.

The Journal continued to run its superficial love stories with their unfailing clinch illustrations, but it also ran popular novels of superior quality, most often by well-known women authors: Pearl Buck, Edna Ferber, Mary Roberts Rinehart, Margaret Buell Wilder, Mignon C. Eberhart, Susan Ertz, Helen MacInness, Emily Kimbrough, Daphne du Maurier, Anya Seton. . . . It varied these with Nevil Shute, Lord Dunsany, Walter Lippman, J. P. Marquand, and Bill Mauldin.

Laura Lou Brookman, a Dakotan named managing editor of the Ladies' Home Journal, excelled in cutting down book-length manuscripts for serialization or one-shot condensations. Keeping everything in the author's words, she excised 75,000 words to 35,000 or 30,000 and even longer manuscripts to far shorter length. Deleting the extraneous, thus heightening the effect of the essential, she managed to edit to the satisfaction of both the author and the Journal reader.

All of the book-length material the Ladies' Home Journal used was not fiction. It ran Pearl Buck's moving story of "The Child Who Never Grew" and John Gunther's "Death Be Not Proud." It specialized in revelatory biography and autobiography: the stories of Fanny Brice, Ethel Waters, Princess Ileana, and of "The Little Princesses" of England. Some titles it was strange to find in a women's magazine at all. Among these were Henry L. Stimson's "Time of Peril" in which the lawyer and World War II Secretary of War told of his service under three national administrations, and "General Stilwell Reports," Vinegar Joe's story of the China–Burma–India theatre during World War II. Mary Roberts Rinehart, who had once refused the Journal editorship, later ran an editorial page for $25,000 a year under Loring Schuler, came back in with "I Had Cancer" in 1947.

Emotional and biological intimacy was another Journal specialty. The editors could safely assume that all of their readers were married, had been married, or wanted to get married. With "Dr. Spock's Talks to Mothers" it captured for Journal readers the pediatrician whose handbook on baby care had given him, and thus gave the Journal, almost a lien on babyhood. "Can This Marriage Be Saved?" thrilled Journal readers every month. The Journal was not close to home. It lived there. "Tell Me, Doctor" was copulation, menstruation, and obstetrics.

Girls working at Curtis would pick up their monthly issues of the Ladies' Home Journal with a grimace, a moue or some apologetically flippant remark about continuing their sex education or, coloring slightly, toss off a risqué witticism. *Playboy*, with especial attention to the Ladies' Home Journal pilloried the sedate women's magazines for their exploitation of sex under the guise of confidential advice to their readers. "The Pious Pornographers" by "Ivor Williams" accused them of "a furtively morbid preoccupation with the seamier, steamier aspects of sex," and the Ladies' Home Journal deserved the attention.

This Journal intimacy drew fascinated readers, but in its publicity the magazine preferred to emphasize its coverage of political and social events and world concerns. It could boast with justification of the Public Affairs department it started in 1947. The Goulds had accomplishments to boast of, and they seldom missed an opportunity. The Journal made a bright front-of-the-book feature of the doings of its editors in New York or abroad with an expert and generous dropping of names.

Whatever they may say in rationalization, editors edit for themselves. The Goulds did, but they also edited for the American women's pleasant conception of herself that with sweet unction the Ladies' Home Journal taught her to have. "Never Underestimate the Power of a Woman" the Journal told her, its advertisers, and the world at large year after year. Devised by an N. W. Ayer copywriter in 1941, it was an inspired warning, a prideful boast, and a useful slogan. The Journal stayed with it in clever cartoons which showed that women are different, that they spend the family income, that they change men's habits, that blithely and surely women rule the cradle and rock the world. "Never Underestimate the Power of a Woman or the Power of the Magazine that Women Believe In." The changes were rung on that promotional line with unceasing regularity and effectiveness.

In May, 1949, the Ladies' Home Journal celebrated the remodeling of the Journal Workshop with a full-length feature, "How the Journal Lives." It was a lush piece heavy with photographs in full color of Bruce and Beatrice Gould and their subordinates in company with food, fashions, kitchen utensils, Eleanor Roosevelt, Walter Fuller, Jose Ferrer, Helen Hayes, J. P. Marquand, *et al* against a background of exquisite decor and cocktail prattle.

It was a Journal boast that its editors were seldom at their desks more than two weeks of the month. They were out interviewing, attending fashion and decorator's shows, in the literary market, or on safari in Africa. In Philadelphia women Journal editors kept their hats on and their gloves atop their desks. Usually one earring lay there too, removed the first time the telephone rang. Hats and gloves were their mark of rank and distinction, notice to the world that they had come in only to open their mail before flying off into glamor.

"So brave, so full, so complete . . ." the Journal breathed in one promotion piece. The Journal, its editors told the world, was so young, so eager, so breathless with excitement. It was so girlishly fascinated and fascinating. Certainly it was successful.

Bruce and Beatrice Gould gave the Advertising Department the new "first" it needed. They made the Ladies' Home Journal first among all of the women's magazines in repute, circulation, and advertising, and they kept it there for over 20 years. Their Journal lacked the originality and strength of Bok's, but what Bok had done could be done only once. The Goulds' Journal was compelling enough. In 1943 Bruce Gould wrote lyrically:

It is what goes into the editorial pages of the magazine that makes this magazine live and breathe and sing. Each recipe must not only be accurate but enjoyable; each fashion fresh and useful; each decorative picture not only beautiful but faithful to our reader's needs, purse, and way of life. A magazine like ours is not a sales counter nor a peep show. It is a moral force. It must have integrity and respect for American principles, as well as entertainment and utility value. No formula will help us, no balancing of pictures or text, long articles or short, reprints or new. There is no possibility of laying down a pattern then following through. . . . Each issue must be created anew; one best issue carved and sculptured out of the hundred potential shapes that issue might have taken.

Every month during the last six months of 1942 Ladies' Home Journal circulation averaged 4,252,000. It was larger than *Life*. It overtopped The Saturday Evening Post by more than 1,000,000. The Journal now had the largest audited circulation of any magazine in the world. In 1952 it carried $9,000,000 in advertising. Gould prophesied that after the close of World War II this might rise to $1,000,000 a month. Just this once he underestimated the power of the magazine women believed in.

Out of Illinois *via* Princeton, Richard Ziesing joined The Curtis Publishing Company in 1926. He was the strong advertising manager of the Ladies' Home Journal. For many years Ziesing had his difficulties working with Bruce Gould, but Gould gave Curtis Advertising something to sell. As every space salesman knows, nothing becomes a magazine like being first. Nothing else really works.

Their indisputable success brought the Goulds gratifying recognition. On the resignation of Wesley Stout, Walter Fuller offered them the editorship of The Saturday Evening Post. The Goulds accepted—on condition that they also retain the editorship of the Ladies' Home Journal.

Fearful of such a concentration of power or that divided attention could not produce the desired results for either magazine, perhaps appalled by the greed, The Curtis Publishing Company refused the condition and looked elsewhere for a new editor for The Saturday Evening Post.

Chapter 15

New Editor and New *Saturday Evening Post*

The National Broadcasting Company operated both a Red and a Blue Network until 1941 when by a ruling of the Federal Communications Commission it was forced to divest itself of part of its operation. It offered the Blue Network to The Curtis Publishing Company.

Curtis refused the NBC offer, and the Blue Network was sold to Edward J. Noble in 1943 for $8,000,000 and became the American Broadcasting Company, Inc. Later Curtis could have purchased the Columbia Broadcasting System for about $10,000,000. It resisted the temptation without difficulty.

Dominated by the Curtis trustees and top Curtis executives dependent upon them for their tenure, the Curtis board of directors sat tight. It did not so much resist change as ignore it. It knew nothing of radio and with what a later editor of The Saturday Evening Post described as "its usual toplofty attitude" wanted no part of it.

Farm Journal had been founded in Philadelphia by Wilmer Atkinson in 1877. It flourished, then declined badly. A victim of the Depression, it was picked up by Joseph Pew of the Sun Oil Company to use as an anti-New Deal paper to help get the farm vote out for Alfred M. Landon in the Presidential campaign of 1936. After Landon's defeat its owner offered *Farm Journal* to The Curtis Publishing Company for nothing if Curtis would fulfill its unexpired subscriptions.

NEW EDITOR AND NEW POST   165

After brief consideration the Curtis board of directors rejected the proposal. After all, Curtis published Country Gentleman. It did not need *Farm Journal.* Curtis consistently avoided diversification and chose concentration. It declared for integration, not dissipation. Later these and comparable decisions would be looked upon as classic errors. At the time they appeared sound, or at least safe, judgment. The company knew how to create and distribute mass magazines. It did not know how to produce radio shows or sell air time. It had no wish to be in competition with itself—and Country Gentleman, then largest of the farm magazines, was usually in enough trouble to make tampering with it distasteful or even dangerous.

Curtis had restored the Ladies' Home Journal to preeminence. Now something had to be done about the difficulties which beset The Saturday Evening Post. Curtis looked around for an editor, but, as usual, stayed within itself. Other candidates were considered after the possibility of Gould was dismissed. As it had done before in selecting editors for its two bigger magazines, Curtis went to Country Gentleman and as its third choice took the editor who had succeeded Philip Rose only two years before. The editorship of The Saturday Evening Post was offered to Ben Hibbs.

Ben Hibbs was born in Fontana, Kansas, in 1901, but brought up in the tiny village of Pretty Prairie on the Kansas prairie. His fate was decided early when at the age of ten he broke into print in the *Pretty Prairie Times* and decided on journalism as a career. He edited his high school paper in Kingman, the county seat, edited the student daily at the University of Kansas, where he was janitor in a Methodist church, and during his senior year broke into the money as assistant to an English professor at $75 a month.

After graduation Hibbs went to work on a daily paper in Pratt, Kansas, population 5,000. He taught English and journalism briefly at Fort Hays Kansas State College, and by the time he was 27 was managing editor of the *Arkansas City Traveler* in a town of 15,000. Hibbs worked 12 hours a day six days a week on the *Traveler* and loved it. He had the job he wanted and William Allen White of the *Emporia Gazette* for hero. Like most young newsmen in Kansas, Hibbs heard White speak at meetings of editors, came to know him, and stood in awe of the national fame he had achieved with his small paper. Part of Hibbs' job on the *Traveler* was to prepare a daily half page of editorial paragraphs. It was these that brought him the astounding invitation to join the staff of Country Gentleman in 1929. Eleven years later he became its editor.

Six feet two inches tall, stoop-shouldered, shy and serious—a Kansas countryman after William Allen White—Hibbs did not leap at the chance to become the editor of The Saturday Evening Post. He was awed. The job was beyond his dreams. To him it meant that he would wear the mantle of Benjamin Franklin and sit in the seat of George Horace Lorimer. It seemed at the same time presumption and glory. Yet Hibbs knew magazines and their instability. He knew the precarious position of the Post at the time, the work that would be involved, and that, particularly under wartime conditions, there was as good a chance of resounding failure as of success. He hesitated. He asked Walter Fuller for 24 hours in which to make up his mind.

That midnight he telephoned Robert M. Fuoss, who by this time was doing a spectacular job as promotion manager of The Saturday Evening Post. He told Fuoss that he had been offered the Post editorship and that he would take it if he would go with him as his managing editor, a position which had not existed before. Fuoss agreed. The next day Hibbs said to Fuller, "I accept, and God have mercy on my soul!" He decided then and told his wife that he would keep the job for 20 years if he succeeded. Then, if he was still alive and in good health, retire.

The name of Wesley Winans Stout appeared as editor for the last time in The Saturday Evening Post of March 28, 1942. His associate editors were A. W. Neall, E. N. Brandt, Richard Thruelsen, Stuart Rose, Alan R. Jackson, Garet Garrett, De-

Maree Bess, and Jack Alexander. W. Thornton Martin was still art editor.

The names of Ben Hibbs as editor and Robert M. Fuoss as managing editor appeared for the first time the following week under the round Franklin medallion and "George Horace Lorimer, Editor 1899–1937," which Stout had promised would be kept on the Post masthead forever. The names of Neall and Garrett disappeared. Adelaide Neall had ended her long and important tenure, and Garet Garrett his long influence on The Saturday Evening Post.

Post Editor Ben Hibbs, standing, with Managing Editor Robert Fuoss. Courtesy of *Business Week*.

Another name, that of George Horace Lorimer, disappeared with the issue for May 23. By May 30, W. Thornton Martin was out of art and into letters. He was listed as an associate editor, and the page opposite the masthead carried an article on walking your way to health in wartime by "Pete" Martin. Frederick Nelson's name was added. He would write the Post's conservative editorials for years.

The change of editorship from Stout to Hibbs was not mentioned in the magazine nor did the new editor signalize his accession by any statement of intent and promise of performance. Hibbs was modest and wise enough not to jar his readers with any alarm of abrupt change or any promises he might not be able to keep. He stated his principles and purposes clearly and at length within the company, but not in Post pages. There was one statement, though, which he could not avoid. Over his fascimile signature he wrote in the issue for May 16, 1942, a half-page editorial titled "The Saturday Evening Post reaffirms a policy."

The carefully worded editorial, obviously prompted by Curtis uneasiness, expressed regret that the Martin Mayer article on the Jews which had provoked such a furor and unseated Wesley Stout had been "widely misunderstood." Hibbs wrote:

> The Post has never been, is not now, and never will be anti-Semitic in belief or expression. . . . we have always believed that a good American is a good American regardless of race or creed . . .
> That one misunderstood article in the Post should have caused so much anxiety in the minds of its readers is a matter of very real sorrow to the new editor. He regrets, above all, that some hurt may have been done to America at a time when national unity is needed as it was never needed before. He asks all Post readers to believe that these words are written in the deepest sincerity.

The repetition of the words "America" and "American" was characteristic of the Post. It was also characteristic of Ben Hibbs. He was deeply emotional about America. The rare reference to his personal feelings also described him accurately. As Post editor he was a quiet man who felt deeply about the values he valued. Though Hibbs was a Phi Beta Kappa of Kansas University, his response was always more emotional than intellectual. That was the Hibbs strength. He made his simplicity and sincerity pervasive in The Saturday Evening Post.

Hibbs looked upon the editorship of The Saturday Evening Post as a trust. Lincolnesque in appearance, he was the American of the prairie. His friends suggest that he has always felt a little alien in big cities. As Norman Rockwell phrases it, "Ben never threw his weight around at the Post." Even more than Curtis or Lorimer, Hibbs was self-effacing, but, unlike Curtis management and its board of directors, he was never averse to change, journalistic change, at any rate. On assuming the Post editorship he pledged allegiance, as it were, to the principles for which the Post had stood since 1899. He then described the "New Post" which he intended to produce. His plan was bold and comprehensive, and his statement of 1942 was detailed. It was both credo and blueprint.

I believe firmly in the American system—freedom of living—freedom of enterprise. Above all I believe that it is the patriotic duty of the Post to help keep alive in the minds of the people that free enterprise literally has made America—that it is the *only* system under which we can prosper and enjoy the fruits of democracy. . . .

The problems that confront the American people are staggering.

It is our responsibility to weigh, analyze, and explain these problems.

America's life will be affected by what happens in Brazil—Turkey—in Hong Kong—in Russia.

To the greatest degree in its history, the Post will report *and* interpret these happenings.

So much for generalities. The Saturday Evening Post would maintain its position. "America" and "American" reappeared. The word "patriotic" was used without apology or self-consciousness. Bulwark of the Curtis–Lorimer world, weakened by the New Deal, threatened by World War II, already suspect in many quarters, "free enterprise" would continue to be the religion of The Saturday Evening Post. It would defend it to the death.

Time and *Life* did not have to bother. *Life* had reached the magazine forefront with the speed of a rocket. It was smart, spectacular, and exciting. Its circulation shot higher and higher as the new magazine sped into popularity. World War II was made for *Life's* pictorial reporting. Whatever the magazine became, it was a picture book during the war.

It seemed to have more correspondents and photographers accredited by the War Department than all of the other magazines put together, and they sent back pictures from the various fronts which brought the actualities of the world conflict vividly to the American public. People looked at *Life* and listened to the radio, and it was almost as good as being there themselves. Glamorous and compelling, *Life* thrived. It did not have to explain America or the world or defend free enterprise. It had only to show what it saw.

By comparison with *Life*, The Saturday Evening Post appeared dull and stodgy, a fact as evident to advertisers as to readers. Lorimer had never had to combat *Life*. A year old when Stout took office, it sneaked up on the Post during his five-year term. Hibbs knew that he had to do something about the Luce competition.

Some changes will be made in the Post—new types of material will be introduced—we will make fundamental changes in typography—layout, style of illustrations, sub-titling, descriptive titling—

Frankly I do not see how any magazine can ignore the tremendous strides which the pictorial art has made in recent years.

Thirteen years in magazine work have taught me that authors can be thorough without being interminable.

We shall handle many of our subjects in much shorter length and we shall cover more subjects.

But let me emphasize that the introduction of short material doesn't mean that the Post will become shallow. Superficiality and brevity are too often synonymous; they are in some periodicals, but they won't be in the Post.

We shall publish more material to interest younger readers—avoiding trivialities—seeking a common ground in the issues that affect and influence youth.

We will give the Post more woman interest, but that does not mean we will become another women's magazine.

The Post will devote more attention to stories of American business.

The Post will devote more attention to informative war articles.

. . . it will do everything in its power to bring the ultimate victory that must be won if this world is to be a decent place in which to rear our children.

Hibbs and Fuoss redesigned the magazine. The Post's familiar script logotype was abandoned. In its place came POST in large black capitals, with "The Saturday Evening" over it in much smaller script type. Like *Life, Time, Tide, Quick,* and all the others, the Post now had a monosyllabic name.

Lorimer had put out a predominantly fiction Post. Articles predominated two to one under Hibbs. An issue usually contained eight articles to four short stories and two serial installments, and the articles, as Hibbs had planned, were shorter. The long-winded Garrett-type piece disappeared. Bright filler and a plenitude of cartoons—long a popular *Collier's* device—enlivened the back of the book.

Flouting a Lorimer edict, The Curtis Publishing Company had doubled the cover price of The Saturday Evening Post two weeks before Ben Hibbs took over. Lorimer had disliked pictures. Hibbs put in more and more photographs, some of them in color. He observed a convention and illustrated articles with photographs but fiction with original illustrations.

It *was* a new Post, with something of the old Post lost. It stoutly maintained the Curtis–Lorimer position, but it showed a new freshness, an alertness. Its shorter articles were more to the point. Its depleted fiction deteriorated. The magazine had a capable fiction editor in Erd Brandt, brother of Karl Brandt, the New York literary agent, but Hibbs liked boy, dog, open country stories, and westerns à la Clarence Budington Kelland. The Post had always run them, but Lorimer had published more substantial fiction as well. His generation of novelists and short story writers had mostly disappeared. Some were dead; others were no longer writing.

Robert Fuoss quipped that he fully expected to see a Post cover showing a 16-year-old boy walking through a Kansas cornfield with his dog. He teased Hibbs by saying that he looked like a benevolent funeral director. Certainly Fuoss did not. Born in Saline, Michigan, Fuoss, who was 29 in 1942, went to high school in nearby Ann Arbor and graduated from the University of Michigan in 1933. As tall as Hibbs and as spare, Fuoss was blunt, often caustic. He was sharp, decisive, and quick. Hibbs and Fuoss complemented each other perfectly. Fuoss was the Post's editorial executive. He was visible. Hibbs was not. Curtis people saw him, head bent, gaze downcast, walking to or away from the building, always at night or in the morning with a bulging bag filled with manuscripts. Even regular contributors to The Saturday Evening Post often saw him only in profile through the open door of his office, head bent over a manuscript, under a handsome banjo clock that probably was one of Lorimer's antiques. It was Bob Fuoss they dealt with.

Stuart Rose, horseman and man of British fashion, and Erd Brandt, tall, gently spoken Civil War buff and antique car fancier, ran back and forth to New York bringing back story and article manuscripts. At this point Marty Sommers, who had been made article editor, was back in the army, a major, then a lieutenant colonel on domestic and foreign assignments out of the War Department.

The Post was covering the war and supporting the government's wartime programs. It ran a series of full-page advertisements in full color to support the National Nutrition Program of the Office of Defense. In April and May, 1943, in conjunction with the U. S. Treasury Department, it staged an exhibition in Washington of Norman Rockwell's paintings of The Four Freedoms. The show sold $1,005,875 in war bonds and stamps. It ran a series of five poems, one with artwork to a page, as "Tributes to the Unconquerables," people who had been overrun by the Germans. The poems were used in a promotion with 280 department stores to open the Fourth War Loan.

The Curtis Publishing Company was much in evidence in the capital during World War II. Curtis men were stationed there in the Army, Navy, and Marines. Others were in the Treasury, the Office of Price Administration, the Office of War Information, and the War Production Board. Walter Fuller headed a paper production and reclamation drive.

Curtis already had its huge forest acreage in Pennsylvania and in Canada, but with magazine paper rationed during World War II, it undertook to increase the production of woodpulp for paper. It worked for the growing and harvesting of trees on small privately owned farms and organized community groups to collect old paper.

As housing and hotel rooms were at a premium, Curtis rented a house on Connecticut Avenue near the Calvert Street Bridge from a retired general, who left his cook and house-keeper there. Sommers, Dr. Alfred N. Watson, and Frank Strohkarck of Curtis Research, both in the army, were there part of the time. Many others were in and out. E. Huber Ulrich, special assistant to Walter Fuller, was in charge. Later Curtis took an office and a large apartment at 2400 16th Street, N.W., and in September, 1945, Ulrich opened a Curtis public relations office in the Public Ledger Building in Phila-delphia. Don A Brennan, Caskiet Stinnett, and Frank Har-rington, all just out of service, were the first men hired.

In Philadelphia, Hibbs and Fuoss were tightening, experi-menting, trying to revitalize The Saturday Evening Post and the public's attitude toward it. Their days went to planning, conferences, interviewing authors, making final changes in manuscript or proof. Hibbs in Narberth on the Main Line and Fuoss in Wayne, a few miles farther out, read manu-scripts every night six nights a week. Occasionally they could relax with their families at the weekend but not often and never fully. A weekly magazine comes out every week. There is always a new deadline. For safety the Post carried enough material in lead, set up in galleys, for two or three issues ahead, but this was always dateless material, articles, stories, and filler. A magazine made up from it alone would be deadly. It is a truism that any magazine is only as good as its latest issue, and the corollary is that every issue must be a little better than the one preceding.

Hibbs gave The Saturday Evening Post its principles and its tone. Fuoss contributed his alertness and perhaps gave it more immediacy. In 1944 Hibbs signed another editorial. It was nostalgic and sentimental. It was Ben Hibbs and his Saturday Evening Post. It was also an effective piece of prose. William Allen White had died. He had been an old-fashioned liberal who fought for the underdog, an optimist convinced that things would somehow be better, a man who loved men—and a Kansan. In The Saturday Evening Post with its millions of readers Hibbs made his tribute personal.

> . . . Bill White is gone from this earth, but he is not gone from my heart. And I can still be comforted by the primary tenet of his faith. I can still believe, as he did, that deep within humankind there is an ancient nobility which in the end must emerge—tarnished perhaps, but triumphant—from the darkness and anxiety of the years we now live.

An editor can edit only from what he is. He cannot deliberately and successfully edit up or down to his readers. Sarah Josepha Hale, Joseph Dennie, H. L. Mencken, DeWitt Wallace, Henry Luce, Harold Ross are a few cases in point. Hibbs learned his journalism on homespun small newspapers in the Middle West, then his magazine lore on Country Gentleman. As a mass magazine striving to please millions of readers and all the advertisers it could entice into its pages, The Saturday Evening Post had never been an intellectual publication. It could not be, and Hibbs could not edit for intellectuals. No more could he edit a showy and pretentious magazine. It was not in him.

The essence of the Hibbs Post lay in what he disclosed of himself in his farewell to William Allen White of Emporia. He had already said as much in an editorial memorandum to his staff: "All the shrewd planning and slanting in the world won't win readers . . . not the kind of readers the Post wants . . . unless a magazine is honest and unless it has a heart."

Hibbs shaped and warmed the Post. Fuoss managed its staff and gave an edge to the organization and the magazine. Within four years they had The Saturday Evening Post back on its feet and running hard and steadily again. Circulation was nearly 3,500,000. It would go over 4,000,000 in 1947. The Post stood number one in number of advertising pages, with gross advertising revenue of $24,368,000 for the first six months of 1946.

Largest of all the women's magazines with a circulation of 4,110,000, the Ladies' Home Journal grossed almost $19,000,000 in advertising in 1946. Even Country Gentleman was doing well. Its circulation over 2,800,000, it took in just about the same amount in advertising for the first seven months of 1946, $2,810,000.

Editing hard, promoting hard, selling hard, making the most of its completely integrated publishing business while some of its competitors were still plagued by wartime shortages, The Curtis Publishing Company was thriving again.

Chapter 16

Reader Traffic

In their reconstruction of The Saturday Evening Post, Hibbs and Fuoss had a new mechanical aid.

On the retirement of Charles Coolidge Parlin in 1938, Fred Healey recalled Donald M. Hobart from Cleveland to head the Commercial Research Division of the Curtis Advertising Department. Hobart had worked with Parlin from 1923 to 1928 and had done independent research in Cleveland in preparing his sales presentations.

During his tenure of 27 years Parlin had not only conducted many basic studies but also had helped refine the techniques by which they were made. The Curtis example had been followed by other magazine publishers and many business organizations. No longer a novelty, marketing research had become standard operating procedure. Survey methods had been improved. Questionnaires were more carefully prepared to avoid ambiguities or distortions in the answers of respondents. Interviewers were more thoroughly trained.

The greatest advance had been made in sampling. The findings of this kind of research are only as dependable as the methods used, and the sample had to be an accurate representation of the entire body of people or opinion reported upon. Quota sampling, asking questions of a specified number of people in various occupations, age, and income groups, and the like, had proved its unreliability in the *Literary Digest* poll of 1936 which showed that Alfred Landon would win the Presidential election by a wide margin. Area sampling, random sampling on an area probability base, was gradually taking its place. Marketing research was becoming more technical and more dependable.

The Commercial Research Division continued with its industry and consumer surveys, market studies, and studies of people's magazine habits. "Are You a Statistic?", 1939, was an analysis of Saturday Evening Post homes as markets for advertised products. Research made a Country Gentleman Reader Survey in 1940, and made studies of Quick Frozen Foods, Trucks, and Food Markets, all in a continuing effort to provide the Curtis Advertising Department with facts the salesmen in its various offices could use effectively in their selling.

Late in 1939 Research conducted an unusual survey. It supplied the Bureau of the Census with the names of 10,000 buyers of one issue of The Saturday Evening Post which represented a national sample of subscribers and newsstand buyers. As it conducted the 1940 census the Bureau located these families and supplied Curtis with all the tabulated census information for the 10,000. This gave Curtis a broad and accurate picture of Saturday Evening Post families compared with the national average. Published as "Sample Census of Post Families," this was the first use of U. S. Census material in this way.

All of this was research done for advertising purposes. Hobart brought in industry experts to strengthen his staff. He started a special library in advertising and economics which became one of the best in the Philadelphia area. Made up mostly of vertical files of clippings from government sources and from some 300 periodicals regularly read and received, these filed under 3,000 subject heads, the Curtis Research Library came to be used almost as much by university students of business and faculty members in the Philadelphia area as by the various Curtis departments and Curtis advertisers. Hobart expanded his statistical section to handle the mass of data brought in by personal interview, telephone, and mail surveys. An art section prepared the charts and graphs based on this material.

At the same time research of other kinds was being conducted.

As another special assistant to Walter Fuller, John Daley of Curtis Circulation had started the rudiments of a kind of editorial research. Herbert C. Ludeke, an M.I.T. civil engineer whom Hobart had brought down from the Boston office was placed in charge of this. Essentially this editorial research was intended to find out what readers liked in the Curtis magazines, what they did not like, what kinds of articles and stories they wished to read and what kinds they did not. The results of this product research, which is really what it was, were not broadcast. They were confidential and for the eyes only of the top Curtis editors. Hibbs used some of these findings of editorial research in redesigning Country Gentleman when he became its editor in 1940. He and Fuoss used much more of it in reconstructing The Saturday Evening Post in 1942.

To bring the various research activities of the company together and free them from the suspicion of bias inevitable while they were still under the control of Advertising, Curtis founded an independent Research Department with Donald M. Hobart as manager in 1943. On the table of organization this was a major department reporting directly to the company president and on a par with Editorial, Advertising, and Circulation, but it had a fundamental weakness. It had no operating funds. Appropriations for all surveys and studies had to come from the Curtis departments that wished or agreed to have the work done.

The Research Department was set up with a number of industry specialists in automotive and aviation, food and drugs, housing, and other categories. It had its media men, one attached to each of the principal Curtis periodicals who worked in Research but for the advertising department of a given magazine. The department had three divisions: Commercial Research, the Development Division, and the Management Planning Division. The last existed only on paper. It consisted really of the advice of Hobart—who became national president of the American Marketing Association, a Curtis vice president, then senior vice president and director of research—using the facilities of his department as they were needed in company councils.

Herbert C. Ludeke was placed in charge of the Development Division. With a small staff he conducted reader surveys on a regular basis on all the Curtis magazines with the exception of Jack and Jill, which did not have the money to spend and felt it knew its readers and what they liked without need for tabulated statistics. Findings of the reader research were turned over to the editors, who were free to accept and use them or to reject and ignore them. Stout called the effort "Hobart's mumbo jumbo," and would have nothing to do with it. The Goulds used it to check results but, generally, not in planning. Country Gentleman, edited now by Robert Reed, was always glad of any help it could get. Hibbs approved, and Fuoss, who liked facts and their utilization, watched the findings of editorial research with sharp interest.

Both men made it clear that they could not and would not edit by arithmetic. They considered reader research an aid to editorial judgment. Always as hyper-cautious as he was tall, Ludeke was careful to make no extravagant claims for his work. The Development Division did it. The findings went to the editors, and there it ended. Ludeke and his assistants devised several means, some of them novel, to test reader reactions, but the Research Department's best device was the regularity with which it conducted what it called its "Reader Traffic" surveys. They were conducted on every issue of the Ladies' Home Journal, every other issue of Country Gentleman, on two issues each month of The Saturday Evening Post, and, after it was founded, on every issue of Holiday. Thus a fund of information was built up, a continuous case history. This obviated some of the difficulty inherent in survey procedures where questions are asked by fallible human beings of other fallible human beings, and moods, weather, digestion, stupidity, and even deliberate falsification can distort results.

Before it could proceed confidently with its reader surveys the Curtis Research Department had to have the answer to one always bothersome question. Who is a reader? It could not use the mere lookers, scanners, or liars. It decided that a reader was an individual 15 years of age or older who showed that he had at least looked through the issue of a magazine under study. Research then needed some test which would indicate the reliability of reader answers to questions asked. The Development Division solved this one ingeniously.

Research built a laboratory designed to look like a living room, then asked a group of people to help with a test of eye fatigue from reading. Test subjects were given an examination on a telebinocular instrument, then seated in the room with a receptionist, given a pre-publication copy of a Curtis magazine and asked to read for an hour and a half. Their actions were observed through windows with one-way glass and recorded. At the end of the hour and a half the unsuspecting subjects were given a second eye test.

Between 24 hours and 14 days later, still before the magazines they had read were released, interviewers were sent to find out what the subjects remembered having read in the living room laboratory. Their answers showed a remarkably close correlation between observed and reported reading. Thus editorial research could be conducted with some confidence in its findings.

This much established, reader traffic surveys were begun. Each time personal interviews were held with several hundred readers who constituted an accurate sample of the magazine's readers. Interviewers showed the reader a copy of the magazine's issue being studied, then went through it with him, item by item asking: Do you recall seeing this item? Did you happen to read it? How much of it did you read? What did you think of it—excellent, good, fair, poor, or very poor? Using the same scale, interviewers also asked readers' opinions of the issue as a whole and their opinion of the cover. Re-

spondents were classified by age, sex, income, education, occupation, and family composition.

Whether or not they believed in the value of research of
this kind, editors followed traffic survey results eagerly. They
discovered for each editorial item the percentage of "read all."
The higher the percentage, the more popular the feature had
been. If it was high, it verified their judgment and they felt
triumphant. If it was low, they usually felt that the research
was at fault.

Readers research gave Curtis editors clear indication of
what types of articles and stories had consistent popular appeal and what other types would, in all probability, obtain
only low readership. They could be fairly sure that—provided
it was adequately written—if they bought and published this
piece with fitting illustrations, the public which read their
magazine would like it, but that if they bought and published
this other piece, the reaction would be unfavorable. With
enough research findings behind them, they could publish
safe issues with few failures.

This was the danger. Research could not appraise the
unusual piece in advance. Uninspired statistics could not create an inspired article. The blind following of reader traffic
findings could produce a profitable, perhaps, but a standard-
ized and lifeless product. There were times when it did, just
as there were other times when it helped avoid pitfalls.

Occasionally reader research wrought significant and successful innovations. There had been few medical articles in
The Saturday Evening Post. Traffic surveys and special studies showed that they had high potential reader interest. The
Post tested this finding with some trial articles. Their acceptance verified the research. The Post installed a science editor
and began to run medical and scientific articles with some
regularity. Research showed that people were interested in
Post covers and wanted to know the stories behind them. An
editorial item about the cover became a regular Post feature.
Reader interest in letters to the editor was checked. People
liked them so letters columns were instituted in all the Curtis

magazines. Research discovered that while readers tolerated serials they preferred stories complete in one issue. The Saturday Evening Post and the Ladies' Home Journal began to run more one-shot condensed novels and novelettes.

It was found that people liked larger illustrations, illustrations in color, explanatory subtitles—but liked them better if they were placed before the title as pre-titles. Readers wanted informative picture captions placed close to the picture. They liked cartoons as separate items, not as illustrations for an article or story. Women readers liked illustrations of a boy or a girl and courting couples in Journal fiction, and they liked close-ups.

In an overall report Ludeke summed up much of the results of this continuing investigation into reader preferences. It showed that people generally preferred the straightforward, simple, and orderly presentation of editorial material. Ludeke said, "We believe in and make practical use of editorial research at The Curtis Publishing Company, research that is not intended to supplant but rather to supplement editorial judgment and skill. There is nothing mandatory about using the results of research. Quite often an editor must fly in the face of a known popular appeal if he is to maintain the character of his publication. But with research to keep him informed, an editor can be bold with his eyes open." [1]

Obviously, reader research often merely supported the conclusions of ordinary common sense, but it did give some certainty to hunches. As one Curtis editor remarked a little unhappily, "Reader research is a great leveller among editors." Sometimes it could do a little more. With many of the other resources of the Research Department it was brought to bear on a new Curtis venture at the end of World War II.

[1] Ludeke, Herbert C., "Magazine Editorial Research, a Progress Report" (Philadelphia: The Curtis Publishing Co., 1956).

Chapter 17

Holiday

World War II ended. The manufacturers of tanks and tank treads, machine guns, LST's, K rations, gasses, ammunition, G. I. medals and caskets, and of thousands of other items of military and naval material switched back as quickly as they could to beating out shiny new plow-shares. Geared to wartime production, industry raced to reconvert to civilian production and profits. In feverish competition, advertisers had to regain lost markets, build new ones, and convince and sell them before the other fellow could.

It was a sellers' market. There was a pent-up hunger for everything and anything, preferably with chromium on it. People had gone without new cars and the fuel for their old ones or the tires to roll them on. Household appliances were antiquated, and many of them were worn out. New families needed new houses as the armed forces discharged their millions. Out of uniform, men wanted cuffs on their trousers again, white shirts, bright ties, and some wanted their waistcoats back. Women wanted all the wonderful, wonderful new clothes. Food rationing had people slavering for food and plenty of it and drink and plenty of that too.

Radio could prate of the super-heated desirability of the new cars, refrigerators, condiments, watches, soups, and wonder drugs, but it was only talk. At best, it was only song in catchy commercials. Radio could not show the driveability, edibility, and drinkability of all the joys it touted. It could not depict the enticing new products in gorgeous full color. It could not depict them at all. Only the magazines could do that, and they were doing it with abandon. Magazine circulations had gone higher and higher during the war. Now, swollen with advertising, the magazines thrived as the world returned to a kind of peace and Americans burst into riotous purchasing.

Curtis was not caught unprepared. Its postwar committee had been planning strenuously. It was willing to meet the demands of advertisers and reap the new fortune. As soon as the restrictions were lifted, Curtis designated all its newly released supplies of magazine paper to the use of the advertiser. Conversely, *Life* squandered its sudden wealth of paper on enlarging and improving its editorial content. Curtis made the immediate gain, but at the end of a year, *Life*'s circulation was a million more than that of The Saturday Evening Post.

Curtis also formed and implemented other plans. It meant to publish several new magazines. One, Magazine Z, would be a weekly news magazine after the manner of *Time*. Magazine X would be a pictorial magazine comparable to *Life*. Imitativeness, and it would become more apparent, was a characteristic of the second Curtis generation, but the idea for its third new magazine, Magazine Y, was not imitative at all. It came straight out of Curtis management. Curtis editors, and they resented it, were not consulted at any point.

One of the most attractive and widely advertised concepts to come out of World War II was that of the "New Leisure." Industry had developed new techniques. Mechanization and automation would take over all the work of the postwar world. It would take all the work out of work. The powerful labor unions were all writing more and longer vacations, more paid holidays, earlier retirements, larger pensions, and shorter work weeks into their new contracts. Government and private organizations adduced millions of statistics to prove that the United States would henceforth wallow in *dolce far niente*. People would have oodles of money to spend on all the accoutrements of inaction—cameras, bathing suits, travel, food, swimming pools, toothpicks, cars, lollipops, avant garde letters and paintings, liquors, and the appropriate costumes to enjoy them in.

Walter Fuller was fired by all he heard of the New Leisure at the CED, the NAM, the MPA, and the other forecasting or trade bodies which vied with each other in issuing optimistic prophesies. It was law at Curtis that the editors of its magazines work without interference from the business department. Editorial integrity was a Curtis fetish, and to a remarkable degree editorial sanctity was seldom profaned on Independence Square. Yet, as editors know too well, everybody is an editor, and management, always a little envious and convinced it could do better, is often particularly eager to try. Here was its chance.

It became obvious to Walter Fuller and his advisers that the manufacturers of all of the accessories of the new leisure, from imported trinkets through cars and cosmetics to domestic toys, would desperately need a slick magazine in which they could tell people newly enfranchised from effort of all the things they could buy to make their new lifelong holiday supportable. Fuller's speech-writing assistant, Frank Beaman, was assigned to prepare a dummy for such a magazine.

Beaman concocted his dummy by clipping and pasting sports, travel, and art material from other magazines and photographs showing happy people being happy. Thus Holiday was born. From the start it was not an editorial or journalistic idea but a commercial grappling for the spilling-over spoils of a postwar bonanza. Holiday was mechanically contrived. It came out of a cold incubator. Planned as a major Curtis venture, it was to be a "class" magazine with as much circulation as could be obtained for a periodical with a fifty-cent cover price and content designed for appeal to the consciously discriminating afficionados of the New Leisure.

From all available sources the Research Department gathered and painstakingly analyzed consumer expenditures for travel, entertainment, hobbies, and acknowledged recreation in general. The market for the proposed magazine was defined as including not only monies expended for amusements, sporting goods, theatre tickets, and the like, but also for all the indirect expenditures involved, such as those for food, drink, clothing, hotel or motel accommodations, and everything else incidental to the conscientious pursuit of pleasure. This generous definition, of course, produced proof of an almost illimitable market.

Curtis Research then conducted two large personal-interview surveys, each with 2,500 respondents.

The first survey was on travel. Its findings showed that 76 per cent of the sample interviewed expected postwar summer vacations, and that 90 per cent of them expected to travel inside or outside of the United States. There was a definite travel market.

The second survey was on sports and recreation, hobbies and entertainment. Again the findings were convincing. Everybody wanted all of them and would spend liberally to get them. The new magazine would show them how.

To this point the proposed publication was called "Magazine Y" or "Go" or "Play." After hard individual and conference cerebration the name "Holiday" was adopted. Beaman was named editor, and the nucleus of an editorial staff was formed. A second and more elaborate dummy was prepared.

The Research Department analyzed it item by item. Space salesmen who had been hired for the new magazine toted copies to advertisers and agents. Circulation showed copies to wholesalers and subscription agencies and indoctrinated its own sales staff. In November, 1945, Research conducted a Holiday "Acceptance Test" in selected cities. Copies of the dummy were left in magazine-reading homes so that interviewers could call back, ask questions, and record answers which would give Curtis some idea of the possible impact of the new magazines.

Final decisions were made on book dimensions, paper weight, and initial print order. Curtis made a cost and income analysis for the first five years of publication. The first issue of Holiday went on sale to charter subscribers and newsstand buyers February 20, 1946.

The Research Department now checked results of the appearance of the magazine it had helped bring into being. Editors and advertisers wanted to know what kind of people bought and read the new magazine by age, income, sex, and the other demographic characteristics.

This time Curtis Research sent mail questionnaires to subscribers. More questionnaires were inserted in the April, 1946, issues distributed from Curtis Circulation offices in 101 cities geographically representative. Returns from both subscribers and newsstand buyers betokened a high degree of interest in Holiday. As far as Research could discover Holiday was going to be all right, probably a little better than all right. Reader traffic surveys were instituted and more specific research was undertaken to delineate the Holiday audience.

No other magazine had ever been so carefully pretested and post-tested. Replete with creative satisfaction, Curtis management predicted a flourishing and profitable life for Holiday. It was a little too sanguine too soon. The trouble was that the first issues of Holiday were flaccid. The magazine seemed to have no point or purpose. Physically splendiferous, it read like a chamber of commerce brochure. The photographic layout was a jumble. Curiosity and snob appeal had sold the first copies.

In New York, Magazine X, which never eventuated, was in preparation under the direction of Ted Patrick. Born in Rutherford, New Jersey, Patrick had been a Young & Rubicam copywriter for 14 years, then, 1942–1944 chief of the graphics section of OWI. He had come to Curtis after a short period with the Compton advertising agency. Curtis brought Patrick to Philadelphia and made him the new editor of Holiday. With him Patrick brought Harry Sions, a Philadelphian and 1928 graduate of the University of Pennsylvania who had been editor of *Salute* then a combat correspondent with the Italian edition of *Yank*.

Patrick took Holiday in hand after the appearance of its third monthly issue. From then on for most of the years of its publication under Curtis, Holiday was the product of Patrick with Sions, who became senior editor, then editorial director, and Frank Zachary, originally from Pittsburgh and an OWI feature editor whom Patrick brought in as art director in 1950. A geographer and a graduate of Clark University in Worcester, Albert Farnsworth was hired early to build and run the Holiday editorial library which was established in Philadelphia. Some years later he became assistant to Patrick.

For a long time Holiday was an unsure entity. Research might be able to define its advertising market, but Holiday did not have and did not discover any firm editorial identity. Patrick and his aides made it lush, gave it an exciting appearance, and suffused it with a kind of surburban glamor. Holiday was never for the vulgar, yet it was never for the cognoscenti.

Handsome, pretentious, expensive looking, it hung suspended somewhere between something that was not quite and something else that was not at all. Patrick was bedazzled by the fashionable and the famous, the jet set, the resort crowd, the very rich in the fabled resort areas of the world. He celebrated the joie de vivre of the bon vivant in the beau monde, or something like that. Sions dealt skillfully with name and no-name authors. Zachary gave Holiday its sound design. None of them could give Holiday substance or ordinary reality. In avoiding the ordinary Holiday impinged on the unreal—of which it was, perhaps, the magazine reflection.

It was ten years before Holiday was solvent, and even Patrick himself could not quite describe it except in vague negatives. He tried more than once when Circulation and Advertising needed statements they could use.

Patrick insisted—probably because Curtis insisted he insist —that Holiday was not a travel magazine. That would limit its market. It could not be a hobby magazine. What hobbies? It was all of them. It was not just fun and games. It had meaning. What meaning? Holiday, Patrick said, was the magazine of "creative leisure," though what creative leisure was neither Patrick nor anyone else knew. Patrick tried:

Creative use of leisure time includes travel, but also other activities . . . all sports, the theater, movies, television and radio, music, painting

or writing indulged as a pastime, the reading of good books, the preparation and pursuit of food, party-giving and attending, the fixing of one's
home to make it more rewarding and relaxing to live in and the making of
acquisition of the clothing best designed for any of these activities.

Patrick sounded badgered in this promotional blurb which
Curtis used in its advertising. His mission was not to define
but to live graciously and to tell Holiday readers what gracious
living was wonderfully like. He did show, as he was supposed
to, that the market for Holiday advertisers was boundless.
Food processors, airlines, railroads, travel agencies, the manufacturers of baseball bats, tennis rackets, and badminton sets
could all cash in. So could the makers of the proper clothes
for listening to radio or watching television. Purveyors of
correspondence courses in writing or painting would find an
appreciative audience of amateurs in Holiday.

Patrick looked upon European aristocracy, celebrity-fre-
quented New York restaurants, American inherited wealth,
smart jazz spots, the French and Italian Riviera, Rome, Paris,
London, and the way-stop capitals of the continent and found
them good. He felt about them in the terms of an ace copywriter. He loved the things that excited him, and his magazine conveyed his excitements over wines, foods, new places
if they were for the correct people, and the savoir faire that
he admired.

He obtained manuscripts from New Yorker writers whom
he knew. He got Pulitzer and Nobel Prize winners into Holiday—Faulkner, Sandburg, Steinbeck. He made Ludwig Be-
melmans, Sean O'Faolin Santha Rama Rau, and Jerome Wied-
man Holiday writers. He got Joyce Cary for a fine piece on
Oxford, J. P. Marquand to do the late George Apley's Boston,
Hamilton Basso to write about New Orleans, James Thurber
to do bloodhounds, William Carlos Williams for a piece on his
New Jersey home town, and John Steinbeck and his dog to
travel the United States in a camper and report on it.

Patrick featured Clifton Fadiman on books, Lucius Beebe
on sybaritic enjoyment, Leonard Lyons for smart chitchat,
and Silas Spitzer on gourmet dining. Smartness, urbane so-

phistication, and cosmopolitan knowingness were the Holiday idea. Every issue was rich with fine color photography. Holiday used Tom Hollyman for many of its travel stories. It used the still lifes of Arnold Newman, the society portraiture of George Aarons, the aerial photography of Lawrence Lowry, the character studies of Henri Cartier-Bresson.

Some of the muzziness of Holiday's rhapsodic approach was cleared by the place pieces which became a staple offering. Holiday did all of the major American cities in impressionistic rather than statistically factual treatments, then it went back and did them again. One of Patrick's policies was to use novelists to write these non-fiction pieces. He felt that the imagination and creativeness of the professional story writer gave lift and added depth to the result. Place pieces led to place issues. Whole numbers were devoted to Paris, Italy, Rome, London. Frank O'Connor's full-length treatment of Ireland in Holiday for December, 1949, was notable. The photographs by Tom and Jean Hollyman were superb, and the article was both evocative and trenchant. E. B. White did the brilliant study of New York in 1949. The Paris issue of April, 1953, was a full-dress presentation, and Holiday's depiction of London in April, 1956, was rich and sturdy.

Holiday ran good writing by good writers, yet some of the text in most issues, even when by well-known writers, was unreadable. Articles lacked substance or point. Perhaps because Patrick usually paid less than the going rate, perhaps because Holiday, writers felt, demanded something different but they did not know quite what, their work in Holiday sometimes lacked clarity or direction. Readers looked at the profusion of excellent illustrations, enjoyed the look and feel of the magazine, then discovered they could find little in it to read with interest and attention and put the copy aside or on the coffee table for display. They had a feeling that visitors would be impressed. The casual presence of Holiday in the living room indicated that you were traveled or artistic or a man or woman of distinction, at least that you could afford a fifty-cent magazine.

Holiday produced outstanding issues, but it was usually the
dilettante reveling in his dilettantism. The splendid looking
magazine did not focus. Holiday celebrated its tenth anniversary with éclat and large amounts of self-congratulatory
appreciation. The cover for March, 1956, was a birthday cake
bearing ten flickering candles. Type surprinted on two layers
of the tall cake said: "For the past decade this magazine has
been the voice of the biggest change in our times, crier of the
new leisure in which you live more fully, live better, enjoy
more personal rewards. With this edition we bring you a
significant portrait of your own golden present . . ."

It was not Holiday's fault if many who read the lines did
not realize that they were enjoying more personal rewards in
their golden present, but, just in case, the Holiday editors
explained once again in oversized display type inside the issue.

The human animal consists of three living entities: the body, the mind
and the soul. Each must be sustained; each must be given its food, its
exercise and its pleasures. For an individual to learn how to provide
these necessities of life to his own three entities is to learn the secret of
constructive leisure. . . .

Holiday's start, 10 years and 121 issues ago, was coeval with the start
of this era of New Leisure. It was our reason for being and has always
been our dominant editorial philosophy. We feel it fitting, therefore,
that it become the theme for this entire 10th Anniversary Issue.

It was evident that the Holiday editors were sincerely
moved. Holiday seldom mentioned the soul or acknowledged
the Y.M.C.A.'s eternal triangle of body, mind, and spirit. It
seemed almost out of character even in the sentimental mood
engendered by a tenth birthday.

On the same occasion a Curtis copywriter struggled with
his assignment. Perhaps in his determined rhapsody he came
a little closer than the editors in pinning down the elusive
magazine.

Holiday is pleasure anticipated, pleasure experienced, pleasure remembered. . . . Holiday is catholic in its tastes; pagan in its enjoyment . . . a poet's appreciation of Rome, an artist's delight in the Rhine
Valley or the farmlands of Iowa, a philosopher's appreciation of Greece,
a boy's excitement at a county fair. It is a debutante's thrill at her
coming-out, a hunter's quickened pulse as he stalks big game in Africa,

the sloth of a fisherman dropping his line in the Mississippi. Holiday is appreciation of the genius of Toscanini and a fat man's mouth-watering happiness as he orders his dinner at Antoine's.

Holiday was started with commercial and editorial research. None of the Curtis magazines ever got further from it. Its nebulosities confounded. Holiday did not sound like Curtis. It was not Curtis, and Holiday never really became Curtis. As a "class-mass" (or "mass-class") magazine it could not compete in circulation with The Saturday Evening Post, the Ladies' Home Journal or even Country Gentleman. The Circulation Company found it desperately hard to sell. During the ten years celebrated Holiday circulation just about doubled, but it went only from 427,000 in 1946 to 856,000 in 1956. Advertising did come in, and it rose from $1,707,883 in 1947, its first full year, to $5,859,135 in 1956. This was fractional in comparison to the advertising revenue of the Post, the Journal, or, again, even Country Gentleman. It was also expensive to obtain.

Chapter 18

Dynastic Change

A big man physically, Fred Healey had been an athlete at the University of Illinois and was an enthusiastic alumnus. At the Army–Illinois football game in 1947 with Arthur H. Kohler, another big man who had been an athlete at the University of Michigan, Healey was stricken with a fatal heart attack.

Fred Healey had been the strong man in Curtis advertising and management for years. He was the last of the giants. No man of comparable stature followed him. A perceptible decline in the quality of top executive personnel set in. It was almost a regular regression and marked through the late 1940's and the 1950's. It was also noticeable that—quietly observing a practice familiar in many companies—men in prized Curtis posts made sure that their associates and assistants constituted no threat to their tenure. On the business side The Curtis Publishing Company was staffed in many key positions by second-rate men and men who could not aspire to that classification. Curtis had no second line of defense. Added to the absentee landlordism which made this situation possible, this weakness kept Curtis contentedly and innocently vulnerable. Though they seemed to occur more through the impersonal operation of the laws of chance than through management planning, there were, of course, exceptions to the general rule.

Arthur Kohler was appointed director of advertising in Healey's place. It was a natural appointment. Born in Lansing, Michigan, in 1890, Kohler had joined Curtis in 1925 as a space salesman for the Ladies' Home Journal in the Philadelphia office. An outstanding salesman, he had become Philadelphia manager, then manager of the important New York office, then manager of The Saturday Evening Post.

As advertising director Kohler had at first only one major problem. Mainstay of Curtis, The Saturday Evening Post was second to *Life* in circulation. The Post had always been first. Curtis and Curtis salesmen were not used to the secondary role and did not quite know what to do about it. There is only one comfortable place for a mass magazine to be—first. It has to be the biggest. Curtis Research and Promotion were hard put to it to prove that the Post was biggest in everything but circulation.

People, Research proved and Promotion shouted, believed what they read in The Saturday Evening Post. People loved and trusted the Post. The Post was "Big, Believed, Beloved." The Post had more readers who owned their own homes, had two cars, played badminton, held executive positions, invested in stocks, believed in astrology, or whatever the claim, than any other magazine. Media buyers did not care that The Saturday Evening Post was first in war, first in peace, and first in the hearts of its countrymen. They wanted the magazine with the largest circulation.

Curtis certainly had the biggest printing plant. From the start on Arch Street Curtis had done its own printing and presswork, and its typographical standards were high. Cyrus Curtis had made it a point that his magazines be well printed. The Curtis Publishing Company was justly proud of the physical excellence of its products. Composition was done by fine craftsmen in the Curtis Building on Independence Square, and the presses roared there day and night.

In 1892 Cyrus Curtis, anxious to make the advertising as well as the editorial pages in the Ladies' Home Journal attractive, placed a want ad in the Boston *Herald* for a typographical expert. In his experience, good men came from Boston. John Adams Thayer applied at the Boston office of the Journal and got the job in Philadelphia. After Thayer resigned, Curtis went to Boston again and from a type foundry hired John B. Williams, who became Curtis manufacturing head. These men and those who followed them were typographical experts, jealous of their profession. They brooked no interference from editorial, advertising, circulation, or any other Curtis department. They placed the composing room and the press rooms out of bounds to amateurs. When he became vice president and superintendent of manufacturing, Lewis W. Trayser set his department completely off limits. The usual comment at Curtis was that Manufacturing operated behind a Chinese Wall.

Trayser wanted only the best, insisted on it, and got it. Curtis spurned rotogravure, offset, and any of the newer methods of printing. It stayed with the finer and much more expensive letterpress. The Curtis Publishing Company went further. After long planning and in the flush of wartime and postwar prosperity, it spent $1,000,000 in technical research, then went ahead with construction of a mammoth printing plant which would be one of the largest and most modern in the United States.

Like most of its magazine publishing competitors, Curtis could have contracted for its printing. This would obviate huge capital expenditure and be cheaper, but the work might not be up to Curtis standards. The company would have to depend on outsiders for prompt and adequate performance. With the tremendous volume of Curtis presswork this would be risky. The Company also wanted to continue its policy of investing Curtis funds in Curtis and to further its vaunted complete integration. There was the added argument that it was economically unsound to continue to conduct a huge manufacturing operation in the Curtis Building in an expensive downtown Philadelphia location.

In Sharon Hill, a few miles outside Philadelphia, construction was started of a 15-acre plant on a 108-acre site. The

The Curtis Plant at Sharon Hill.

Sharon Hill plant began operation in 1947. The plant, the presses, and the entire operation were a marvel of technical efficiency. Curtis Public Relations—grown to a body of a dozen men with their secretaries and assistants—pointed out that two football games could be played at the same time with umpty-ump spectators looking on in the Sharon Hill plant. Public Relations conducted daily tours of the new facility, and the sight was awesome.

It took a year to build one of the high-speed, four-color YY presses, and in time there were 12 of them turning out millions of copies of Curtis magazines every working day. The YY presses, three stories high, ran at speeds up to 18 miles an hour. Once they were set up—and makeready took several days—and the proper buttons were pushed, these presses, seemingly, could go on forever. It was cheaper to overrun by a few thousand copies than to stop one. One-ton rolls of paper from the Curtis Mills in Johnsonburg and Lock Haven, Pennsylvania, went in one end; magazine sections, printed, dried, and folded flashed out of the other. Conveyors took the sections through the bindery and the completed magazines to the loading platforms. The monster presses were served by 1,000 men and women working in eight-hour shifts. In all of its operations, including its wholly owned subsidiaries, The Curtis Publishing Company employed some 10,000 people, about 8,000 of them in the Philadelphia area for Curtis itself.

Later a huge offset press, known at Sharon Hill as "The Green Hornet," was built to print Reader's Digest Condensed Books under contract. It spilled out 12,000,000 copies of books of 600 pages each a year. A "Little Green Hornet" was installed to print Jack and Jill. The main roller got out of round, and for about a year Jack and Jill went back and forth from offset to letterpress.

The capacity of Sharon Hill was enormous. Just one of the YY presses could print 18,000,000 magazine pages in two, four, or even five colors every 24 hours. Even all of the Curtis books could not sop up this capacity which was one of the severe limitations of the mammoth plant. Presses were often idle. They were marvels for producing magazine pages in color at high speed; they were anywhere from uneconomical to impossible to use for short runs or black and white. They were practical only for manufacturing the Curtis magazines.

Another and more severe liability was soon sharply manifest. Printing The Saturday Evening Post, the Ladies' Home Journal, Holiday, and later American Home at one point on the east coast and having to distribute all copies from there for release nationwide on the same date meant long closing dates for both editorial and advertising material. In general the editors could get around this competitive disadvantage by pat timing of their articles, but advertisers could get their sales messages into print and before the public more quickly in other periodicals. Some of the multimillions spent in construction and operation of Sharon Hill were invested in building strict limitations into the business operation of The Curtis Publishing Company.

Walter Deane Fuller moved up to become chairman of the board in 1950. He relinquished little of his power, in fact he added to it, but the presidency was open. There were immediately numerous strong claimants to the throne with not a whispered *nolo episcopari* among them.

One was Benjamin Allen, who had built the Curtis Circulation Company into one of the most powerful periodical distributing organizations in the country. Another was Lewis Trayser, who had triumphantly engineered the building of the Sharon Hill plant. A third was Arthur Kohler who as director of advertising was in close touch with the sources of Curtis profit. Significantly, no editorial man was considered to lead the company. George Horace Lorimer was the last Curtis editor who was also company president. No outsider, of course, was considered.

There was a fourth candidate. Robert Ernest MacNeal, company secretary and in effect its business manager, was a Fuller protegé. Ben Hibbs used his strong influence with

the Bok family in his favor. Added to Fuller's recommendation, this was enough. MacNeal was made fourth president of
The Curtis Publishing Company.

Son of a glassblower, who perforce turned salesman during
the Depression, MacNeal was born in sandy, piney South
Jersey in the small town of Medford in 1903. He went to
school in larger nearby Glassboro then, of necessity, went to
work in one of the area's large glass factories when he was 13.
He worked at various jobs and became an installer and tester
for Western Electric when he was 18. Friends told him that
Curtis was a good place to work. They arranged an interview, and, aged 20, MacNeal was hired in 1923.

His first job was in Scheduling, estimating the press runs
for issues. Mechanically ingenious, he redesigned a folding
machine for the Post binders. He decided that an outmoded
press could be made to work as well as the one which supplanted it, had parts of two old presses made into one machine, and proved his point. He did some photographic work.
He liked target shooting. Early, he built his own television
set. MacNeal did other things, but he had one overriding
interest, The Curtis Publishing Company.

From Scheduling, MacNeal moved into Standardization,
the Curtis time-study operational engineering department,
where he was just one of a number of men with desks in a
large room. This job enabled him to take a hard look at
almost every corner of The Curtis Publishing Company. Attracted by his energy and competence, Fuller sent him to San
Francisco to hunt down new and growing companies that
could be developed into Curtis advertisers. In two months
on the coast MacNeal found none—but then no one else did
either. He was made manager of Standardization in 1934,
assistant secretary of The Curtis Publishing Company in 1937,
a director in 1942, and secretary in 1943.

Robert MacNeal was the complete company man. He had
come up through engineering, manufacturing, and accounting.
He carried on the Curtis–Fuller tradition of the self-made
man, even to the Fuller correspondence course. Strictly an

inside man, a factory man, he was an untiring worker who liked and understood detail. He had traveled, but his world was Philadelphia, where he had an apartment with his wife, who had been a Curtis girl, and Ocean City, New Jersey, where he had a summer home, but mostly the massive Curtis Building on Independence Square. He reached it early every day, and he left it late. MacNeal's appointment guaranteed continuance of Curtis's insularity from New York, Washington, and other points and points of view without the pale.

Unlike Fuller, Bob MacNeal had a sense of humor and a quick wit, dangerous indulgences in an executive. He had no side. Because he had been one of the workers and knew their problems, he understood printers, pressmen, shipping clerks, and the ordinary run of Curtis employees. For internal direction Curtis could not have found a better man. For the development of plans that entailed working in the outside world he lacked education and experience. No one at Curtis worked harder—or perhaps as hard—as MacNeal, but for the first seven years of his administration he had a frustrating handicap. Walter Fuller had merely changed his title.

Herself an indefatigable worker, Jack and Jill's Ada Rose came in early one morning in 1954 to rush some revised proof to the composing room. She found MacNeal already there.

"Morning, Bob, how's the boss?" she called breezily.

MacNeal looked at her soberly. "I don't know. I haven't seen him yet this morning."

MacNeal liked to swap things. Once it was a rifle for a camera he wanted. He got the camera. "Of course," he reflected, "the guy didn't know it was a left-handed gun." MacNeal had defective vision in his right eye. He swapped his cars until he had a Cadillac. MacNeal was quick, and he was a realist.

In 1954 Country Gentleman with General Foods celebrated the 25th aniversary of quick-frozen foods with a big black tie dinner and cocktail party in Washington. Both the processor and the magazine had a stake in the industry, hence the promotion. The Secretary of Agriculture spoke. Dignitaries of government, business, and publishing sat at the head table. The press was there in force. After it was all over and Milton L. ("George") Peek and his staff could relax, MacNeal sat with Donald Hobart, Trudy Dye, women's editor of Country Gentleman, and a few others in the Statler bar. A group of happy college-age revelers came in. MacNeal looked at them.

"Oh, to be young again!" he said.

The Country Gentlewoman touched his arm reproachfully. "Oh, go on, Bob!"

"Go on and what," MacNeal asked her, "Shoot myself?"

It was comfortable at Curtis as MacNeal took over. The Saturday Evening Post was taking in about $60,000,000 a year from advertising. The Ladies' Home Journal led all the women's magazines. Jack and Jill came pattering sturdily after. Holiday was costing money, but a great future was seen for it in the halcyon world of moneyed leisure. Curtis employees had not noticed the leisure yet. For all but manufacturing units, office hours were from nine A.M. to five-fifteen P.M., not five o'clock as in lesser companies. In almost every department everyone, even highly placed executives, punched the time clock. Salaries were paid in cash brought by armored trucks, not by check. There were a minimum of paid holidays, six a year. Even then, these were not guaranteed. Each time as the day approached, an official memorandum made the rounds. It said that if all work was caught up The Curtis Publishing Company would be closed on Christmas Day, or whatever the feast.

Privileged employees rode the front elevators. "Second Registry" workers came in the Sansom Street side entrance and rode the back elevators. Dean of the elevator men, Buford Tighlman ruled the lobby elevators. Tighlman heard all, knew all, and told all to his intimates. If Tighlman counted you one of his friends and you were allowed to call him by name, you were in at Curtis; if not, you remained an outsider. No messenger with a package ever got into one of the two front elevators next to the white marble bust of Benjamin Franklin when Tighlman was on duty, and Tighlman was no respecter of rank. He ignored editors or management men he disliked and was pointedly cordial to lesser mortals of whom he approved. He would stare past self-important personages, slam the heavy bronze doors shut behind them, and his car would ascend viciously, no one venturing to speak if Tighlman showed that grim silence was expected of them.

At Curtis there were none of the frivolities, such as Christmas bonuses that marked fly-by-night enterprises like banks, department stores, or ordinary companies. Curtis was national, permanent, as safe as the Bank of England. It seemed as solid as its building, and that was unshakable. Curtis had overflowed the structure. It had offices in the Ledger Building, and Advertising, Research, and Holiday were housed in seven floors of the Penn Mutual Life Insurance Building, diagonally across on the southeast corner of Sixth and Walnut, but the Curtis Building was the castle of the feudal Curtis domain.

Curtis in these years seemed to partake of the nature of Independence Hall and the old American Philosophical Society in the square across from it. Independence Square was green under tall old trees. It had its characters whom most Curtis people knew. "The Silent Talker" walked its paths. He addressed the trees with impassioned gestures but uttered no sound. Then there was "The Dancer." Rouged and painted, exquisitely dressed, dark eyes burning, he swung his hips as he minced past. Then, to the delight of cheering boys and the amusement or sympathetic repulsion of older onlookers, he would break into his stately dance. No one molested him. Like The Silent Talker, he belonged.

In spring, summer, or fall the humid Philadelphia air outside the Curtis Building was thick with rich odors. It was easy to tell whether Campbell's, just across the river in Camden, was canning tomato or split pea soup. The smells of the Delaware itself rolled up Market, Walnut, and Chestnut to meet the heavy sweetness from the Whitman's chocolate factory near the Philadelphia entrance to the Benjamin Franklin Bridge.

For years Curtis had two men who, according to a Post editor, were there for just one reason. They were Eberhard Mueller and Frank Stiefel.

Mueller had served under Funston in the pursuit of Aguinaldo, then became a meteorologist in government service in the Pacific. He had become a sharp practical economist and a securities expert who, as assistant treasurer, worked on the Curtis investment portfolio.

A big man who, like most construction men, was seldom seen with his hat off, Stiefel was the iron-willed building superintendent. According to the Post editor, the two men were there to tell you that whatever you wanted to do could not be done. Mueller would explain that it was financially impossible and Stiefel that it was physically impossible.

An amateur painter and an unbridled decorator, Stiefel rose to glory each year in decorating the Curtis lobby for Christmas. The Curtis Choir sang its carols almost buried in stars, spangles, greens, toy trains, and ornately framed originals of Post and Journal covers. Crowds of Curtis workers listened happily at noon of Christmas eve before returning eagerly to unsanctioned parties in their own departments.

After he became president—he would hardly have dared before—MacNeal liked to boast of his one victory over Frank Stiefel. He suspected that an exhaust fan in the kitchen of the dingy employees cafeteria on the tenth floor was not working properly. Stiefel insisted that it was. MacNeal ordered it taken down for inspection. It was found then that the fan faced into a solid brick wall built during some forgotten reconstruction.

The Curtis trucks, well-kept big green electrics of World War I vintage, rolled noiselessly through the narrow streets of downtown Philadelphia at tops speeds of ten to 15 m.p.h. They were as familiar a sight as Franklin's grave or Elfreth's Alley and looked almost as old. They carried huge rolls of paper or stacked bundles of magazines. Sometimes they carried people. During the recurring street car strikes in Philadelphia they picked up loads of Curtis employees from various gathering points and carted them slowly but irresistibly to work. Pleased with the idea, one young woman said she felt like Marie Antoinette in her tumbrel on the way to the guillotine.

She spoke in jest for Curtis was no guillotine. It was home. There were often flash fires, quickly extinguished, in the press rooms where some of the old presses were still used for Country Gentleman. One which caused more smoke than usual emptied the whole building into the street and brought the fire engines. It was lunch time. Crowds of workers enjoyed the excitement from the street. The Curtis research librarian, Louise Moore, was not so fortunate. She was caught alone with the operator in one of the two front elevators when the power was cut off. Smoke poured up the shaft. Sirens screamed and the bells of the Philadelphia fire apparatus clanged in the street below. Freed finally through the escape hatch in the elevator roof, she dashed not into the street and the open air but back to her desk on the eighth floor of the almost empty building. Safety seemed to lie not in escape but in return to Curtis. It affected people that way.

Because there was no sharp competition among them there was little infighting or sycophancy among major and minor Curtis executives. Discouraged by Curtis gentlemanliness, the unpleasantly ambitious and aggressive went elsewhere. Curtis was not their kind of place. It was old and conservative Philadelphia. At the same time it was Middle Western.

The editors of The Saturday Evening Post, the Ladies' Home Journal, Country Gentleman, and even little Jack and Jill had all been born and bred in the Middle West. They retained their freshness, honesty, and innocence, their belief in the simple virtues, and their distrust of Yankee shrewdness, big business, big labor, big government, and the big world that menaced the United States. This was correct, for they were editing for the great American middle class to which they belonged. They had an unconscious rapport with their readers that was stronger than their deliberate attempts to give them what they thought they wished.

It was tranquil, even modestly buoyant at Curtis. Under a reproduction in color of the board-room portrait of Cyrus H. K. Curtis, The Saturday Evening Post ran proudly, June 17, 1950, an editorial which opened with these paragraphs.

Recently a Post reader ended a pleasant letter to the editor by saying: *If Cyrus Curtis were alive today, I feel sure he would approve of the way The Saturday Evening Post is being edited.* We hope it is true. At any rate, whether the reader knew it or not, it was the finest compliment that could have been paid to the editorial staff of the Post. For Cyrus Curtis, who was born just 100 years ago, on June 18, 1850, was perhaps the most discerning and exacting magazine publisher this country had ever known.

Because Mr. Curtis was a man vitally alive, he inspired vitality in his magazines. Because he was a man of great integrity, he insisted upon honesty and decency in his publications, both in the editorial contents and in the advertising pages. Because he was a human being and was enormously interested in people, and also because he possessed a shrewd, intuitive understanding of popular reading tastes, he was able to build a group of magazines which now go into millions of homes every week and every month.

In other words, very little had changed. "Honesty" and "decency" had lost some of their standing, but Curtis was still for them. Reading was becoming outmoded too, supplanted by looking. Television did not, like radio, start slowly. Held up by the war, it galloped ahead. There were 3,000,000 sets in use by the end of 1948; 18,000,000 by the middle of 1952 with 110 commercial transmitters operating. By 1956 the numbers were 37,000,000 and 450. The networks had been established for 30 years. Television was a strong advertising medium from the start.

A few in Curtis had foreseen its promise and threat. In Research, Bremier urged a study. Hobart agreed. Though it was not too impressed, Advertising provided the funds. Five thousand personal interviews were conducted on a random sample base. Respondents were asked in 1947 whether they had seen television, liked or disliked it, whether they planned to purchase television sets. The response showed an overwhelming interest in radio gone animatedly pictorial. People would rush to buy receivers as soon as they were available in quantity. Magazines had a new and strong competitor for the time and attention of the public as well as for advertising.

Curtis mimeographed the results of this survey for internal use but did not publish them for general distribution. If what the survey showed was true, Advertising did not wish to publicize its electronic foe. It was better to mark the report "confidential"—the usual practice when a survey did not come out favorably for Curtis magazines—and bury it in the files.

Bremier then made a still more confidential report to the Curtis board of directors, presenting the startling highlights of the survey and, in view of the evidence, urging that Curtis get into the new and promising field quickly. Though he had agreed to conduct of the survey, Walter Fuller just sat and listened. He made no comment, offered no suggestions, and provided no support for the recommendation. Some of the other board members asked polite questions.

Then the Curtis board shook its communal head and repeated its standard declaration. "We're in the publication business."

Chapter 19

Postwar *Post* Writers and Editors

Lorimer had worked with a small editorial staff, giving assignments to regular contributors to The Saturday Evening Post who remained independent writers. Hibbs and Fuoss enlarged the staff. *Time, Life,* and some of the other newer magazines were entirely or almost entirely staff written, and the Post went part way. It added men who were listed as editors but who were in reality the magazine's own writers. Less of the Post's nonfiction came in from outside sources; more was produced by Post editors who were writers in Curtis employ.

An associate editor of The Saturday Evening Post for more than 20 years, Harold H. Martin was as consistent and characteristic a writer for the Hibbs Post as Kenneth Roberts had been for Lorimer's. Born in Converse, Georgia, Martin was one of Dean John E. Drewry's graduates at the Henry W. Grady School of Journalism of the University of Georgia in nearby Athens. He got a job on *The Georgian,* the Hearst paper in Atlanta. When it was sold to the Cox interests and combined with the *Atlanta Journal,* Martin went along, and Ralph McGill put him to work as obit editor of *The Atlanta Constitution.* Martin was writing a column called "Dreams and Dust" for the *Constitution* when he did his first piece for the Post in 1942 just after Hibbs became its editor.

It was a colorful little back-of-the-book piece for which the Post paid Martin $350. At a weekend the commanding officer of an artillery unit at Camp Stewart, Georgia, got orders to move out quickly. Army funds for the troop movement were in a bank with a time lock on its vault, and, because it was Robert E. Lee's birthday, the bank would not open on the Monday. The worried officer called another banker whom he knew. The second banker could not provide the money, but he had friends who could. Gamblers, lottery operators, and madames turned in all their take, cash in bills and change amounting to $66,000, and the artillery went rolling along.

A big man, Martin got restless as the war progressed. Most of his friends were going into service. He quit the *Constitution* and for a short time managed the Roxy Theatre in Atlanta—30 Beautiful Girls! Count 'em! 30!—and hated it. He applied for Navy officer's training but was turned down because of a deviated septum. His surgeon father-in-law undeviated it, but the Navy said it was not sufficiently healed for it to take a chance on him. Martin went down the hall to the Marine Corps, which did not care one way or another about his nose, and it sent him to Quantico. He emerged an intelligence officer, who exercised his intelligence by writing color bits about the Marines and sending them back to the *Constitution*. Impressed, an obliging superior officer had orders cut so that Martin could ply his trade in a larger area and more usefully for the Corps. These orders gave Martin a roving commission to cover the Pacific. He could fly anywhere he wished and do anything he liked as long as he wrote about Marine Corps Aviation. He filed his stories from Guadalcanal, Okinawa, and where else the Marines had landed.

The Marine Corps sent them to Captain Patrick O'Sheel, a literary agent in civilian life who had been wounded on Guadalcanal and sent back to New York to use his skill and experience. O'Sheel placed Martin's stories with *Harper's*, *Collier's*, other magazines, and one with The Saturday Evening Post. A pig was "The Fat Lady of Okinawa." When Japanese planes bombed the island on schedule every night, the men leaped for their foxholes. She had learned the routine quickly and crowded in with the nearest man. Martin excelled in the human-interest, local color piece.

He was in Peking when the war ended and the Marine Corps finally caught up with him and sent him peremptory orders to come home. At Pearl Harbor on the way back he picked up $2,700 in checks for the stories he had written. In New York he called on some of the editors who had printed them. They were courteous to cordial, but that was that. Martin started back to Atlanta and the *Constitution,* but from the 30th Street Station in Philadelphia he called The Saturday Evening Post and heard for the first time what would become the familiar "Sommers!"

Martin explained who he was.

"You the guy did the Fat Lady? Come on down."

Sommers took the discharged Marine to lunch at the Downtown Club atop the Ledger Building and asked him if he could do some assignments for the Post along with his regular work on the *Constitution.* Harold Martin thought that would be the end of it, but he did not yet know Marty Sommers.

A newsman and a soldier himself, Sommers knew a reporter when he saw one and a story when he read it. Marty Sommers's world was not bounded by Walnut to Sansom and Sixth to Seventh Streets. He was one of the Post's few contacts with the outside world. He had the complete confidence of Hibbs and Fuoss, and he knew what he was doing. Sommers read *The New York Times* thoroughly every day with an eye for stories that might develop weeks or a month or two later. He seemed to have editorial prescience born of his early newspaper experience, and he could handle writers. Wherever they were, and he had Post writers about the world in his charge, he looked after his men. He understood writers, encouraged them, commiserated with them, drank with them when they turned up in Philadelphia. All of them swore by Marty Sommers and what he called his "cabinet work." No one could cut, rewrite, and polish a piece like Marty. His ear was perfect.

Within two weeks after his return to Atlanta and his newspaper job, Martin received a manuscript article from Sommers with a request to rewrite it. Martin researched it over again and wrote it over completely. It became "The Gay Banker of Rock Hill."

The Saturday Evening Post then gave Harold Martin a contract for ten articles a year at $1,750 each, allowing him at the same time to write three columns weekly for the *Constitution*. The price for each article was raised by $500 every successive year. When the first contract came, Martin took his family to Rich's Department Store in Atlanta to celebrate. His small daughter Marion made the most of the occasion by asking loudly, "Daddy, now that we're rich can I have a double sundae?"

On Post orders and expense account Martin started to re-visit places he had covered during World War II. Because he had never been there he made a detour to Samoa to write up the island chieftains. Several weeks later at another South Pacific spot he found a cablegram from Ben Hibbs waiting. It read, "All agree story needs more work." It was a bad start, but Martin rewrote the piece with a new lead describing the Samoans as the Texans of the South Pacific, and the Post was satisfied. He filed 14 stories from Samoa, the Philippines, and other Pacific points before he ended a seven months' trip in Bangkok. He decided he wanted to see Patrick O'Sheel, who was then in London, so Sommers sent him more expense money, and Harold Martin returned to Atlanta via England with a way stop in Philadelphia.

Martin was on Okinawa when the Korean War broke out. He sailed on the first carrier sent with planes to bomb North Korea. The Post sent Demaree Bess, Robert Sherrod, Nora Waln, and William Worden as well as Martin to cover that conflict.

In all Harold Martin wrote more than 200 pieces for The Saturday Evening Post, with just one rejection and five that called for rewriting. Wherever he went, and he went many places, including Russia to do a piece on Khrushchev's birthplace and, much later, Vietnam for an article and a visit to his son, he could always call Philadelphia. It was comforting, he says, in out of the way places half way around the world to hear "Sommers!" at the other end of the line.

Whatever his title on the masthead, and it was at various times "Article Editor" and "Foreign Editor," Marty Sommers was in effect the city editor of The Saturday Evening Post. He gave it wide coverage, vigor, and good writing. Once Martin despatched a 5,000-word cablegram sent by a South Pacific native operator who did not know English. There was no punctuation. Sommers wrote the complete piece from it.

Hibbs was keeping his promises and putting out the kind of Saturday Evening Post he had planned. It was attracting women readers as well as men and more younger readers. In 1945 it published "What Really Happened at Teheran" by Forrest Davis, its Washington correspondent. Until its publication the public had known little of what transpired when Roosevelt, Churchill, and Stalin met for the last time. Hibbs paid $60,000 for "Admiral Halsey Tells his Story"; $102,000 to General Beetle Smith and his collaborator for six articles— "Six Great Decisions"—summing up the high points of the war in Europe; and $175,000 for Navy Captain Harry Butcher's "My Three Years with Eisenhower," which the Post ran in six installments.

Hibbs found a new hero in that other Kansan. He bid $500,000 for all rights to Eisenhower's "Crusade in Europe," intending to sell off the book rights, but Curtis was outbid by the newspaper–magazine–book publisher syndicate formed to obtain and exploit the book. Breaking all precedent, The Saturday Evening Post declared for Eisenhower even before the World War II commander-in-chief was nominated for the Presidency at the Republican convention in 1952.

At the same time the Post was running lighter material. It began a "Cities of America" series which Arthur Baum suggested. The idea did not seem promising because, the editors felt, only the city featured would be interested. They were wrong. By various writers, graphically illustrated, light in touch, often superficial, the series proved popular. It ran for well over 100 issues before it stopped to be continued as the equally popular "Cities of the World."

Pete Martin suggested that he do a series on motion picture celebrities. Again, there was no great enthusiasm, but Martin was despatched with his tape recorder for interviews with the Hollywood great. Movie-magazine pieces, often poorly written, they were a great success, circulation builders which shot newsstand sales way up for the issues containing them.

Hibbs scored a coup when he bought Whittaker Chambers' "I Was the Witness," story of his involvement with communism and the Alger Hiss trial. He broke the turgid prose-poetic account February 9, 1952, with an issue which bore no picture on the cover, only a large-type blurb for "One of the Great Books of Our Time." The Post ran it in ten installments.

Even *Time* published a congratulatory article when Hibbs and Fuoss had edited the Post for ten years. *Business Week,* March 15, 1952, featured their picture on the cover and ran a full story in the issue. These commendations had been earned.

The circulation of The Saturday Evening Post was up almost a million from the time Ben Hibbs assumed editorial control. It averaged 4,220,178 for 1952 and went over 5,500,000 in 1953. Advertising sales were high: $75,372,127 in 1952 and almost $81,000,000 the next year. More than half the gross advertising revenue of The Curtis Publishing Company came from The Saturday Evening Post.

Early in 1953 the Post began publication of the story of one of the country's most durable heroes. The first installment of "33 Hours to Paris" by Colonel Charles A. Lindbergh, heralded as "the literary event of 1953," began April 11. The Post moved on and up. The first installment of Bing Crosby's "Call Me Lucky" (as told to Pete Martin) shot Post circulation to a new high. The Bob Hope story proved another such success. It took Post circulation over the 5,000,000 mark for the first time. Arthur Godfrey disliked Martin's write-up and proceeded to rewrite it. What finally appeared in the Post was Ben Hibbs's rewrite of Godfrey's rewrite of Martin's writing, but with the popular Godfrey at the height of his radio and television career and much in the news for publicized disputes with the cast of his show, it was a third smash hit. Martin went on to do Marilyn Monroe. Hollywood was staggering under the onslaught of television, but its gods and goddesses, especially if they played on television too, still enthralled.

Curtis had a triumphant year in 1953, and MacNeal as well as The Saturday Evening Post shared in it. It had been his declared intent to pay a dividend on Curtis common stock, and he did. The gross operating revenue of The Curtis Publishing Company in 1953 was $174,773,718. Net profit after taxes was $4,868,027, a satisfactory ratio. Curtis paid $7 on its preferred stock, $3 and a contingent dividend of $1 on its prior preferred, and 20 cents a share on its common stock. To lessen the liability it constituted, the company was buying back its prior preferred stock as fast as it could. It paid out $4,580,364.77 for all it could acquire between July, 1951, and the end of 1953.

Forecasts for 1954 indicated that The Curtis Publishing Company would continue to flourish. They were a little off. Circulation of the Post was up but that of the Journal down. Holiday was down, and even Jack and Jill was slipping. Country Gentleman about held its own in circulation, but its advertising revenue fell for the third straight year. The gross income of The Curtis Publishing Company in 1954 fell more than $1,000,000.

The real difficulty was with The Saturday Evening Post, chief support of the entire Curtis structure. Despite its breadth of coverage, the variety of its offering, and its popularity with a growing number of readers, advertising revenue fell almost $2,000,000 in 1954. The Saturday Evening Post was beginning to lose favor with advertisers.

There were a number of reasons, but the overriding reason was television. Television hypnotized advertisers as well as simple viewers. It was big, gargantuan. It reached audiences no magazine could hope to reach. Not only was it big, it was also profitable. It was profitable for the advertising agencies because 15 per cent of huge sums is larger than 15 per cent of smaller sums. It was popular with corporation heads who could see their products celebrated by even more celebrated screen personalities, and might even get to meet some of them some time. It was popular with everybody.

The mass magazines existed to purvey information and entertainment. Television provided masses of mass entertainment and more information than many people could absorb; and they could get both without even the effort of reading or the bleak necessity of paying for the magazine. People did not have to wait for printed reports and comment about wars, sporting events, labor disputes, musical comedies, murder mysteries, and assorted disaster. They attended them by television.

Yet not television but simple social and economic change was responsible for the troubles which beset one Curtis magazine.

Chapter 20

Death of *Country Gentleman*

Country Gentleman which had suffered badly during the Depression recovered somewhat as European war orders strengthened American industry and the manufacturers of farm implements and machinery began to advertise again. MacKinlay Kantor was in the magazine with a short story in 1940. DeKruif was still a featured contributor. Erle Stanley Gardiner was in with a serial, "The D.A. Calls a Turn." All this was hardly bucolic, but, as in World War I, Country Gentleman emphasized the importance of the farm and farmer in defense during World War II.

Months before Pearl Harbor, Secretary of Agriculture Claude R. Wickard wrote "Our Food Is a Weapon." The magazine kept insisting that "Farm Work Is War Work." In 1944 Charles F. Kettering tried to distinguish between postwar thinking and postwar dreaming. Robert Reed, another Kansan, faithfully imitated the successful features of the other Curtis magazines. He continued the "Washington Roundup" which Hibbs had inaugurated. Like Hibbs on the Post he ran more articles and fewer short stories. As Bok had done in the Ladies' Home Journal years before, he began to publish plans for modern homes, but these all farm homes.

Reed built up the women's interest material in Country Gentleman with recipes and patterns. As a subscription promotion scheme Country Gentleman had started a Country Gentlewoman League in the 1930's. The league had 13,500

215

member clubs and a page in the magazine which told of their activities. Like the Ladies' Home Journal, Country Gentleman operated a testing kitchen and promoted it. It added a beauty editor to its staff.

The Gent shared in the immediate postwar prosperity enjoyed by most of the magazines, but the respite was short-lived. Advertising fell off again, and issues grew markedly thinner. Country Gentleman no longer called itself America's oldest agricultural journal or its foremost farm magazine. It was not sure what it was. It was no longer the largest in circulation. Through the purchase of the *Farmer's Wife* and adding its circulation to its own, *Farm Journal* had outstripped it, though not by much. Both Country Gentleman and *Farm Journal* circulations were over 2,000,000. Circulation was not the problem. Country Gentleman no longer wished to be considered merely a farm publication for a very simple reason.

There had been 6,518,000 farms in 1920. There were only 5,648,000 in 1950, and the number was falling every year. Farm population was 31,974,000 in 1920, but it was down to 23,048,000 in 1950 with every evidence that it would continue to dwindle. The move from the country into the city then into the suburbs had been going on for a long time. Two world wars had sent farmers and their sons, and often their wives and daughters, scurrying into town for high-paying war production jobs. "How You Gonna Keep 'Em Down on the Farm" was no longer the rhetorical question of a World War I ditty. It was actual, and there was a clear answer. You couldn't.

There were fewer family farms, fewer subsistence farms. Large farms were owned as often now by corporations as by individuals. Except that it had more money from government subsidies, the farm family was no longer distinct from the urban or suburban. It had all the conveniences of electricity, the telephone, plumbing, cars, trucks, tractors, radio, and television. The farmer and his family no longer needed the vocational advice the farm papers had once disseminated. The agricultural colleges for which these publications had pled existed in profusion. Crop and market reports came daily over the air. Swelling as farms diminished, the U. S. Department of Agriculture was one of the largest and strongest bureaucracies in Washington.

Country Gentleman called itself now "The Magazine for Better Farming—Better Living." It was straddling an issue which bedevilled most of the farm papers. It could return to being completely an agricultural journal for a shrinking number of readers who no longer needed it, or it could transform itself completely—it had already done so partially—into one of the so-called "shelter books" like the very successful *Better Homes & Gardens* published by the Meredith Publishing Company in Des Moines.

It would then be a periodical not for the farm and farm family but for the suburbanite or the country dweller with suburban tastes. There were difficulties in either choice. The advertisers of farm machinery, feeds, seeds, stock, and other purely agricultural appurtenances would not advertise in a shelter book. They had no market among exurbanites who commuted to city jobs. Conversely, the advertisers of luxury merchandise for commercially sophisticated tastes would not advertise in what purported to be a farm magazine. The dilemma bristled with horns.

Country Gentleman, literally, tried halfway measures. January, 1953, was the last Saturday Evening Post size issue. It contained only 84 pages. In it an editorial signed by Robert Reed announced "a new and greater Country Gentleman for you." It would be of a new handy size, easier to read. Its covers would tell a story. It would carry more profit-making articles, regional reports, and brilliant new pictures. It would still be edited for the family-sized farm and for every member of the farm family.

When the February issue appeared the page size of Country Gentleman had been cut just about one-half to 429 lines. There was no longer a separate Country Gentlewoman section, but a Country Living section ran throughout the issue. There were 14 general articles and just one story—by Clarence Budington Kelland. The masthead was choked with names, including those of professorial consultants, and there was another signed editorial. In it Reed pled for just one favor, "That each of you read this first issue of the new Country Gentleman from cover to cover."

Reed then asked humbly for suggestions on how to improve his magazine. Using the old appeal of two for the price of one, he said that Country Living would be a magazine within a magazine. Though he did not say so, it was also the compromise which made Country Gentleman at least one-half a shelter book. Indecision was rampant throughout Reed's eloquence when he urged, "We earnestly invite you to go adventuring with us into our second century, as the stirring story of Better Farming and Better Living unfolds."

The Gent was struggling to get advertising. It was having just as hard a time now to get the kind of readers advertisers demanded, farm subscribers, subscribers with Rural Delivery addresses. To make a special effort to get them, circulation effort for the magazine was taken from under the Curtis Circulation Company's Subscription Division and set up in a special division under Robert M. Goshorn.

Goshorn had already recommended controlled circulation, a decrease to about 2,000,000 in line with the decrease in farms and the increased selectivity of the farm market. This would remove Country Gentleman from the ruinous circulation race and save on the inordinate expenses of the effort to obtain new subscribers. His recommendation was not adopted.

With a small staff and under some difficulties Goshorn's unit had some success in obtaining additional circulation of the kind required, but not enough. Country Gentleman's space salesmen intensified their efforts but the results were discouraging.

More editorial attempts at the appearance of change were made. February, 1953, through July, 1954, the cover bore only the title "Country Gentleman." In August "The Magazine for Better Farming" was inserted in large type at the bottom of the cover. The September issue carried this slogan directly under the logotype. December, 1954, was the last issue called "Country Gentleman." In a desperation move the century-old title was changed in January, 1955, to "Better Farming." In small black type above were the words "Country Gentleman the magazine for."

Kansas-born "George" Peek graduated from the University of Wisconsin, then became a newspaperman in Madison. Because, so he said, he wanted a rug on his office floor, he switched to advertising and became in time Philadelphia Office manager of the Ladies' Home Journal. He was made manager, in effect publisher, of Country Gentleman in 1953. Peek made every effort to stabilize the wobbling magazine. Curtis had a promotional film made in the apple country around Winchester, Virginia, showing the magazine close to the productive soil and readers there. A script was written and an answer print shown to Curtis executives. It looked promising, but no other prints were made, and the film was never used.

A promotional brochure of 1951 proudly listed 613 advertisers who had used Country Gentleman anywhere from 2 to 41 years. January, 1950, through June, 1951, 175 new advertisers came in. All-out effort and a cut of 15 per cent in the advertising rate for the smaller page worked a temporary miracle. The March, 1954, issue carried a record $1,000,000 in advertising from 508 advertisers, but gross advertising sales for 1954 as a whole were down again. They declined steeply again in early 1955 while production and distributions costs rose.

The managers of the seven advertising branch offices of The Curtis Publishing Company were asked what they thought was needed to reestablish Country Gentleman and getting it to operate at a profit. Each of the seven had a different answer, and no one of the answers provided a solution. Their inability to agree helped Robert MacNeal reach a decision.

The August, 1955 issue of "Better Farming" was of 80 small pages, far less than one-half the size of the magazine a year and a half earlier. "Better Farming" had run for eight monthly issues. After 102 years of continuous publication Country

Gentleman died. It was sold to its chief competitor, *Farm Journal.*

The price—not disclosed at the time—was about $5,000,000. This was not an outright payment but the amount involved in a detailed agreement. At the time of the sale the circulation of *Farm Journal* was 2,870,380, while that of Country Gentleman was 2,566,314. Farm Journal, Inc. assumed liability for unfulfilled Country Gentleman subscriptions in the amount of $2,816,145. It agreed to spend $100,000 a year for five years in advertising in The Saturday Evening Post and to give Curtis free advertising space in *Farm Journal* or in *Town Journal,* which it was publishing at the time in the amount of $100,000 a year for five years. It would also give Curtis 15 per cent of the revenue from all other advertising in *Farm Journal* in excess of 450,000 agate lines a year for five years, the total not to exceed $2,000,000.

The loss of Country Gentleman was not a severe blow to The Curtis Publishing Company. It got a good price for a magazine which had never really been profitable. Its discontinuance was a practical relief. In a formal statement Robert MacNeal said, "Aside from the fact that *Farm Journal* made us a very attractive offer, we see definite advantages in concentrating our efforts on the other magazines in the Curtis line."

Emotionally the loss hurt. Ben Hibbs, who had spent 13 years on the Gent, said, "It breaks my heart." Men and women who had spent years in Gent editorial or advertising were disconsolate. A number of the editors were taken on by the Post. The Post and Holiday absorbed most of the Gent's space salesmen. Charles Ficke, manager of Country Gentleman for many years became manager of the New York advertising office, then an assistant to MacNeal and survived to be an invaluable aide to his successors. Before seeking another spot in the company for himself, Peek placed all of his men, then became a regional vice president of The Curtis Publishing Company. Goshorn placed his staff members before he became circulation manager of the *American Home* when Curtis purchased that shelter book in New York.

Country Gentleman had been deeply imbedded in The Curtis Publishing Company since Cyrus Curtis called on Gilbert Tucker in Albany in 1911. Privately, perhaps to console himself as well as the other, MacNeal told Goshorn not to feel badly or that he had failed. "It would have taken a miracle. All it proves is that for 44 years we have been publishing the wrong magazine."

A magazine which had been its competitor for all the years since Curtis bought The Saturday Evening Post was in serious trouble—trouble enough to please Curtis but also to cause concern that a general weekly of fiction and non-fiction faced a harsh present and an unpleasant future, if any future at all.

Collier's never had the substance or the polish of The Saturday Evening Post. It did not have the Post's standing with advertisers. Long past its muckraking and crusading days, it was light entertainment in its short and short-short stories and Sunday feature articles. The intent of Collier's, stated and restated, was to entertain. Thus it was particularly vulnerable to television which was hugely engaged in doing just the same thing.

Crowell-Collier Research conducted a major survey based on interviews with 33,452 respondents in 16,000 homes and released the results in December, 1953. The survey showed that Collier's had such depth of reading that it was "Practically TV-proof." It proved to those who believed the findings that it had lost only three per cent of the public's reading time to television where other magazines had lost much more. The Saturday Evening Post, for instance, had lost 13 per cent.

No improvement in Collier's unhappy situation resulted. As popular entertainment only the magazine had really lost its raison d'etre. It had difficulty maintaining its circulation, and advertisers did not believe that it reached an audience profitable to them.

William Ludlow Chenery, who resigned in 1949, was the last important Collier's editor. He was succeeded by a string of touted but ineffectual men, none of whom lasted very long. In 1953 Crowell-Collier imported Paul C. Smith from California where he had been editor of the San Francisco

Chronicle. Smith was made a Crowell-Collier vice president, then president, then chairman of the board, then—setting a precedent—editor-in-chief of all three of the company's magazines: *Collier's, The American Magazine,* and *Woman's Home Companion.*

To cut production costs *Collier's* went from weekly to biweekly publication with its issue for August 7, 1953—thereby setting another precedent. It was offered to advertisers with an average circulation guarantee of 3,500,000, which meant a bonus of some 500,000 readers, and a minimum of 112 pages an issue. The move to biweekly publication took the magazine out of direct competition with *Time, Life,* and The Saturday Evening Post and placed it in competition with the then weaker biweekly *Look.* None of this worked. *Collier's* lost $4,000,000 in 1953, and *Woman's Home Companion* lost money for the first time.

Collier's tried spectacular editorial tactics. Smith said he wanted "scope not scoop" but did not explain. The magazine ran more fiction and more of it with appeal to women. Then it published sensational exposés—setting a third precedent. When this did not work, it returned to optimism and escape. In a statement issued August 7, 1953, Crowell-Collier said: "Collier's is a popular magazine, first and last, and it means to remain one. It knows that a major function of a popular magazine is to entertain. All of us have to have some escape in these troubled times. . . . it is just as important to appreciate and perpetuate all that is good in our national life as it is to correct what is wrong."

If this was the new formula, it was no more successful than any of the earlier approaches. Three years later, after borrowing $10,000,000 to keep its magazines going—thereby setting a fourth precedent—Crowell-Collier was forced to drop the long popular and still solvent *American.* The circulations of *Collier's* and *Woman's Home Companion* were strengthened, but Crowell-Collier lost $7,500,000 in 1956. Smith talked now of "total communications" rather than mere magazine publishing, but he was unable to raise the $15,000,000 needed to buy control of seven radio and television stations. He also planned purchase of newspapers and publication of a weekly news magazine.

Continuing to establish precedents and provide a preview of things to come, Crowell-Collier made a Chicago financier chairman of its executive committee and loaded its board with five new members who were executives of outside corporations. These moves attracted press attention but more attention was paid to rumors that *Collier's* and *Woman's Home Companion* would be closed down. Crowell-Collier denied the rumors. Its director of public relations declared, "What the members of the advertising community—and the publishing industry—should remember is that we are in the magazine business . . . and that we have never announced that we are getting out of it."

The announcement that had not been made came a few days later. Though there was nothing in either magazine to indicate that the issues were the last that would ever be published, *Collier's* ceased publication as of January 4, 1957, and *Woman's Home Companion* in January, 1957.

Nearly 500 Crowell-Collier editorial, advertising, and management employees lost their jobs just at Christmas, 1956, and got no severance pay. Men and women on Independence Square in Philadelphia felt sorry for them and felt grateful that they worked for Curtis. Ben Hibbs said that the *Collier's* failure was "one of the tragic stories of publishing." There was natural sympathy for what had been a colleague as well as a competitor but the comforting belief that "It can't happen here."

The Curtis magazines were losing advertising, but The Curtis Publishing Company was still making money. As for all magazine publishers, hit by television, rising production costs, and crippling increases in second-class mailing rates, the ratio of net profit to gross income was diminishing, but the picture was not unpleasant.

In round numbers net profits of The Curtis Publishing Company were the following.

1954—$4,516,000
1955— 4,080,000
1956— 6,340,000
1957— 6,239,000

The fully integrated company with its valuable physical assets on Independence Square and in Sharon Hill was bulwarked by an assortment of wholly owned subsidiaries. At this time they were:

American Home Magazine Corporation, purchased in 1958.
New York & Pennsylvania Co., Inc., pulp and paper producers.
Curtis Circulation Company.
National Analysts, Inc. Founded in 1943 as an offshoot of the Curtis Research Department, it did survey research for outside clients as well as for Curtis.
The Premium Service Co., Inc. It supplied incentive merchandise for Curtis Circulation and for other companies.
The Moore-Cottrell Subscription Agencies, Inc. This was a large catalogue agency for subscriptions to many magazines.
Keystone Readers' Service, Inc. Another field selling subscription agency.
Colonial Electrotype Company.

In addition The Curtis Publishing Company also owned part interests in Science & Mechanics Publishing Co., Bantam Books, Inc., Treasure Books, Inc., Wonder Books, Inc., and National Magazine Service, Inc.

The activities of this complex were directed by the Curtis board. In 1956 it consisted comfortably of Walter D. Fuller, chairman; Mrs. Mary Curtis Zimbalist, Cary W. Bok, Robert E. MacNeal, Robert Gibbon, Brandon Barringer, Walter S. Franklin, Walter R. Reitz, and M. Albert Linton. All but the last named three were officers of the company. Mrs. Zimbalist was senior vice president as well as majority stockholder. Her son, Cary W. Bok had resigned as treasurer shortly after World War II but was a senior vice president and chairman of the finance committee from what he called "The North Pole Office" in Camden, Maine. Gibbon was a lawyer and company secretary and assistant treasurer, Barringer was treasurer.

Among the outsiders, Linton was chairman of the board of the Mutual Life Insurance Company of Philadelphia, Reitz board chairman of the Quaker State Oil Refining Corporation, and Franklin a director of the Pennsylvania Railroad.

Presence of Mrs. Zimbalist's gray Bentley and her chauffeur before the pillars of the Curtis Building was the signal that this board was meeting to hear glowing reports of circulation gains and editorial plans, learn of more new equipment being installed at Sharon Hill and of the profitable operation of the Curtis subsidiaries. It sat assured that, as nearly as possible, everything was going exactly as when Cyrus H. K. Curtis was alive.

Chapter 21

New Men, New Ventures

If the Curtis board was content, Curtis management was uneasy. Circulation of its magazines was being maintained and even enlarged, but at a price. Big advertisers were allocating most of their appropriations to television, giving the magazines what was left, and they had to scramble for the tossed coins. Food advertising deserted the Post. It was losing the largest share of automotive advertising, of which it had had a virtual monopoly, to television and losing advertising in other categories to *Life*. "As Advertised in Life" was what dealers wanted now.

Walter Fuller retired as Curtis board chairman in 1957, but remained on the board, on its executive committee, and a Curtis trustee. He had opened an employment agency for retired executives as Walter D. Fuller Company, Management Consultants, but with offices in the Ledger Building he was still in evidence almost daily next door.

Curtis had always refused to diversify, but it needed additional sources of income and MacNeal found a way to stay with periodicals but add to the Curtis line. It was also his turn to act as editor. He planned and started two new magazines, both imitative.

The spectacular success of *TV Guide*, published in Philadelphia by Walter H. Annenberg of the Philadelphia *Inquirer*, was an irresistible temptation. Issued in many regional editions it seemed as much a household necessity as a television

226

set itself. In 1955 the Curtis Circulation Company began production and distribution of *TV Week,* another program listing in many editions of the same size and general appearance as *TV Guide.* There was some editorial content but the basic inducement was the detailed listing of network offerings on stations across the country. It did not take long to discover that the editorial chore was considerable and that people stubbornly preferred the well established *TV Guide* which, in their minds, was the official organ of the fantasy electronic world.

In mid-1955 Curtis established a new subsidiary with Mac-Neal as president. Bride-To-Be was established as a $1 a copy quarterly with editorial offices in New York and advertising offices in Chicago. Its woman editor gushed, "The magazine proposes to take each reader figuratively by the hand, and lead her directly and authoritatively toward everything she has been dreaming of, from satin gown to silverware, from bridal veil to honeymoon and home, counseling all the way. It will help the bride and groom with their early marriage problems, their marriage manners and philosophies for happy living."

Translated, this meant that Bride-to-Be, again in many regional advertising editions, was an order catalogue tailored to the desires of all the advertisers who cater to the marriage market, and there are many. When it appeared, the first issue was thick, glossy, and looked promising, but the magazine had built-in limitations. Many young women are brides only once and did not need a second $1 copy of Bride-to-Be. Even the most ambitious or carefree seldom marry more than half a dozen times. Advertisers needed to reach her only once or rarely. Bride-to-Be did not survive its honeymoon.

"I don't know how many more of these the Post can support," said Marty Sommers, shaking his big head.

The Post was being pressed hard enough so that in 1958 it took a daring and almost impious step. It broke its own Curtis Code of 1910, overrode the objections of Ben Hibbs, and announced that it would accept liquor advertising. There were horrified outcries, and some affronted readers cancelled their subscriptions, but Curtis hoped to gain an additional $5,000,000 in advertising. The liquor advertising came in slowly for distillers had no facts on the alcoholic capacity of Post readers, but it came and eventually The Saturday Evening Post realized just about the forecast figure.

As deaths and retirements made it possible, MacNeal made new appointments to key Curtis posts, hoping to revitalize the company's operations. Many of his appointments were surprising, and some of them were almost inconceivable to Curtis personnel.

When Arthur Kohler retired in 1956, Edward Von Tress, who had been Holiday manager, was made Advertising Director of The Curtis Publishing Company. Originally a Holiday space salesman on the west coast, Peter Schruth was made advertising director of The Saturday Evening Post. E. Kent Mitchell was made manager of Holiday, then, after its purchase, of American Home. On the retirement of Lewis Trayser, John M. Downs was appointed director of manufacturing. When he died within the year, he was succeeded first by Henry M. Chestnut, and Chestnut by Leon Marks.

Most of these positions carried the title of vice president and some of senior vice president. The second title was adopted to distinguish between actual operating heads and the numerous vice presidencies newly created, after advertising agency fashion, as job titles for sales executives to add to their prestige in meetings with clients or in soliciting new business.

In October, 1958, Benjamin Allen, president of the Curtis Circulation Company who was on leave for health reasons was found dead in the garage of his summer home in Stone Harbor, New Jersey. Allen had built Circulation into a formidable engine. At its peak its subscription division had about 3,500 representatives soliciting subscriptions by telephone, 400 door-to-door magazine salesmen, some 25,000 part-time agents, 50 field managers, and about 50 men and their assistants in the home office on the tenth floor of the Curtis Building. The single copy division with about 70 in the home office and a staff of about 400 in the field offices in many cities across the country dealt with about 750 magazine wholesalers and 110,000 newsstand dealers.

In addition to selling the Curtis magazines, the Curtis Circulation Company had the entire and very profitable distribution of about 100 client magazines. Among others it distributed *Look*, the *Atlantic, Harper's, Esquire, Coronet, Vogue, House and Garden*, and *Field and Stream*.

Circulation also had about 150 School Plan men, independent operators, many of them former teachers or school administrators, who organized magazine subscription campaigns by students in thousands of high and junior high schools. Profitable for the school men and the schools—which received about one-third of all the money collected for a long list of magazines—this was one of the chief sources of Curtis subscription production. Crowell-Collier had operated such a plan, purchased for *Look* when *Collier's* closed. It was later absorbed by the Quality School Plan, owned jointly by the Reader's Digest Association, Inc. and Time, Inc.

Circulation was distinct at Curtis. From the viewpoint of the advertising space salesmen in their Brooks suits, button-down collars, and regimental ties, and the editors in their tweeds and flannels, the circulation men were different. They were the hard-headed, hard-working, hard-drinking nickel and dime boys in their carefully pressed dark suits, starched white shirts, and department store ties who probably spent their spare time bombing newsstands. Their manners were more formal than those of the casual editors or wisecracking salesmen. They were courteous with each other and deferential, if perhaps cynical, toward editors and the eggheads of Research, but they were suspect. They were continually in conference. They kept record sheets filled with mysterious figures.

That they knew their business thoroughly was obvious. It was also obvious that, very politely, they could baffle any outsider who asked too many questions. The competence of the circulation men was beyond dispute, but they were realists.

There was always the suspicion that they had real muscles under their padded shoulders. It did not pay to buck Circulation. Just by being polite but by lessening sales effort imperceptibly here or there they could make an editor look foolish and leave a space salesman hanging in the air.

On Allen's death, MacNeal appointed E. Huber Ulrich, Curtis public relations director, to the presidency of the Curtis Circulation Company. When Don Van Metre, a close associate of Allen's who spent millions of dollars every year in advertising the Curtis magazines, left, MacNeal appointed Hamilton Cochrane, writer of action historical novels, of Post Promotion to be manager of Circulation Advertising.

One of MacNeal's surprise appointments came when Ada Rose, its founding editor, retired from Jack and Jill in 1959. He appointed Karl K. Hoffmann to a new post as publisher of the children's magazine. Hoffmann, who had joined Curtis Circulation in 1933 and become single-copy branch manager in his native Columbus, Ohio, had spent 12 years in Philadelphia as a promotion man for Holiday, then the Ladies' Home Journal.

Hoffmann had approached Walter Fuller with an idea for what he considered a new and different children's magazine. The Jack and Jill appointment gave him a chance to put what he called his "new concept" into practice. Jack and Jill circulation had been slipping. It was off more than 100,000. Profits had diminished. Hoffmann went quickly about righting this situation.

He struck the literary quality which Ada Rose had so carefully built into Jack and Jill and scratched the magazine's book look in favor of a more journalistic and colorful appearance. Dismissing both new editor and managing editor, he took over editorial direction himself. He cut staff, cut already minimal payments to contributors, cut paper costs and the other small costs of Jack and Jill production. Hoffmann retained enough simple articles, stories, games, cutouts, puzzles, and things-to-do to keep Jack and Jill reasonably intact. He expanded the pages of children's letters, always strenuously solicited, and children's drawings. There was no cost for this editorial material. Then he focussed on what was basic in his plan.

Hoffmann featured a television story in each issue of Jack and Jill. Prepared, generally, by the network, the studio or the producer's staff, the story gave behind-the-scenes details of children's shows, bits about the actors, and glimpses of forthcoming attractions. There was no editorial cost for this publicity material, and the originators gladly supplied excellent photographic illustrations, usually in color. Each story was, implicitly, a deal whereby the show received cover mention and four or five pages of free publicity in a national magazine in return for exposure of Jack and Jill on the air.

Hoffmann proved an astute promotional publisher. This exploitation got attention for Jack and Jill while it cut editorial costs and gained the goodwill of the networks and producers. The "new concept" was based on a simple but oft proven expedient, "If you can't beat 'em join 'em." As Hoffmann had correctly forseen, "the kiddies," as he always called them, knew television shows and personalities better than they knew the family scene and their brothers and sisters and ate up entertaining tidbits about them just as their adult counterparts relished the movie magazines. In a very short time Hoffmann had Jack and Jill circulation and profits up again.

The littlest Curtis magazine was safe for a time, but big brother was uneasy.

Robert Sherrod, another Georgian and another Drewry graduate, had been a newsman in Miami, then a *Life* and later a Post correspondent in the Far East. He was made managing editor of The Saturday Evening Post in 1955, Fuoss moving up to the new post of executive editor. While continuing to function as an editor and Post editorial executive, he took on additional duties which were really those of a publisher.

Saturday Evening Post circulation was booming. It reached 4,000,000 in 1947, went over 5,000,000 in February, 1954, and crossed 6,000,000 in February, 1959. It had to in the bitter race with *Life*. Post advertising revenue was $90,930,000 in 1957. It set a record with $3,364,417 in the issue for April 4, 1959. These were gratifying figures, but they did not represent profit entirely, and the competitive position of the Post was deteriorating.

In 1957 Fuoss, who saw difficulties ahead, decided to resign. Ben Hibbs was hurt and distressed. Hibbs and Fuoss worked closely together but, as it should be, it was Hibbs's principles and philosophy which governed. After 15 years Fuoss chafed somewhat. He was cut off from making what he thought were necessary fundamental changes in the magazine and he feared for the future of the Post.

Hibbs reminded him that he had always said he would resign after 20 years as Post editor. He reiterated his intention to retire then. The editorship of The Saturday Evening Post would be Fuoss's as of January 1, 1962. Fuoss remained.

"One stinking hot day in the summer of 1957"—the words are Ben Hibbs's—Hibbs, Fuoss, and Sherrod met to discuss a problem. It seemed to all of them that in its competitive effort the Post was getting out of balance. Each year it was moving a little farther to the light side. It needed more substantial material. Fuoss, who followed editorial research closely, believed that the magazine had to establish its identity more firmly and shore up its image. Three days later he presented Hibbs with the idea that became the Post's "Adventures of the Mind."

The idea was to try to establish communication between intellectuals and the ordinary readers of a mass magazine. It was a daring attempt for the Post and a risky one. It seemed ridiculous to the scholars and scientists they first approached. They had never respected The Saturday Evening Post. "What? Me write for the Post?" They changed their minds when they learned that their writing would not be tampered with—and the prices the Post would pay.

Started in the spring of 1958 after heavy promotion, "Adventures of the Mind" was a resounding success. The Post introduced a different kind of big names and their ideas to the public, and the public was impressed. Scholars wrote of their specialties: physics, art, religion, philosophy, poetry, criticism, and kindred subjects usually avoided in a mass magazine. Edith Sitwell, J. Robert Oppenheimer, Lewis Mumford, Loren

Eisley, Aldous Huxley, Bertrand Russell, John Ciardi, C. P. Snow, C. Day Lewis, C. Northcote Parkinson, and Henry M. Wriston were typical of the thinkers presented.

Their articles were unedited, and a number of them were lucid and enlightening. The reader felt that he really had adventured with his mind and was pleased with himself. This was self-improvement on the highest level. Many of the articles were far too long, murky, and bumbling. Their authors could not write, hence what they wrote was unreadable, but there was still for the reader the fine aura of high intelligence about their pieces; and the authors were just as pleased to "make the Post," mingle with the common people, and accept large payments as any professional journalist. Sixteen publishers competed for the first anthology of "Adventures of the Mind." The series ran for five years, and eventually three volumes of the articles were published.

Fuoss did not make many speeches, but he spoke to the space salesmen of The Saturday Evening Post when they met in Boca Raton, Florida, April 30, 1958. He knew they needed all the encouragement they could get. The Post was slipping. Net earnings of The Curtis Publishing Company were dropping sharply and suddenly—from $6,239,000 in 1957 to $2,786,000 in 1958.

According to Ben Hibbs, Fuoss was "often frighteningly outspoken." He was not gentle with television, the Post's magazine competition or American indolence in "an era in which we Americans convinced each other that everything is easy." His point was that The Saturday Evening Post had consistently refused to run with "the tide of triviality and easy values that made it a cinch for our competitors to describe us as bumbling, stodgy and old-fashioned."

Fuoss reminded his space-salesmen listeners that they had only one thing to sell—the editorial integrity of The Saturday Evening Post. It observed what he called the two cardinal rules of publishing.

1. To warrant its readers' loyalty a publication must have a reason for being other than the desire to return a profit for its owners;

2. The best advertising medium is that publication which was not designed to be one.

> . . . this business of preparing a nation to meet its future, of giving it the spirit, the fiber, the resolution, the knowledge, to face its greatest challenge—these are not mere matters of corporate rivalry, or who gets a schedule from Jello. These are the proper concern of an editor —in fact the only proper concern of an editor.

With a mingling of common sense and idealism, Fuoss was enunciating sound editorial doctrine. He was also saying what he thought might encourage dispirited Post salesmen. At the same time, perhaps not consciously, he was isolating the Post's essential handicap. At a time when it was increasingly unfashionable in the United States at large and in magazine journalism in particular, The Saturday Evening Post still stood for something. It had convictions and a discernible attitude toward the world, its readers, and itself.

Yet millions still swore by the Post. Its repute was high. President Dwight D. Eisenhower was among its staunch admirers. In late 1960, when Eisenhower was nearing the end of his second term (and the net earnings of The Curtis Publishing Company were tumbling again, from $3,960,000 in 1959 to $1,079,000), Ben Hibbs went to the White House. He offered Eisenhower $25,000 an article for four articles a year.

Eisenhower said immediately, "I accept. The Saturday Evening Post is the kind of magazine I want to appear in." Then he told Hibbs that a competing magazine, which he would not name, had offered him twice as much but placed a two-year limit on its offer, feeling, evidently, that after that time he would have nothing of importance to say. Eisenhower followed a precedent set by many Presidents and ex-Presidents in declaring for the Post, and he and Hibbs worked together on a series of 18 articles, the later ones appearing at a higher price in *The Reader's Digest*.

Chapter 22

Competitive Magazine Research

The Curtis Research Department completely changed direction in the late 1950's. It ceased to make major industry surveys. Advertisers were now equipped to make their own marketing studies. Most large companies had research departments, and business had about all the statistics and compilations of sales percentages it could manage. The Curtis Advertising Department did not need and was unwilling to pay for significant research of this kind. What it did need and would pay almost any price for was research that would enable it to sell space in a market that was getting more viciously competitive all the time.

The big magazines were feverishly engaged in a ruinous circulation race in which Curtis was losing. A bronze medal was no good. It had to be gold. The answer seemed to lie in "Media Research." Whether it did or not, that was what the magazine publishers were using as a weapon in a pitched battle and what Curtis management would pay for.

Media research was far from disinterested fact-finding. It was conducted to amass statistics, some significant, some niggling, and many that passed ordinary understanding, which would give a publication promotional advantage in the struggle to obtain advertising.

In the early competition with radio *Life*, with Alfred M. Politz, a German emigré who successfully and profitably sold new media research concepts to magazine after magazine, adopted the total audience count. Since 1914 advertisers had been content with the certified circulation figures provided by the Audit Bureau of Circulations. These figures were woefully small compared with radio's reports of the numbers of its vast audience. *Life* adopted the idea of the total readership of a magazine. The figure included not only the original subscriber or newsstand buyer, but also pass-along readers in the purchaser household or outside of it. A copy, and thus the advertising it contained, might be read by four, five, six, or even more people. Research proved this multiple reading and established a large total audience figure for *Life*. *Look* liked the idea, took up the research, and proved that it too had a huge total audience.

Curtis refused to accept the concept. It stuck with ABC figures and sold the selective market. Instead of telling advertisers and their agencies that its magazines reached vast numbers of readers it proved by circulation breakdowns, market area maps, city market maps, "Sales Opportunities" and allied studies that they reached the high-income, well educated, able-to-read, able-to-understand-what-they-read, and able-to-buy consumers. By implication the advertiser's message was wasted on the under-educated, inattentive, primary, secondary, and tertiary audiences of other magazines who had not the means or discrimination to buy the advertised products. The Post sold audience quality rather than quantity.

The Research Department made studies of Post impact which were intended to show that people paid more attention to advertising in its pages because they believed in the editorial quality of the magazine. Herbert C. Ludeke summed up some of the results of these studies in depth at a Post sales meeting in Spring Lake, New Jersey, September 12, 1955. He warned that such research was in the field of attitudes. It dealt with the human mind. It took time to develop research techniques which would stand up to criticism. Experimentation and sampling had produced only certain feelings and impressions. Then he said,

The overriding impression I get is one of deep loyalty, almost fierce loyalty. The Post is not only a friend of the family, it is practically a member of the family!

Post readers repeatedly stress that there is "something in it for all of us." They say the Post is clean and decent. . . . Frequently they mention with pride the length of time they have been Post readers. They speak with sincere affection of the Post as a friend.

The Post exerts its influence on its readers, it seems, by transmitting to them reading material in a relaxed, enjoyable setting. The Post differs from picture magazines in that the reader's association with the Post is an absorbing rather than a superficial experience. That appears to be the root of its influence.

Impact studies led to sociological research in 1957, and out of it came the "Post Influential" promotion. The contention was that The Saturday Evening Post was read by and influenced community leaders. They in turn influenced people on their own social and cultural level and that influence seeped down to levels below. In this way Post influence, editorial and advertising, spread far beyond its original readers. The "Post Influentials" were celebrated in elaborately staged presentations held before advertising audiences in city after city, in space salesmen's spiels, and in newspaper advertising—even on neckties. Silhouettes of men and women who typified Post Influentials were imprinted on ties in a half dozen assorted subdued colors, worn by Curtis advertising and circulation men and by everyone else who could be persuaded to put one on.

"Sell the Post Influentials—they tell the others!" Curtis newspaper and trade magazine advertising adjured.

All of this was exciting and some of it was effective, but more was needed. Advertisers have always yearned for—and not yet received—arithmetical answers as to the actual effectiveness of the large sums they spend in advertising. Through Politz, the Curtis Research Department embarked on a series of elaborate, and very expensive, surveys designed to give them some approximation.

The number of days on which an average issue of The Saturday Evening Post was picked up and looked at by readers was measured. These were dubbed "Issue Exposure Days."

Out of this research came in 1958 a thick report titled "Ad Page Exposure." It showed how often a page of advertising in The Saturday Evening Post was exposed to readers and what these readers were like. Post advertising was exposed to the reader not just once but on several occasions. It could make repeat impressions.

Curtis space salesmen were indoctrinated with the new research at a 1958 sales meeting in Cherry Hill, New Jersey. "Ad Page Exposure is a simple count of the number of opportunities to influence and sell the consumer that the advertiser obtains from his advertisement in the Post. It is a vital measure of the magazine's ability to bring people within visual range of an advertisement so that it can then attract, influence, and bring him finally to purchase. It is a concrete measure of the power of the magazine itself."

Post salesmen applauded enthusiastically and wondered if they could ever understand the research and its findings well enough to explain them to an advertising prospect and whether he would care anyway. They wished the money had been spent in buying circulation that would put the Post ahead of *Life*.

What Curtis Research and Advertising felt was needed now were comparative and competitive findings. A new giant Politz study was underwritten jointly by The Saturday Evening Post and *The Reader's Digest*. Ad Page Exposure was measured in the Post, *Life*, *Look* and the *Digest*. Hobart, now a senior vice president as well as Curtis director of research, broke the findings to a huge audience of expectant agency and advertising men in New York, January 22, 1960. The Starlight Roof of the Waldorf-Astoria was crowded for an elaborate luncheon and disclosure of the long-awaited results of the gilded study.

Personal interviews had been held with 32,000 respondents in a national area probability sample. Heavy with the technical explanations, the voluminous report gave audience size, issue exposure, advertising page exposure, and frequency of advertising page exposure for 12 classifications of the entire population of the continental United States aged ten and over, and gave it for each of the four magazines singly and in combination.

Using color slides, Hobart showed the exact findings for advertisements in different industries and the total number of exposures obtained. In combination the four magazines produced 152,000,000 ad page exposures for a Campbell Soup advertisement; 152,000,000 for a 7-Up advertisement; 116,000,000 on people with incomes of $4,000 or more annually for the Ford Motor Company; 50,500,000 exposures on suburbanites for Chevrolet, etc. Every advertisement placed in all four of the magazines scored 152,000,000 exposures.

At current rates this meant that the advertiser paid only 77 cents per 1,000 for black and white magazine advertising exposures, only $1.06 for his advertising in full color. Using the Post, *Digest*, *Look*, and *Life* he paid about one-tenth of a cent per ad page exposure.

At last the magazines had numbers. They had figures that dwarfed those of television, and the magazines were not reaching just the undifferentiated mass that might or might not have their sets turned on when an advertiser's message was being beamed but the college-educated, the high income brackets, the young, the large families. The advertiser knew now exactly what he was getting for his money in the pages of these giant magazines and how little he was actually spending.

A new day should have dawned. One did, as one always does, but it was murky. As Hobart and other research men knew, Curtis management did not really believe in what it supported. Post salesmen admired the research but from a safe distance. As far as they—and most of the advertising community and certainly the general public—were concerned, ad page exposure was an extravagant exercise in statistical virtuosity on themes which few understood and almost nobody could put to practical use. The elaborate surveys had intrinsic excellence but little extrinsic value. They were pretentious competitive ploys, and they could be easily refuted. All the proofs in percentages faded away before, "But my wife likes

Life better" or "The client never reads magazines. He watches television, and he loves Egneria Slithers in 'Biĸinis Are for Baby' so we're buying in three nights a week."

It was of a different kind and it came from a different quarter, but the Ladies' Home Journal was in as much trouble now as The Saturday Evening Post.

The Journal had queened it almost unchallenged for years. It was without dispute the dominating women's magazine. Though the Goulds had announced early that their magazine transcended formula, the formula was very evident now: good popular fiction, feministic articles, recipes, obstetrics, architecture, pediatrics, and ooh and ah gossip about the Journal editors were its staple. Every issue contained one highly promotable piece, usually the latest and most marvelous diet.

McCall's had waned until it was mostly thin romantic fiction and unending serials. Otis L. Wiese, who became its editor in 1928 when he was 23 years old, checked its downward course by insisting the magazine's editors be free of management interference and turned it into a woman's service book. *Mc-Call's* was doing all right with main sections on news, fiction, style and beauty, and homemaking. Wiese was made publisher as well as editor in 1950.

In 1956 west coast financier Norton Simon obtained control of the McCall Corporation of which the magazine was a small part, and Arthur B. Langlie, a former Washington governor was made president. In November, 1958, Wiese and eight top editors and executives of *McCall's* resigned in a body and without public explanation. More resignations followed. Inevitably there were strong press rumors. *Tide,* December, 1958, attributed the resignations to a new policy announced by the McCall Corporation which called for integration of editorial planning with advertising and circulation. It was editorial freedom which Wiese had insisted upon 31 years before. Thus his position and that of his like-minded associates, most of whom he had hired, was untenable.

Herbert R. Mayes, for 20 years editor-in-chief of Hearst's *Good Housekeeping,* was appointed editor of *McCall's.* Cost conscious and determined, Mayes threw out *McCall's* promotional slogan of "Togetherness" under which it had been striving for male as well as female readers, He replaced it with "The First Magazine for Women." It was not in size or in repute, but it sounded as if it were, and Mayes promised he would make it so. A. Edward Miller, obtained from *Life*, was made *McCall's* publisher a few months after Mayes took over. *McCall's* took the Ladies' Home Journal, proud leader in the field, for chosen foe, threw down the lavender-scented elbow-length kid glove, and then began to fight with no gloves on at all.

McCall's boasted that it would pass its competitors in circulation. It would reach 6,000,000. It would reach 8,000,000. The boast seemed ridiculous. In time, *McCall's* announced that it would touch 11,000,000, which was patently absurd.

Mayes redesigned *McCall's* for more vivid appearance. He used a profusion of color photography and bright features. The magazine appeared changed and vital in July, 1959. Curtis was unworried. Research interviewed 200 women readers of the magazine and reported that of this number just five of them had noticed the change and commented on it favorably. Eighty per cent said that as far as they were concerned *McCall's* for July was just about the same as any previous issue. The research reported concluded: ". . . their liking for a magazine is founded on what it has to offer in ideas, information or entertainment. . . . It is apparent that what makes or breaks a magazine with its readers is its editorial content."

This was comforting, but the comfort did not last. *McCall's* drove for circulation, no matter what the cost. It drove for advertising on the basis of this increased circulation, and it got that too.

In actuality, the Ladies' Home Journal was beaten from the start. It had to make a profit. As part of the powerful McCall Corporation with its large printing business and its diversified interests, *McCall's* magazine did not. As circulation rose, it did not raise its advertising rates. It guaranteed a bonus of hundreds of thousands, then a million, more readers than the advertiser paid for. It charged no more for bleed on either black and white or color pages than for pages with conventional margins. In these ways it undercut its rival.

In September, 1959, *McCall's* advertising in the trade press read: "McCall's Is FIRST." The "first" was in letters literally eight and a half inches tall in *Advertising Age*. Copy blocked against a giant numeral "I" said that *McCall's* was first in total editorial linage, four-color advertising pages, total service editorial linage, and food editorial linage. Though the implication was there, it was not yet first in circulation.

The Curtis Publishing Company was forced into this circulation battle at the very time when advertising linage was falling off badly in all of its magazines. No matter what the effort cost it had to maintain the Journal's lead. By November, 1960, *McCall's* had a total circulation per average issue of 5,491,575. The Journal's lead was small. Its circulation stood at 5,755,317.

Bruce and Beatrice Gould professed to be unworried. Though Journal circulation had been pushed up to 7,000,000 in March and April, 1961, they were forced to admit that it was losing advertising. They believed this was only temporary. Bruce Gould said, "If Madison Avenue were run by women, we'd get so much advertising we couldn't take it all." His wife pointed out that *McCall's* was giving women beautiful pictures but nothing they could really use. She said, "Advertising follows excellence. We've done a more serious, solid job. We're putting out a magazine women can believe in . . . the Journal's future is very secure. The advertising will come; the Journal is the magazine of excellence." [1]

In July, 1961, *McCall's* announced that effective in December it would regularly deliver a monthly paid circulation of 8,000,000. Its promotion read as if it had already reached that level. It said, "This represents a bonus of 1 million over McCall's present rate of 7 million and will be delivered at no extra charge through June, 1962. No matter how much Mc-Call's circulation rises during the coming year, no increase in

[1] Quoted in *Advertising Age*, May 8, 1961.

advertising rates is contemplated before July, 1962. And then, when new rates are announced, *there will be no increase in the rate per page per thousand.*"

There is no defense against something for nothing. Robert MacNeal was stung to bitter—and helpless—retort. He issued a press release July 18, 1961. In part it read:

> With advertising rates already unprofitably low in the women's magazine field, McCall's promise of a million bonus circulation free of charge is obviously a hurried move calculated to preserve the illusion of leadership. . . . For McCall's to ascribe their move to enormous reader demand at the very time when they are tempting dealers to 'eat' copies by making whopping bonus offers for extra newsstand sales and extending the sales period in hopes that someone will buy a copy is obviously nonsense. . . . The astute buyer of advertising has, of course, not allowed McCall's hocus-pocus to obscure the fact that they have again bid for leadership by making another unjustified price cut. Emphasis should be on quality and effectiveness of the product rather than merely on price. We consider McCall's move a form of ego satisfaction rather than sound publishing practice and we see no virtue in winning a race to the poorhouse. Therefore, although we will adjust prices competitively, on a delivered cost per thousand basis to meet this latest gimmick, our circulation will not be inflated, but will continue to reflect the true level of reader interest in the Journal's editorial and advertising content.

MacNeal was right, but neither his being right nor the profit-erasing cost of the battle for circulation and advertising helped Curtis. *McCall's* overtook and passed the Ladies' Home Journal, and advertisers wanted the bigger book at the lower price.

The Journal was losing. So was The Saturday Evening Post. The number of advertising pages in the Post fell from 3,687 in 1954 to 2,816 five years later in 1959. There was a pervading sense of decline at Curtis both within the company and in magazine and advertising circles. Robert Fuoss set out to find out what was wrong and what could be done about it.

Chapter 23

The New *Saturday Evening Post*

Circulation could pay top price for subscriptions. Research could prove that advertisements in The Saturday Evening Post were brought before the influential men and women of the country hundreds of millions of times. The Post could stud its pages with "Adventures of the Mind" and the latest Hollywood gossip, but none of it seemed to make any difference.

Advertising managers and agency account executives listened politely to the elaborate presentations and earnest arguments of Curtis space salesmen, but their wives and children liked television. When they looked at a magazine at all, they looked at *Life*, perhaps *Look*. The Saturday Evening Post was getting thin. It looked unimpressive. It had lost important advertising accounts, and, according to Joe at lunch or Bill at the golf club, it was going to lose more. Research was important, of course, but a guy has to keep his ear to the ground and his eye peeled. You have to go to the grass roots. The Post looked like a loser, and you can't go with a loser. The Post was promoting too hard, always a bad sign. Everyone knew that some of its space salesmen were looking around for new jobs. It was too bad. The Saturday Evening Post had been the greatest once—and pretty snotty about it.

Fuoss looked inside Curtis. He worried through the complexities of circulation and emerged with suspicion verified. Every Saturday Evening Post subscription cost more, often much more, to obtain than the money it brought in. He tried

244

to find out what specific difficulties its space salesmen were having in selling the Post and what, if anything, could be done about them.

Fuoss went outside. He traveled talking with advertisers and agency men. They liked the Post. Older men felt an affection for it. Younger men, brought up on radio and television, professed to admire it too. Yet, business is business, and the volatile advertising business is as imitative as it is unstable.

Everywhere he went Fuoss got the same story. The big advertisers had turned to television for mass exposure. What they had left of their appropriations they did not wish to spend in mass magazines to reach the same market. They turned to the small-circulation trade and association publications, the special interest magazines, to reach consumers of given vocational or avocational kinds. If they used mass magazines at all, they went with the largest and those they considered the most popular, and that list did not any longer include The Saturday Evening Post.

Fuoss gave them his word that the Post would come back. It would become more vital, more vigorous. It would compel attention it was not getting. He promised that The Saturday Evening Post would reassume its position of leadership. Now the trick was to make good on his promises. Obviously change was needed. He reported his experiences, and his arguments were convincing. There was an even more convincing argument for change and the attempt to establish a "new image" for The Saturday Evening Post. Increases in advertising rates, new discounts for various space units, repetition, frequency, and joint advertising in other Curtis magazines, the acceptance of liquor advertisements, and regional issue advertising brought Post advertising revenue to a record $97,456,146 in 1959, but advertising linage was steadily declining.

The Saturday Evening Post had been redesigned and appeared in new dress with the issue of October 1, 1955. A new body type, different layout, greater use of white space, and changed title display were adopted. Each issue featured a two-page spread of bleed color to depict "The Face of America" in photographs. This had been bold revision. It was revolutionary change that Fuoss planned now and to which Hibbs—who reiterated his determination to resign at the end of 1961—agreed.

Hibbs asked Fuoss whom he wanted to work with him in producing the "New Post." Fuoss asked for Kenneth Stuart, the Post's art editor, and Clay Blair, Jr. Recommended by Robert Sherrod who had known him when both worked for Time, Inc., Blair, a Virginian, had been hired in 1957 as Washington correspondent for the Post. According to both Hibbs and Fuoss, Blair did an aggressive job in Washington, provoking rather than writing colorful and even powerful articles. As a result he was brought to Philadelphia and made an associate editor when Jack Alexander was seriously ill. In 1961 he was made one of three assistant managing editors.

Hibbs and Sherrod ran The Saturday Evening Post all through the spring and summer of 1961 while Fuoss, Stuart, and Blair worked excitedly on the changed magazine they envisioned. Full-scale promotion of the "New Post" began almost as soon as work on it was started. The promotion mounted in intensity. A tremendous teaser campaign became an enfevered beating of tom-toms as time for its appearance neared. Curtis spent $1,350,000 in the effort. A full-page advertisement in *The New York Times,* September 7, 1961, was ecstatic in large type.

. . . It will be the freshest voice to be heard in the land—springing from deep breaths of the bracing air of new graphic design and inspired by the power of the written word . . . new features whose purpose is to be weeks, months, even years ahead of press coverage. . . . It will speak . . . in the bubbling staccato of youth, whose language our new young men and women editors dig well. . . . It will sing the tune of these changing, challenging times. . . . a constructive force in America . . . Unpredictable, unique and urgent reading. LIKE NO OTHER MAGAZINE YOU HAVE EVER READ BEFORE.

Another full page in the *Times,* September 12, carried "REVOLUTION" in great black type as heading for a shorter outburst.

Suddenly, The Saturday Evening Post explodes with a blazing new spirit. Color runs riot. Imagination is king. The printed word rises to new glory. A new creative freedom comes to magazines—and the roar of excitement can be heard round the reading and advertising world. Vive la revolution! In the new Saturday Evening Post—out today—suddenly reading becomes a new adventure.

The "New Post" dated September 16, 1961, opened with "the blast," the featured feature. Articles were intact on consecutive pages. There were no jumps. Advertising pages were not massed fore and aft but inserted throughout the issue. A new feature, "Speaking Out: The Voice of Dissent," was established in the front matter. Another new feature was "People on the Way Up." There was a humor department of four pages of jokes and cartoons. The editorial page was relegated to the back of the book.

These changes were hardly startling, but the appearance of the new Saturday Evening Post was. Traditional Post dignity had been banished. All formality and restraint were gone from artwork and illustrations. The switch was to what its creators or adopters called "Iconography," symbolism, impressionism. Colors were stark. The inspiration is said to have been phonograph record albums. It looked to be packaging in general. The familiar Norman Rockwell covers were exiled. Color photography, sometimes impressionistic painting, took their place. Photographs, mostly in color, were chosen to show "physical action" designed to arouse "an emotional response."

Given a preview of the New Post, Ben Hibbs said it was not his kind of magazine or one he could edit. He went to MacNeal and asked that the date of his resignation, already set for December 31, 1961, be advanced. MacNeal convinced him to remain.

Fuoss talked to about 150 Curtis executives in a meeting at Pocono Manor about the New Post. "We are battling for our corporate lives and we are battling enemies who think they've got us. But none of us shrinks from the challenge. A new day is dawning—when we can demonstrate again how great is the contribution this magazine can make to the nation. . . . We'll retain our integrity and central character—but beyond that, all shibboleths are out. There's room to be as bold, as daring, as creative as can be."

In a promotional motion picture shown to Curtis advertising and circulation people about the country Fuoss said with an understandable gleam in his eye, "It's my turn now."

When it reached the newsstands and its subscribers the New Post aroused all the attention its sponsors could have wished. Many readers were horrified. The New Post was sacrilege and heresy. Other readers were merely aghast. Some were even tolerant. The New Post was all right if you liked that kind of thing. The point was that it was not The Saturday Evening Post as they knew and respected it. Designers and agency art directors expressed enthusiasm. This was what they considered proper recognition of the importance of graphics. As they knew the first issue would be looked at, advertisers had supported it with 82 pages of advertising. They made polite noises when the September 16 Post appeared, but few bought more space than usual in subsequent issues.

No revamped magazine could possibly have lived up to the raucous ballyhoo that preceded the debut of the New Post, and it was quickly apparent that only the surface of the magazine had been changed. The iconography, action pictures, and new layout had simply been superimposed on a Saturday Evening Post that did not really differ in content from the old. Only in the promotion for it had the touted new glory been achieved. The change ruined the Post's image with its faithful readers and failed to attract new ones.

On its usual sample basis Reader Research discovered that a majority of its readers liked the New Post, but The Curtis Publishing Company received thousands of letters castigating or deploring the change. Their writers may not have constituted an accurate sample of Post readers, but what they lacked in statistical accuracy they made up for in vilification.

The back cover of the professionally derisive *Mad* magazine, March, 1962, was a parody of the annual Benjamin

Franklin cover of The Saturday Evening Post, published that year as of January 20, 1962. Ironically, *Mad* saluted "all them dizzy layouts and bold editorial ideas that are supposed to make reading a new adventure in the allegedly revamped—but actually the same old tired Saturday Evening Post." Then, adding malice to insult, it showed the bust of Franklin with a clothespin over its nose, and in the usual box on the traditional Post cover quoted its patron saint. "I cannot but wish that our American printers would in their editions avoid those fancied improvements and thereby render their works more agreeable."

Certainly the New Post was not the sole cause, but its gross advertising revenue fell almost $18,000,000 in 1961 from 1960 —from $103,930,304 to $86,442,603. At the same time the Ladies' Home Journal dropped from $28,336,234 to $26,511,-007. Holiday slipped by almost $2,000,000, and even American Home was down to $8,125,499.

The situation was far worse than these advertising revenue figures indicate.

Every year from its founding in 1890 through 1960 The Curtis Publishing Company had shown a profit, in its golden years an enormous profit. In 1960 it had had an income of only $1,079,361 on a gross of $248,607,091, but a profit. Then came the collapse.

In 1961 for the first time Curtis showed a loss, and the loss was substantial. It reported a net loss of $4,193,585—and the loss would have been more than twice that amount had it not been for a federal tax refund and the sale of more than $3,000,000 in company securities.

In the annual report for 1961 Robert MacNeal wrote that the huge deficit was directly attributable to the loss in advertising linage and that two major factors had contributed to that loss.

. . . One was the growth and multiplicity of rumors suggesting drastic change in ownership and policies of the company, elimination of one or more of its magazines, sales of its paper mills or manufacturing plant and, finally, doubt as to its financial stability. To appreciate the insidious effect on this campaign on placement of advertising it is essential to realize that, unlike other manufacturing enterprises, magazine publishing deals basically in intangibles. The product is a new one each week or month. Its effectiveness for advertising is a function of its reader acceptance and trust. Its character and reputation are as important as solvency to a bank. None of the dire consequences implicit in the rumor have materialized, nor are any included in our plans for the future.

The second major factor contributing to reduced advertising linage has been the natural hesitation of advertising agencies and advertisers to place firm schedules in the face of dramatic and far reaching changes in The Saturday Evening Post. . . .

MacNeal was whistling with desperate courage in the dark. Once again, he was right. There had been malicious and damaging rumors, and they were multiplying. The New Post had certainly aroused a "natural hesitation" on the part of advertisers and agencies. Once more, his being right was of little help.

Its cover price raised to 20 cents, the two year-end issues of The Saturday Evening Post were combined to save production and distribution expense. Even in good times these issues contained little advertising. With that combined issue, December 23–30, 1961, the Post went over 7,000,000 in circulation.

The Curtis Circulation Company went all out to achieve this record for the Post's retiring editor. In the issue was Ben Hibbs's final editorial, titled "Let's Stand Up on Our Hind Legs and Be Americans." In it Hibbs spoke of his boyhood on the Kansas prairies when everything was serene and America was generally considered the Land of Opportunity. He mentioned his 20-year editorship of The Saturday Evening Post, then deplored the changes that had come over the United States.

The seeds of doubt—doubt of ourselves—are becoming too strong within us. . . . I think it is high time that we all started saying a few kind words for Uncle Sam. . . . These are bewildering times, fearful times . . . our only safeguard is to remain strong, strong in heart and fiber as well as in arms . . . I think we still have it in us to dream and achieve, to be gallant and proud, to stand up on our hind legs and be Americans.

This was pure Ben Hibbs. It was Kansas, sentimental, and decent. It was not his fault or the fault of The Saturday Evening Post that moral fiber in the individual had become an anachronism or that Uncle Sam, an imperious figure on World War I recruiting posters, was now almost entirely a cartoon figure.

Robert M. Fuoss became editor-in-chief of The Saturday Evening Post with the issue for January 6, 1962. His opening editorial was almost defiant. The Post would be non-partisan. Under his editorship it would back no party but the best man. Fuoss struck at journalism which always provoked "a predictable response" and at "push-button Americans." He said he would make The Saturday Evening Post "an island of free expression" and wished to help "make our nation a show-case of liberty."

Fuoss wrote that he would uphold the American free enterprise system against every challenge. He continued, "I feel that we, collectively, have grown fearful and hesitant in our commitment to America. There is a danger that we have become tired and cynical, over-zealous for security, afraid to live and afraid to die." He felt reassured when he heard the booming of the clock in the steeple of Independence Hall outside his office. It spoke of men who loved, believed, dared, "and said to a hostile world, 'We believe these truths to be self-evident' . . ."

Fuoss spoke, comparatively, as a liberal. The hesitancy and fear he noted were certainly there. The Americanism he upheld was the same as that of Hibbs—or Lorimer. The difficulty was that "free enterprise" existed as little more than an ideal of the NAM or a fiction to which public speakers paid dutiful obeisance. Many of his readers might feel as he did about the excessive pursuit of security, but Americans had been demanding and getting more and more of its from government for 30 years.

Despite its $4,000,000 loss, The Curtis Publishing Company was still big business. The circulations of its magazines were tremendous. It had a score of active subsidiaries. It was printing more than 1,000,000 magazines a day. Long lines of freight cars moved across the country packed floor to ceiling with copies of The Saturday Evening Post, the Ladies' Home Journal, Holiday, American Home, and Jack and Jill. Curtis was one of the largest customers of the United States Post Office. The fully integrated magazine publishing company was big, but its very bigness was now a handicap. It meant huge outgo on diminishing income.

In an effort to cut costs, MacNeal ordered the dismissal of scores of clerical and lower echelon employees at the end of 1961. He curtailed expenses in every direction, then looked about to accomplish further savings. Early in 1962 he decided to cut the number of editorial columns in The Saturday Evening Post which had always been held to a minimum of 220 an issue. He also decided to cancel publication of costly seasonal editions of the magazine. His plan was to continue combination of the last two December issues, then to combine the first two issues in January, and to publish only five issues during the ten-week period between July 4 and Labor Day. This would mean dropping from 52 to 45 issues a year, charging the same subscription price and the same 20-cent cover price.

MacNeal informed Fuoss of his decision. There had already been persistent rumors that, like the badgered *Collier's*, The Saturday Evening Post would sink to biweekly publication. Everywhere he spoke Fuoss had promised consecutive weekly publication of a revitalized magazine. He felt that he had made a personal commitment to advertisers and to readers. He told MacNeal that he could not agree to the suggested schedule. He would agree to any "predictable pattern of publication"—weekly, biweekly, even monthly—but not to this hit-or-miss issuance for which it would be impossible to edit. He would have to resign if it was adopted. MacNeal was adamant. Old friends, they agreed to think about it overnight.

Robert E. MacNeal.

The next day MacNeal asked Fuoss if he had changed his mind. Fuoss said that he had not and asked him if he had changed his. MacNeal had not. Fuoss resigned. His name was on the Post masthead as editor for just three months, appearing for the last time April 7, 1962. In a statement issued March 26 MacNeal announced that Robert Sherrod,

53, would replace "Robert Fuoss who has voluntarily resigned because of a completely friendly but irreconcilable difference of opinion with management on matters of policy" and that Clay Bair, Jr., 36, had been appointed managing editor of The Saturday Evening Post.

The real Saturday Evening Post ended with the retirement of George Horace Lorimer in 1937—or on the appearance of the "New Post" in September, 1961—or at this point in 1962. It was of the essence of The Saturday Evening Post that it brought Saturday evening to the United States every Thursday afternoon. The Post that followed Hibbs and Fuoss was not even a reasonable facsimile of the magazine which Curtis had published since 1897; and The Curtis Publishing Company as it had been known and respected for 72 years—or for 79 years if the 1883 founding of the Ladies' Home Journal is taken as the beginning—ceased to exist in 1962.

Chapter 24

The Sea Change

Even those who did not hate it unduly often called it the "do-nothing" Curtis board of directors. Sometimes they used the term almost affectionately. It was accurate. Dominated by the Curtis trust and the Bok interests, the board was complacently inert. If prodded, it resisted by digging in its toes. There were mild stockholder protests now and then, but they were parried. For a long time, except when death removed someone who was supplanted by someone else much like him, the board was intact. Curtis won one proxy fight but was forced to admit a single outsider. Then it settled down comfortably again. In 1962 it was driven to disturbing concessions.

J. R. Williston & Beane & Co., Carl M. Loeb, Rhoades & Co., and the Peter Treves Co., brokerages which controlled about 600,000 shares of Curtis common and preferred stock, demanded representation. M. McLean Stewart, and Milton S. Gould, a New York lawyer who represented Treves, were seated on the Curtis board. At a meeting, March 18, 1962, they assured the officers of the company that they did not constitute and did not plan to become a "wrecking crew." The trustees and Bok interests still held financial control of The Curtis Publishing Company with 32 per cent of its outstanding stock, and Walter D. Fuller was still on the board and on its three-man executive committee, but board control

255

was shifting, and, when more newcomers were added, was lost to the old guard.

Still protesting the damaging complexity of rumors, saying that loss of advertising revenue was principally responsible for "the temporary inability to show a profit," MacNeal expressed confidence in the reconstructed Curtis magazines and a multi-million cost reduction plan just instituted. In a policy statement dated March 26, 1962, he said Curtis would encourage newsstand sales and de-emphasize cut-price subscriptions. For many years Curtis had disdained such cut-price enticements, but all of the big magazines were engaged in them now. A *McCall's* maneuver, he said, forced the Ladies' Home Journal into continuance of a ten per cent discount on its advertising rates.

MacNeal also disclosed the resignation of Bruce and Beatrice Gould as editors of the troubled magazine. They were succeeded by Curtis Anderson, 34, who had come from *Better Homes & Gardens* and had been managing editor of the Journal. Bruce Gould said elsewhere that he and his wife resigned when they saw they could no nothing more to save The Curtis Publishing Company.[1]

MacNeal's statement was meant to be reassuring. The facts were not. The Curtis magazines, particularly the pamphlet-thin Saturday Evening Post were losing advertising at an accelerated rate. Manufacturing costs were increasing. A strike at its paper mills cost Curtis $2,400,000 in outside sales. Between 1958 and 1962 Curtis's mailing costs had risen $8,000,000. Against a gain of over $2,000,000 in the first quarter of 1961, Curtis rang up a loss of $4,000,000 in the second quarter of 1962.

The situation at Curtis was involved, confused, feverish, and verging on panic. Mrs. Zimbalist was 85 years old. Cary W. Bok was divorced from actual company operations. There was no direction from the principal owners of the company. Peter Treves journeyed down from his offices in the Paramount

---

[1] Gould, Bruce and Beatrice Blackmar, *American Story* (New York: Harper & Row, Inc., 1968).

Building in New York to tell MacNeal he should resign. He did not.

MacNeal went to Europe on business for the company. He was in Spain in April, 1962, when he received notice that he had been summarily dismissed from the job that was paying him $131,700 a year. Two weeks later the Curtis board of directors elected Matthew J. Culligan, 44, president of The Curtis Publishing Company.

A product of Manhattan's Washington Heights and a graduate of a Christian Brothers school there, Culligan was a supersalesman who had become sales vice president of NBC radio, then gone on to become a "general corporate executive" of Marion Harper, Jr.'s New York advertising complex, Interpublic, Inc.

Wearing a black patch over his left eye which had been destroyed in the Battle of the Bulge, Culligan galloped into Curtis like a young Lochinvar from the east, though his steed was the Curtis helicopter which he used to commute from his home in Rye, New York, to Philadelphia. Energy-charged, fast-talking, exuding optimism, Culligan signed on at about $130,000 a year under a five-year contract with a guarantee of further payments in the unlikely event of failure. Over a fanfare of steam calliope publicity Culligan promised to restore Curtis immediately to its former greatness.

With him he swept in a completely new crew of executives, mostly from NBC or RCA. One was J. M. Clifford, an RCA vice president from California. With him he brought from RCA Gloria Swett, who was made secretary of The Curtis Publishing Company. Maurice W. Poppei, an accountant who had become an RCA vice president in data processing, was brought in. There were many more, almost none of them with any magazine publishing experience. Vice presidencies with lucrative contracts attached multiplied like maggots in cornmeal. Following the pattern set by Paul Smith at Collier's, Clay Blair, Jr. became both a vice president and editorial director of all the Curtis magazines. Marvin D. Kantor, who had been a Treves partner, then president of the J. R.

Williston & Beane brokerage before it was dissolved, was made another vice president somewhat later.

Culligan flew off on a barnstorming tour of the 100 top advertisers and the top 30 advertising agencies. It was a carnival progress. He pled for Curtis. He promised new life, new blood, young blood, dynamic marketing. He prophesied wonders, new purpose, new brilliance. Most of them in their late 30's, the newcomers pounded their chests with Tarzan-like cries, boasting of their youth and drive and deriding the tired old men whose senility they had supplanted with their irresistible vigor. They forgot—more likely never knew—that Cyrus Curtis was 33 when he founded the Ladies' Home Journal, Bok 26 when he became its editor, Lorimer 31 (he liked to say 30) when he was made editor of The Saturday Evening Post, Hibbs just 40 and Fuoss 29 when they came to power.

If they had no experience neither had the new executives any interest in mere magazine publishing. They made it clear that they came from higher and more rarefied realms. Their self-appreciation was matched only by their naïveté, but one thing was sure. The Lilliputians had Gulliver spread-eagled and staked helpless to the ground.

The contrast between the new Curtis men and the old was painfully ludicrous. In reality there was no contrast because there were no points of resemblance between them in appearance or manner. Younger men who had served the old regime hurriedly sought jobs elsewhere. Older men, who had spent anywhere from 20 to 40 years in Curtis and had slight chance of employment anywhere else at anything like the levels they had attained, were paralyzed by fear.

Blair was made head of an all-powerful committee with representatives from Editorial, Advertising, Circulation, and other departments, to review the work of every department in The Curtis Publishing Company. Robert MacNeal served on the committee. Heart-broken and bitter, MacNeal could not quit the company where he had spent his life without trying his utmost to help. That Curtis should fail or vanish was incredible to him. The holocaust he was forced to witness horrified him.

It was a Star Chamber proceeding. Arbitrary decisions followed on committee inquisition. Curtis service departments were wiped out. Every department was decimated, then decimated again and again. Some men were forcibly retired. Others were discharged with due notice and severance pay. Many got neither pension nor severance.

Followed usually by sycophantic henchmen the new dictator stalked the Curtis offices and corridors exercising the power of job life and death over those to whom Curtis was home as well as livelihood. It was rumored that he represented one, sometimes another, of the brokerages which were now dictating Curtis policy. It was said he represented Admiral Lewis Strauss, head of the Atomic Energy Commission, who was thought to own large investments in Curtis. Strauss later assured Ben Hibbs that he had never invested so much as a dime in The Curtis Publishing Company.

Marty Sommers looked at some of the new appointments and could not believe what he saw. Of one newly exalted figure he said, "Why, the s.o.b. can't even spell!" Other sins Marty might be able to forgive. Another Post editor with 20 years of hard and honorable service behind him, said, "It could pucker a man's soul." A third said, "Godammit it!" and left.

By mid-1962 Curtis was antic revelry loosed. A vice president or manager one day and jobless the next was commonplace. The guillotine went up slowly and fell with its decapitating crash. Reprieve was almost worse. It was announced that the editorial and advertising departments of The Saturday Evening Post would leave Philadelphia for New York and that the other Curtis magazines would follow. Somehow geography would erase the ills that even the new management could not cure. Post editors and executives were asked to move to New York—or they were not. A man found out in that way whether he was to be retained and suffer only the inconvenience and expense of moving and an uncertain future or to be left where he was and thus dismissed. Few enjoyed the waiting to be invited or the invitation when it came or the lack of it when it did not.

The brave new Curtis announced its firings jubilantly and the press reported them zealously. How the mighty fall is always happy news. After his retirement as editor of the Post, Ben Hibbs remained as a senior editor. He wanted occupation and to help Fuoss and Sherrod as he could. As far back as his days on Country Gentleman, Hibbs had been sought by DeWitt Wallace for *The Reader's Digest*. Wallace renewed his offer. Not yet ready to give up on the Post, Hibbs remained until he could stand the debacle no longer. He resigned a second time and went to the *Digest* as a senior editor.

Giving an unnamed top Curtis executive as its source, *Newsweek* published, November 26, 1962, a list of men newly discharged from Curtis. It named Ben Hibbs as one of them and carried his picture only with the story headlined "Dismissed." Already badly hurt at the collapse of what was to him the country's greatest magazine, Hibbs was angered. He objected violently, and *Newsweek* duly printed his letter with a retraction, but, as usual, the displayed initial story made its impression while the correction went virtually unnoticed.

Many at Curtis had long seen disaster approaching, for it was impossible not to see it, but they could not believe it when it came. Suddenly right had become left and up was down—everything was down. It had always been up and upright. You got up in the morning, took the Paoli Local, and went to Independence Square. You saw the green Curtis trucks looking as much like horse-drawn drays as mechanized vehicles could. You walked through the white marble lobby past the bust of Benjamin Franklin expecting to see Tighlman as you took the elevator. Life was lived at Sixth and Walnut. Suddenly it was not there any more.

Some 2,000 Curtis employees were wiped out in the 1962 purge. Some discovered their fate in strange ways. The Curtis medical director found out that he had been dismissed when he saw the name of his successor listed in a program he received in the mail as speaker at a forthcoming medical convention. The pogrom had its refinement.

Culligan issued a command invitation for Robert Sherrod and Norman Rockwell to appear at his home. They obeyed. He then enthusiastically suggested a round-the-world trip, Sherrod to write up and Rockwell to paint world celebrities. When Sherrod objected that he could hardy leave his desk for that long, Culligan reassured him. Perforce the editor and artist left and did as directed. When they returned, Sherrod found that he had been supplanted as editor of The Saturday Evening Post by Blair. Sherrod was made Post "editor at large."

Chunks of Curtis and crowds of personnel were disappearing so fast that no one could keep track. From his home in St. David's Martin Sommers wrote a friend, October 18, 1962, "Until I phoned yesterday I didn't know (at least I think I didn't know, the goings and comings have blown up such a fuzzy whirlwind I wouldn't take my oath on what I know and what I don't know) that you had taken off. . . . I can't recall whether or not I told you that when Curtis moved the SEP editorial offices to New York I was invited to go along, but decided to take advantage of early voluntary retirement instead."

In 1962, eight months of the year under its new management, The Curtis Publishing Company lost $18,917,000, beggaring its loss of a mere $4,193,585 in 1961.[2]

The new editor of The Saturday Evening Post announced that the magazine would go in for "sophisticated muckraking." It may not have been sophisticated, but it produced results and got all the free publicity its public relations department could ever have wished. Undisputed leader in the magazine world, Curtis had ruled for years with almost absolute power. It had been arbitrary and sometimes contemptuously insolent. The press has a long memory. It headlined Curtis's troubles day after day and often could hardly conceal its glee. Journalistic pundits offered condescending condolences and sage

[2] To make this staggering loss look less a collapse, the annual report of The Curtis Publishing Company for 1962 listed $9,004,000 as "loss from operations" in 1961.

advice. The press was delighted with the results which Post muckraking soon displayed.

"The Story of a Football Fix," March 23, 1963, brought libel suits for $10,000,000 from Wallace Butts, ex-coach of the University of Georgia, and Paul Bryant, coach at the University of Alabama. The Post story had reported an overheard telephone call in which, supposedly, the Georgia coach gave his rival information which resulted in a football victory for Alabama. Bryant accepted a tax-free settlement of $300,000. After prolonged litigation and a series of appeals, Butts collected $460,000 which accrued interest brought to a total of $600,000. After appearance of "The Automakers and their Mighty Works," September 19, 1964, the ex-president of the Chrysler Corporation sued for $2,000,000. Suits for libel or invasion of privacy are routine in magazine publishing, but the muckraking Post was setting new records. Though some suits were dropped and others settled out of court, libel suits against Curtis reached a reported $40,000,000.

This exceeded the loan of $35,000,000 which Curtis obtained in November, 1963, from a syndicate of five banks spearheaded by Serge Semenenko, vice chairman of the First National Bank of Boston. Semenenko, who described himself as a constructive financier interested in making sick companies well, thus became another behind-the-scenes power in The Curtis Publishing Company.

Culligan's whirlwind salesmanship and the wholesale firings were beginning of pay off. Curtis loss in 1963 was only $4,393,000. Compared to that of the year before this was improvement. The multi-million loss was hailed as a triumph, and great things were prophesied for 1964. They came, to more and larger newspaper headlines, but not quite in the way the loquaciously optimistic Culligan and his obedient chorus foresaw.

Chapter 25

The Circus—Maximus

The *annus mirabilis* of this travesty on magazine publishing was 1964. Played extravagantly to a national audience which far exceeded the combined circulations of all the Curtis magazines, the farce gamboled through tragi-comedy to grotesque denouement.

Harold Martin met Matthew J. Culligan for the first time when Culligan dashed into Atlanta on his crusade to save The Saturday Evening Post. The man who introduced them said he hoped the new Curtis president would allow Martin to continue writing his column for the *Constitution*. Culligan, who probably was not too sure at that point who Martin was, said abruptly, "I don't care who he writes for."

For Harold Martin, as for several other writers, The Saturday Evening Post died when tough-minded, warm-hearted Martin Sommers left. As an associate editor, Martin kept on writing for the magazine, but for him the real Post was gone. For the Post of August 24–31, 1963 he wrote a full-page editorial which he would have been glad not to write. Bordered with a thin black rule, the editorial was headed simply, "Martin Sommers." Sommers had died in Philadelphia, July 17.

It was a piece in which, had the subject been any other man, Marty Sommers would not have changed a word. Martin said that Sommers was the friend of Wall Street bankers, Hong Kong bartenders, Main Line matrons, and fat old

Frenchwomen who ran small restaurants in Paris. He loved writers. He hated phonies.

. . . From a head that looked too big for his short, bandy-legged body there poured a daily torrent of story ideas, both foreign and domestic. He knew writers all over the world, both good ones and bad ones, and he had a genius for keeping the good ones producing at top performance and for spurring the bad ones to write better than they knew. When they turned in a piece that pleased him, his praise was unstinted. When they failed, his criticism was gently phrased, and his suggestions were so clear and sensible a child could follow them. When only a little carpentry was needed, he did the job himself, running his hands through a mop of silver-blond hair that gave him, in his younger days, the look of a lost angel, he would stab at a manuscript savagely with a big black pencil, muttering incoherent phrases of anger or approval. With masterly craftsmanship he excised the useless word, clarified the muddy sentence, smoothed the awkward transition, cut out the soft spot where the writer had spread a compost of verbiage to conceal a lack of facts. . . .

In late September, 1964, Culligan knew who Harold Martin was. He sent out an urgent call for him, Robert Sherrod, and Stewart Alsop to meet him immediately in his New York apartment. When the three got there, he told them that he had been faced with an ultimatum. Clay Blair, Jr.—now senior vice president, editor of The Saturday Evening Post, editorial director of all the Curtis magazines, a member of the Curtis board of directors—and Marvin Kantor, also a senior vice president and owner of 4,000 shares of Curtis common stock with options on another 30,000 shares, were demanding his resignation. They led a group of 17 editorial and executive dissidents who backed their demand.

This was on a Friday. The Blair–Kantor ultimatum was that unless Culligan resigned none of them would report for work on the following Monday, and there would be no Saturday Evening Post three weeks hence. Months of friction, infighting, and cut-throat conflict inside Curtis had preceded this ultimatum.

The charges made by the two men whom Culligan had placed in positions of power and given almost unlimited license were shrill but vague. They accused Culligan of maladministration. They did not like him. They felt they were stronger than he. They wanted him out, and they wanted his job.

Culligan now proposed that Martin, Sherrod, and Alsop take over editorship of The Saturday Evening Post. Sherrod had been editor and may well have wished the job back, but that was not suggested. Alsop was on the Post staff as political writer and columnist. He did not wish the job, nor did Martin who told Culligan that he was a writer and would remain one. He had no wish and he doubted that he had the ability to edit. Martin then proposed a counter ploy.

The rebels were holding a meeting only a few blocks away. Martin suggested that he go to talk with them. While Culligan, Sherrod, and Alsop waited, he did. Martin faced the determined and indignant rebels who felt they had their victim by the throat. He told them that except for Blair and Kantor, backed by Gould and presumably by Treves, the Curtis directors were scattered for the weekend. It would be impossible to reach them for decision, thus no action could be taken. Would they continue to act like children or appear for work on Monday and wait for the scheduled meeting of the Curtis board on October 1? The men he addressed murmured, muttered, and renewed their threats.

When Martin reported back, Culligan demanded excitedly what the answer was. Martin told him there was none yet. Sherrod, Alsop, Martin, and the enfevered Curtis president waited an hour, then telephoned. The rebels agreed to return to work on the Monday and await the board's decision. They despatched a letter to M. Albert Linton, chairman of the board's executive committee, charging Matthew J. Culligan with gross mismanagement of The Curtis Publishing Company.

The New York Times broke the story of the revolt with a three-column spread on its front page, October 9, 1964, disclosing that the charges against Culligan had been aired at the Curtis board meeting on October 1. The story was taken up and got headline attention throughout the press. At a special directors' meeting October 19, the board resolved the situation neatly. Blair and Kantor were dismissed from Curtis employ. Culligan—who had the backing of Serge Semenenko —was removed as president but retained as chairman of the board. After the meeting Culligan triumphantly took ten of the board members to lunch in the Downtown Club. Blair and Kantor left in a waiting Lincoln.

Immediately, Blair, who had been getting $75,000 a year, and Kantor, who had been getting $80,000, filed suit against The Curtis Publishing Company. They claimed that they had been wrongfully discharged and demanded $36,250 as accrued deferred compensation and unearned sums for the balance of their contracts totaling $500,000. In settlement, December 28, 1964, each man accepted $75,000. In the language of a Curtis notice of the annual meeting of its stockholders, April 21, 1965, "Under the Settlement Agreement Mr. Blair and Mr. Kantor have agreed not to take voluntarily any action directly or indirectly injurious to the Company for a period of two years." After that, presumably, they were free to do as they pleased.

Culligan had lasted as Curtis president just a little over two years. He resigned as chairman of the board and left the company March 4, 1965. He had presided over most of the loss of nearly $19,000,000 in 1962, the loss of over $4,000,000 in 1963 and a more impressive $13,947,000 loss in 1964. Under the terms of his contract he would still receive $110,000 in 1966 and for ten years would receive $20,093 annually. Curtis found the Blair–Kantor–Culligan extravaganza expensive.

The Curtis Publishing Company had bought a full 20-page supplement in *The New York Times* of Sunday, October 11, 1964, to plug its magazines and celebrate the new "Saturday Evening Post Building" in which it had leased office space at 641 Lexington Avenue. The multi-page advertisement, which boasted Curtis history, accomplishments, and widespread assets, was rich with illustrations and blazing with promises of future achievement. Curtis had provided even more entertainment than it pledged. The palace revolution which had unseated both adversaries was only part of the program.

Holiday's circulation was about 1,000,000. It had lost and was losing advertising but, proportionately, not as much as The Saturday Evening Post or the Ladies' Home Journal. In Philadelphia, Holiday had never quite belonged. Resented by the other Curtis editors who had not been consulted when it was founded, dependent through most of the 1950's on the earnings of the Post, it had not been fully accepted by the conservative Curtis organization. Holiday itself considered that it was cosmopolitan and metropolitan, of New York, where Patrick spent most of his time when he was in this country, rather than of parochial Philadelphia.

In the 1960's the situation was reversed. The Post and Journal were the immigrant country cousins in New York. Editorially, Holiday was established; commercially it was almost holding its own. The new Curtis management had placed none of its partisans on Holiday, which was thus able to repulse any indications of attack. Smooth enough to deal with gauche pretenders, Ted Patrick was able to keep his magazine out of the general fracas.

Patrick died in March, 1964. Harry Sions, Albert H. Farnsworth, Frank Zachary, and picture editor Louis F. V. Mercier had worked closely with Patrick and helped establish Holiday. They expected, not unreasonably, that one of them or all of them as a group would now edit the magazine. Instead, Blair, still in office, appointed Don Schanche, a recent Curtis arrival who had become managing editor of The Saturday Evening Post.

The original Holiday men were restive under direction by an outsider who, they felt, knew little or nothing of the spirit and policy of Holiday. For eight months they suffered under what they felt intolerable conditions and watched what they considered the ruination of the glamorous magazine they had helped bring into being. In December, 1964, they presented their ultimatum to the new Curtis president. Curtis had been hard put to it to find a successor to Culligan. No one wanted the once coveted post. It went by default to John C. Clifford, whom Culligan had brought in from RCA.

The ultimatum was that Schanche go or they would resign. This time the rebels had the sympathy of the press and of the Holiday writers with whom they had worked. Clifford was a cautious executive responsible to the banks to which by this time The Curtis Publishing Company owed $37,300,000. He was anxious to avoid further unpleasant notoriety for the company. Clifford was politic and went by the book. Schanche, succeeded later by Caskie Stinnett (novelist and Post humorist who had written deft promotion in "Speaking of Holiday"), was retained, and his insubordinate subordinates were allowed to resign. They left with surprisingly generous severance pay in December, 1964.

Even comparatively insignificant Jack and Jill had its revolution in 1964. Culligan had seized delightedly on the children's magazine as the one Curtis magazine property which consistently returned a profit. He held it up as an example of what Curtis could do with its other books and promised to do great things for it. When Jack and Jill published its 25th anniversary issue, November, 1963, Culligan contributed a full-page birthday greeting which he signed as president and board chairman of The Curtis Publishing Company. It ended:

> On this twenty-fifth birthday, I have one great wish for JACK AND JILL, and for all our boys and girls: Like Peter Pan, may each of you be blessed with the lightsome gladness, the curiosity, and the pure joy of those who are forever young at heart. May you keep forever the dreams and hopes and laughter of youth.

Jack and Jill readers knew the names of Ada Rose, Nancy Ford, and Karl Hoffmann. They probably wondered who Culligan was and what he was talking about.

To improve Jack and Jill, which had begun to take advertising, Culligan imported Dr. Frances R. Horwich, nationally known for "Miss Frances' Ding-Dong School" on the air (Culligan had once sold time for the show) as director of children's activities for The Curtis Publishing Company. He brought in a retired New York State public school administrator as editor.

When Curtis bought American Home from W. H. Eaton and Mrs. Jean Austin in April, 1958, it got one of its space salesmen, John J. Veronis. Veronis went rapidly to the top under the new regime. He became a senior vice president and director of the company's new "Magazine Division." Early in 1964 Veronis ordered Hoffmann from Philadelphia, where Jack and Jill had remained, to a meeting in New York. Hoffmann was summarily forced into early retirement and dismissed.

A few months later Veronis himself, caught in the in-fighting and after reported clashes with Blair and Kantor, was out of Curtis. Two years later, largely at the instigation of G. B. McCombs, who had followed Ulrich as president of the Curtis Circulation Company, Hoffmann was recalled. Overlaid with heavy new expenses, Jack and Jill was losing circulation and money. Dr. Horwich had left. Hoffmann discharged the educator editor, became editor himself—later publisher as well—and a second time restored Jack and Jill to material prosperity.

In 1965 a fluke, a freak of nature, perhaps "an Act of God," saved The Curtis Publishing Company.

It had been selling off subsidiaries and physical assets as fast as it could find buyers, but this piecemeal liquidation was not enough to stem the continuing financial drain. In 1963 the Texas Gulf Sulphur Company discovered an ore lode under its lands in northern Ontario. In April, 1964, it announced this discovery of an estimated 55,000,000 tons of copper, silver, and zinc ore. Curtis owned a great tract of land adjoining Texas Gulf Sulphur's holdings. In 1965 Curtis sold Texas Gulf Sulphur 13,000 acres in Kidd Township in Ontario outright. It retained a 50 per cent interest in the mineral profits from another 35,000 acres and a 10 per cent interest in returns from a third parcel of 50,000 acres. It also sold Texas Gulf 141,000 acres of timberlands in Pennsylvania, where it had already sold its Lock Haven paper mills. This sale brought Curtis $24,000,000. Semenenko's banking syndicate could breathe easier.

The bookkeeping and comparatively quiet Clifford administration was cutting costs into and under the bone. There
was wave after wave of dismissals. Departments were cut
to skeletal forces. In some there was no one to answer the
mail which piled up. The giant Curtis Building in Philadelphia, with the editorial and advertising offices of the magazines in New York, was silent. There were rows on rows of
empty offices. Junked equipment lay scattered on acreages
of what had once been busy factory space. When two men
met in the halls it was like a startled Robinson Crusoe coming
on a surprised Friday.

In 1966 Curtis showed an unexpected profit of $347,000—
a little more than normally little Jack and Jill returned. All
of the Curtis magazines except Holiday were up slightly in
advertising revenue.

Advertising Age hailed the "Curtis Comeback," March 6,
1967. In *The Saturday Review,* June 11, John Tebbel took
"A New Look at Curtis." He found that there was hope and
listed the encouraging signs. The signs were false. Curtis
lost $4,839,000 in 1967 and more in 1968; 1961 through 1968
it lost over $55,000,000.

Chapter 26

Last Act

The crumbling of The Curtis Publishing Company in 1961 and 1962 had been incomprehensible to Robert E. MacNeal. He could neither understand nor accept the magnitude of the disaster. His abrupt dismissal as president was a crushing blow, but worse was the spectacle of the shattered Curtis. Proud and seemingly impregnable, it was the helpless prey of exploiters and opportunists and too weak even to resent the machinations of enemies it once would not have deigned to notice.

Critics complained that MacNeal tried to do everything himself and that no man could. To an extent they were right, but Robert MacNeal worked in the only way he knew and by the business standards and practices he understood. He did not bring on the Curtis failure, though he could not avert it. Discarded, he left broken and ill. He never recovered, but he was spared the final shabbiness. Robert MacNeal, 64, died in a hospital in Somers Point, New Jersey, November 2, 1967. Ben Hibbs said, "I think he actually worked himself to death." A broken spirit did not help.

Curtis Bok had died in 1962. Walter Deane Fuller, still a member of the board of directors of The Curtis Publishing Company and of its three-man executive committee, died in 1964. He had spent 56 years with Curtis, most of them at the top making decisions—or avoiding them—for the company.

By 1968 Curtis and its magazines were distress merchandise. As such, it was only natural that they would attract the attention of a specialist.

A native of Rochester, New York, and a graduate of Syracuse University and Rutgers Law School, Martin S. Ackerman worked briefly as a law clerk with Louis Nizer in New York. He then became a partner in a small law firm, Rubin & Rubin. He studied corporate law, byways as well as highways, and, using the almost moribund United Whelan as a base, put together the Perfect Photo Company in 1962, buying 100,000 of its 300,000 shares himself. He developed this company into the Perfect Film and Chemical Corporation of Manhasset, Long Island, a film processor and a mail order merchandiser of vitamins and health aids. Ackerman was its $200,000 a year president.

Ackerman became president of The Curtis Publishing Company, April 22, 1968, and at the same time a creditor. He lent the nearly bankrupt company $5,000,000. Known for mergers, amalgamations, absorptions, and adept use of the mysterious devices of financial wizardry, Ackerman was viewed from the first as intending liquidation of Curtis. This he quickly, loudly, and insistently denied.

Ackerman had had his own car at 16 when he attended Benjamin Franklin High School in Rochester. He had never been poor. He owned two small banks in California. He drove back and forth to work in a chauffeur-driven Cadillac. Money was what he understood. Money was the object, and he made no secret of it. He opened his first formal meeting with Curtis executives by saying, "Good evening. I am Marty Ackerman. I am 36 years old, and I am very rich." He said he would make his listeners rich too.

No ostentation of modesty or undue humility hindered him. There was no idealization of The Saturday Evening Post or of Curtis. He pretended to no altruism, but he professed to be a lover of magazines. "I've always been a prolific magazine reader right from the time I was in school and college. I read every magazine I can get my hands on. On Saturday mornings I go out and buy up $15 worth of magazines at retail. I get everything from analysts' journal to women's magazines. You just name it. I read it." [1]

He was not without the usual layman's wish to edit. In another effort to describe himself Ackerman said, "I'm a stimulator—an idea man in terms of finding people to do things. I do not envision myself running the magazines, but I do say that I think I will give some of the people who run the magazines ideas in terms of approach and where to go." [2]

Ackerman declared he would sell none of the Curtis magazines and that he would not end the Post. As long as he was president of Curtis, he promised, there would not be a last issue of The Saturday Evening Post. He called dramatically for "dynamic marketing" and said he sought "a positive plan." Part of it was to rid the company of its remaining subsidiaries and extraneous activities and concentrate on its magazines. Everywhere he went Ackerman renewed his promise not to sell any of the books and not to close the Post, whose advertising revenue had dropped to $41,270,000 in 1967. Eventually, he said, he hoped to merge Curtis with Perfect Film.

Two days after Ackerman took office, the Curtis Building, a Philadelphia landmark since it had been opened in 1911, was sold to a real estate developer for $7,300,000. Curtis leased back part of the building in which the principal tenants were already the Insurance Company of North America and the J. C. Penney Company. Ackerman subleased the executive offices on the 32nd floor of The Saturday Evening Post Building in New York, where Curtis was paying an annual rental of over $500,000 for all the space that it used in the building.

May, 1968, was a busy month. Ackerman obtained a loan to Curtis of $5,000,000 from Time, Inc. He sold the Curtis paper mill in Lock Haven to the Hammermill Paper Company. The New York Stock Exchange delisted The Curtis Publishing Company as not meeting its assets and earnings requirements. Ackerman bought the thriving Curtis Circulation Company for the very low price of $12,500,000 for Perfect

[1] Quoted in The New York Times, May 27, 1968.
[2] "Curtis: The Last Act," Forbes, May 1, 1968.

Film. Then he came up with what he described as a secret and revolutionary plan to save The Saturday Evening Post.

When divulged, the plan proved to be halving of the Post's 7,000,000 circulation. The Saturday Evening Post would become a class rather than a mass magazine by divesting itself of older, poorer, weaker subscribers with rural or small town addresses or addresses in low income areas. It would retain only the young, the opinion leaders, those with high incomes and good addresses in metropolitan areas.

A number of magazines when hard pressed had deliberately cut their circulations and lowered their advertising rates. There was nothing new in the idea, only in the way it was done. Presumably Curtis selected the names it wanted by close computer scrutiny. Belief in magazine circles was that it simply kept every other name and gave the rest to Life, and subscribers were serviced with that magazine.

The revolutionary plan provoked a new flood of derision, this time mostly good natured. The newspapers pointed out delightedly that Martin Ackerman, Winthrop Rockefeller, the wife of the Dow Jones president, and many other presumably solvent subscribers were dropped. Newspaper columnists hugged themselves for the joy of it all. Each concocted his own tales about the Post "dropouts." Stricken subscribers were not all as amused. Many had read the Post for years. Some had been Post boys. They felt hurt, and others were puzzled. Infuriated complaints sizzled through the mails. As amused as generally less dignified journals, The Wall Street Journal told of one angry dropout who addressed his complaint to Benjamin Franklin and signed it Thomas Jefferson.[3]

The Ladies' Home Journal, Holiday, American Home, and even Jack and Jill fell off in advertising, but the Post maintained its runaway lead. It was galloping toward zero. Curtis deficit in the first quarter of 1968 was $1,600,000.

Ackerman decided to sell the huge Sharon Hill printing plant, then changed his mind and decided to let Curtis keep it. He fired another 450 office workers in New York, Phila-

[3] The Wall Street Journal, August 20, 1968.

delphia, and branch Curtis offices. The company was getting low on people to banish. Editors, executives, secretaries, clerks—anybody—could voluntarily escape or be involuntarily exiled and most days some did one or suffered the other.

August 10, 1968, the first new-new-new Saturday Evening Post, a class magazine with a cover price of 50 cents appeared on the stands. Four days later Ackerman sold both the Ladies' Home Journal and American Home to the newly formed Downe Communications, Inc. Journal circulation at the time was 6,800,000; that of American Home 3,600,000. For both magazines Downe paid 100,000 shares of Downe stock which was quoted then at 54—which went to Perfect Film as collateral on loans to The Curtis Publishing Company. Curtis had received $5,000,000 in less inflated dollars for failing Country Gentleman with its 2,566,000 circulation 13 years before so the price paid by Downe for what was still one of the important large-circulation women's magazines and the shelter book combined was hardly exorbitant. With the Downe stock going as guarantee to Perfect Film, the benefit to the povery-stricken Curtis Publishing Company was slight.

All of its identity gone, the anemic looking once-every-two-weeks Saturday Evening Post with its folksy lead-off editorial was a melange of not much of anything. Whatever it was, it was fluttering now like a shot bird. Obviously it was headed toward a coma out of which it could emerge only into extinction. It had been pronounced dead by the major advertising agencies in 1961. The press had happily taught the public that the Post was dead. The surprise was to find it still on the stands or in the mails.

Curtis had in reality ceased to be a magazine publishing company. It appeared to be just odd lots of bankrupt stock, raw material for deals that might as well have concerned lollipop sticks by the gross or so many carloads of celluloid collars. A newly formed Saturday Evening Post Company, owned half by Curtis, half by Perfect Film, though Curtis alone was responsible for fulfilling unexpired subscriptions, published the remaining Curtis magazines.

Part of the Curtis share in this company had been paid for with $6,000,000 which Ackerman withdrew from the Curtis pension fund. Thousands of Curtis employees who had not worked long enough or were not old enough to qualify for pensions under the Curtis rules had been fired. Their equities had been retained. It was money available and Ackerman used part of it for working capital, part for investment in The Saturday Evening Post Company.

The loss for 1968 broke all previous records. The Curtis Publishing Company had a deficit for the year of $20,900,000.

Though a different meaning was intended, The Saturday Evening Post of December 14, 1968, had in big black letters on its cover, "Are we heading toward the day everything stops." There was no question mark. It was a statement. The December 28 issue was more optimistic. In large primitive lettering the cover said, "Happy Happy Happy."

The Wall Street Journal, January 8, 1969, warned that The Saturday Evening Post might soon cease publication. Official announcement came two days later. Still in press, its final issue appeared dated February 8, 1969.

It had 84 pages, a prose–poetic editorial about winter weather signed "Bill Emerson" in script, a piece about Vietnam, another piece about the rebirth of the blues, and a story by John O'Hara. The second cover was an advertisement for Lark cigarettes, the third for Dodge cars, the fourth for Marlboro cigarettes. Faithful to the last, Campbell Soup was in for its tomato soup. There was not much else.

Nostalgic and patronizing death notices filled the newspapers. The New York Times, January 10, 1969, held what was really a journalistic requiem with four columns across the bottom of the front page and more than a half page of prepared obituary inside. There were reproductions of Post covers of various periods beginning with 1898 and a capsule history. Newsweek, January 20, gave two pages to the "Death of an Institution" together with more pictures of more Post covers, and Stewart Alsop used another full-page column for history and sentimental regret.

Everywhere the press was sad, gentle, and much wiser through hindsight than for some 30 years The Curtis Publishing Company had been through foresight. Editorially, January 11, *The Springfield Daily News* said,

> The demise of The Saturday Evening Post . . . is more than just the end of a venerable and respected publication. It is the death knell of a way of American life for which the Post was a sentimental and articulate spokesman.
>
> This was for more years than any of us can remember a way of life uncluttered by electronics and today's demands for "instant entertainment" and "instant knowledge."

This was the general tenor of the kinder eulogies. Others came to bury not to praise. It all seemed a little belated. The Saturday Evening Post, and Curtis with it, had really died seven unholy years before.

Complete disintegration of the completely integrated Curtis Publishing Company would have set in now had there been much of anything left to disintegrate. There was not. The Saturday Evening Post, the Ladies' Home Journal and American Home were gone. Holiday, Jack and Jill, and the unimportant Status, said to have been picked up in payment of a debt, were all part of Perfect Film. The Curtis Circulation Company was now the Perfect Circulation Company. Six million dollars had been transferred from the Curtis pension fund. Some $9,000,000 in Curtis accounts receivable had been made over to Perfect Film. The liquidator had liquidated quite thoroughly.

Even before the final issue of The Saturday Evening Post appeared there were angry outcries. With all the Curtis horses gone, there was a tremendous banging shut of stable doors.

A Philadelphia lawyer, a minor Curtis stockholder who had tried but failed to get elected to the Curtis board of directors, filed fraud charges against Martin Ackerman in connection with the sale of the Curtis Circulation Company, Ladies' Home Journal, and American Home, the closing of The Saturday Evening Post, and other transactions. His suit in the Common Pleas Court in Philadelphia claimed that except for certain accounts receivable, a paper mill, part ownership of the three remaining magazines, and its printing plant, "Curtis has been fraudulently deprived of all its business operations and assets." He asked dissolution of The Curtis Publishing Company because it was no longer in the publishing business.

Six unions representing about 1,700 Curtis manufacturing employees filed suit charging Ackerman with misappropriation of pensions funds belonging to Curtis employees. Ackerman threatened to close down the Sharon Hill plant if they did not desist.

The most serious charges came from the trustees of the Curtis estate. They demanded immediate dismissal of Ackerman and three other board members: E. Eugene Mason, company secretary; Milton S. Gould; and G. B. McCombs, who under the Ackerman aegis had been made executive vice president. The trustees charged conflict of interest and gave Ackerman until noon of Saturday, January 4 to resign under threat of "appropriate legal action." Ackerman was still in office January 10 when the trustees filed their suit in the U. S. District Court in Philadelphia.

It charged the four men with "defrauding defendant Curtis by causing the transfer of its assets for fraudulently insufficient consideration in breach of fiduciary duties." The trustees attacked the sale of the magazines, the transfer of the others to Perfect Film. They demanded that these and a number of other transactions be rescinded or that fair compensation be paid to The Curtis Publishing Company.

Backed by Gould, Ackerman vigorously denied all charges and pooh-poohed the suits as utterly ridiculous. He pointed out that directors representing the trustees had agreed to all his transactions. One of the trustee directors complained that, despite repeated requests, Ackerman had submitted no board meeting reports after August 1968. *Newsweek*, February 17, 1969, quoted a "source close to the trustees" as saying that they had been "bamboozled." The source said that Ackerman would say he would do one thing then do another.

Wounded, Ackerman screamed that all the attacks against a valiant attempt to save The Curtis Publishing Company from bankruptcy were unfair and legally unsound. They were irresponsible and a gross injustice. He declared that he had saved Curtis and detailed his accomplishments. His resignation as Curtis president was promptly accepted March 3, 1969. He continued for a few weeks as chairman of the board, then resigned that position too, prophesying that The Curtis Publishing Company would be in bankruptcy court within two weeks. Ackerman left Perfect Film within the year.

The Philadelphia lawyer agreed to withhold action on his suit when he succeeded this time in election to the Curtis board and was made a vice president. On becoming president of The Curtis Publishing Company he tried to join in the trustees' suit, failed, then set up in opposition. The situation became so confused that stockholders, the few remaining Curtis employees, and the public were befuddled—and very tired of the interminable and religiously publicized Curtis decay and collapse.

In May, 1969, The Curtis Publishing Company lost its contracts, worth about $20,000,000 annually, to print the Ladies' Home Journal and American Home. Then it lost the printing of even Holiday, Status, and Jack and Jill. In July, Curtis laid off 1,000 of the 1,600 workers at Sharon Hill. It closed the giant plant in August. Its principal customer lost, the Johnsonburg paper mill was forced to close, and the once important Curtis subsidiary of which it was a part, the New York and Pennsylvania Company, was sold.

In the same month the Curtis estate sold the Public Ledger Building to the Massachusetts Mutual Life Insurance Company for $8,000,000. In Philadelphia, of which it had been so much a part for so long, there was hardly a physical vestige left of the world's largest magazine publishing company, virtually inoperative by this time, which Cyrus H. K. Curtis had started with his Ladies' Home Journal in 1883; but there was intricate and enfevered litigation enough to make up for the lack.

This culminated—at least, came to a halt—in early December, 1969, when an out-of-court settlement was reached between the principal litigants. Under the terms of this agreement, Holiday, Status, and Jack and Jill were all returned to The Curtis Publishing Company, which also regained full ownership to the name and all rights in The Saturday Evening Post. Perfect Film retained the Curtis Circulation Company and its subscription subsidiaries which had been transferred to it in June, 1968, but the final purchase price would be fixed by a board of arbitrators. Various sums of money were transferred, and Perfect relinquished all liens on Curtis property.

Terms of this settlement were approved by the United States District Court for the Eastern District of Pennsylvania, January 21, 1970. Five other actions involving disputes between Curtis and Perfect or Bok and Ackerman *et al.* were "dismissed with prejudice."

The Curtis Publishing Company got back a number of properties which had strayed to Perfect Film. It regained what had never been more than its fringe publications: Holiday, Jack and Jill, and the recently acquired and small-circulation Status. It could not recover what really mattered—the Ladies' Home Journal and the living Saturday Evening Post.

There was concomitant action at the time of the settlement. Evidently the "extraordinary contingency" which Cyrus H. K. Curtis had seen as remote to impossible when he drew up his binding will in 1932 had been reached. The Curtis trustees announced that they were placing all of their controlling 1,123,721 shares of Curtis common and their 127,651 shares of its preferred stock on sale. No one rushed to buy them at any acceptable price, so very quickly (by February 5, 1970) the offer was withdrawn.

Curtis now tried to sell its remaining magazines, but only as a package. Any purchaser would have to take all three. No one did. Cowles Communications, Inc., by this time in severe difficulties of its own, is said to have considered purchase of Holiday and Status to combine their circulations with *Venture*. Cowles did not buy. *Parents'* is supposed to have been interested in Jack and Jill. Another large publisher considered adding Jack and Jill to its line. It reconsidered. In the spring of 1970, by which time it was understood that any Curtis magazine could be bought separately, Curtis said it had decided to retail Jack and Jill as a nucleus for possible new magazine publishing acquisitions. By midyear none had eventuated, but Status was sold to *Show;* and the stockholders of both companies approved the sale of the giant Sharon Hill printing plant to the General Electric Company.

With the January, 1970, settlements and the subsequent actions and inactions a period of some kind seemed to be placed to something, possibly to an epoch. Undoubtedly to the relief of those immediately concerned, the widely and loudly celebrated bickering came to an end, though the dribbling and drooling away did not. New Curtis presidents succeeded new Curtis presidents through most of 1970. More editors were dismissed. Yet it all seemed anticlimactic. Reality had fled a long time before.

Chapter 27

Conclusion

The Curtis Publishing Company was a pigmy compared with the corporate giants whose advertising its magazines carried for many years and which The Saturday Evening Post, sometimes the Ladies' Home Journal, helped essentially to bring to their size and earnings. Many larger companies have sickened and died after protracted illness with the public unaware and uninterested.

It was different with Curtis and its magazines simply because, if it is any good at all, a magazine is a living entity with a character, an individuality, even a moral force, of its own. It is a familiar part of the environment. It affects the lives of its readers. When, like The Saturday Evening Post, that individuality permeates the national scene, its influence extending into the homes of a large part of the population over successive generations, its welfare seems part of the country's. More intimately, it is as important as that of a close friend, at least of somebody who has always been around the house.

Press attention was deserved. The subject was newsworthy. Unfortunately it focussed on Curtis' weakening, foundering, and collapse. The real story of a man's life does not lie in the painful details of his exhaustion, senility, weeks or years of intensive care to keep him biologically alive, then his inevitable death and burial. Neither does the real story of a magazine or group of magazines.

The shock of 1961, the bucket o' blood melodramatics of 1964, the long intermission when the victim lay bleeding at every pore, then the terminal spasms of 1968 and 1969 were not Curtis. They were merely its death agony to flourishes and catcalls.

Always an unprofitable business, the attempt to place praise or blame is, in this instance, an impertinence after the fact. The fact is that for nearly three-quarters of a century The Curtis Publishing Company dominated the magazine world. Women lived by Edward Bok's Ladies' Home Journal and enough of them by the Journal edited by his successors. Men lived by George Horace Lorimer's Saturday Evening Post; and the Post edited by Ben Hibbs with Robert M. Fuoss his able associate and successor was a strong magazine.

Hibbs had a right to say in 1965, "We did, I think, get out a weekly magazine crammed with significant information, thoughtful opinion and wholesome entertainment. And we espoused causes which we believed to be right and important —often thereby incurring the wrath of many people who disagreed with us. There were times when it seemed clear that we had influenced the course of events in this country." [1]

The Curtis Publishing Company, firmly and soundly—and quickly—established by Bok's Ladies' Home Journal, rose to the heights and tumbled from them with The Saturday Evening Post. By Curtis legend the last issue of the Post was Number Three in its 242nd year of continuous publication from its founding in 1728. Certainly there had been a magazine named The Saturday Evening Post from its founding with that title in 1821. In actuality, The Saturday Evening Post which the country knew dated from 1899 when George Horace Lorimer became its editor. That magazine was 63 years old when first Hibbs, then Fuoss, resigned. That was the effective life span of the weekly magazine.

During that lifetime The Saturday Evening Post was Presidents, captains of industry, Tish, Little Orvie, Ruggles, Old Gorgon Graham, Potash and Perlmutter, Norman Rockwell,

---

[1] "Journalism, My Way of Life," *Boys' Life*, September, 1965.

Horatio Hornblower, Kenneth Roberts, Little Lulu, J. C.
Leyendecker, Tugboat Annie, Garet Garrett, Old Judge Priest,
Wililam Faulkner, Charlie Chan. . . . It was the memoirs
of World War II generals, admirals, and their aides, and of
Lindbergh, Eisenhower, Whittaker Chambers—Cities of the
World, The Face of America, Hollywood celebrities, Adventures of the Mind. . . . It was much more. It was the vigorous, uncomplicated, hard-driving United States, the romance
of business, and the glory of material success. It was free
enterprise, square-shooting, God-fearing America for Americans. It was confident, optimistic, and decent. The Arrow
Collar Man was clean-shaven and masculine.

The Saturday Evening Post was more than that too.

Cyrus H. K. Curtis had just one purpose in starting *The
Tribune and Farmer* which became the Ladies' Home Journal
and in rebuilding The Saturday Evening Post. It was the
same purpose which had moved Benjamin Franklin to start
his *Pennsylvania Gazette* in 1729 and his *General Magazine*
in 1741—to make money. It was not Curtis's fault that his
magazines became "American Institutions." His family had
been poor relations. As a boy he had used to clench his fists
and say, "I'll show them some day!"

He showed them month after month, then week after week,
in a way which Americans of his time understood, admired,
and applauded. He was an advertising man who published
advertising media, and they liked the advertisements too. In
the Ladies' Home Journal and in The Saturday Evening Post
they saw all the things they wanted and were determined to
obtain. Curtis showed them in a way nobody else could.
Before radio, television, and competition from a different kind
of magazines than he or his contemporaries could envision,
he dominated American advertising just as he and his editors
dominated magazine journalism.

The Saturday Evening Post not only preached and pictured
success every week, it showed it in a day when few people
had anything against it. It was not that they preferred the
profit motive to any others. It was that they could conceive

of no other. They thought of profit in terms of sound American dollars, as legendary now as the Post's derivation from Benjamin Franklin, and what you could buy with them. They went to church where they heard of other values, and they admired them sincerely except that they were not practical. You could not buy an automobile with them, and everyone wanted an automobile. The Post saw to that.

The Saturday Evening Post grew up and flourished with the automobile which its advertising—and stories like Sinclair Lewis's "Free Air"—publicized and glamorized. The Post helped strongly to establish the industry on which so large a part of the American economy and American society depends. With the car now as commonplace as the left thumbnail the industry, as it showed, no longer needed the Post.

Two unexplained and perhaps unexplainable mysteries persisted all during the long Curtis confusion which began in 1962. One was the inaction and seeming indifference of the principal owners of the company. Mrs. Mary Curtis Zimbalist was made a "director emeritus" in 1967 when she was 91. Long a senior vice president, she could have provided, in the opinion of some who knew her well, the strong direction the company needed. Known as a philanthropist and patroness of the arts, particularly music, rather than for her connection with The Curtis Publishing Company, Mrs. Zimbalist, aged 93, died in Philadelphia, January 4, 1970. Her son Curtis Bok had never been active in the company. Her younger son, Cary W. Bok, was a senior vice president and chairman of the Curtis finance committee, but from a distance, and he remained silent.

After Lorimer's resignation at the start of 1937 there was never a controlling intelligence or a firm hand in The Curtis Publishing Company. Strong leadership backed by the power to exert it had really vanished when Cyrus H. K. Curtis, replete with victories, turned his attentions and the power of his millions elsewhere. Fred Healey was a strong man, but he did not have the confidence of the Boks. Fuller kept shop for them, guarding the company zealously under the terms of the Curtis will. Robert MacNeal reaped the whirlwind after it had blown itself out but was punished for the wind's dying. None of his successors did any better than he. They huffed and they puffed but could not start the current moving again.

The other mystery in the Curtis downfall was the conviction of the major advertising agencies, dutifully adopted by the minor, that The Saturday Evening Post was no longer an effective advertising medium.

Cyrus Curtis and The Curtis Publishing Company had done more than any other forces to establish, strengthen, and maintain the agency system of doing business. Gratitude and loyalty are hardly to be expected in business, particularly in advertising, and, arrogant in the 1920's, the Post had made enemies with long memories, but the cold facts did not warrant this dismissal of The Saturday Evening Post. Its readership was little less than that of its two strongest magazine competitors, and the demographic characteristics of its audience were little different. The Post was still bought and read by about 7,000,000 people and looked at and presumably read by all the others who saw pass-along copies. Though its physical appearance differed, the editorial content of the Post was much like that in its flashier competitors. Yet the agencies decided against The Saturday Evening Post. Illogicality is, of course, part—a valued part—of the advertising complex, but here it seemed over-observed.

If there was a reason for the wholesale and almost concerted desertion of the Post by advertisers and agencies, it was the simple one of fear. Inescapably headlined, the financial difficulties of The Curtis Publishing Company were common knowledge. The rumor, which like all rumors gained strength through repetition, was that The Saturday Evening Post would cease publication. Such a rumor can kill a large magazine as an advertising medium almost as quickly and as thoroughly as the actuality. Sales campaigns are planned a year or more ahead. Advertising has to be scheduled many months in advance. Toward the end, advertisers could buy space in The Saturday Evening Post in almost any way they wished and very nearly on their own terms from disheartened Curtis salesmen. They resisted the temptation if they felt it. To have succumbed would have been to admit not being in the know. It would also be a risk. Agencies were afraid to buy lest the magazine fail to appear when it was too late to schedule the advertising elsewhere. Every rejection added to the rumor and convinced others that the Post was through. The Saturday Evening Post was beaten simply because it was The Saturday Evening Post.

George Horace Lorimer was completely right for himself and The Saturday Evening Post when he hated, feared, and fought the New Deal as it came in with Franklin D. Roosevelt in 1932. It was the antithesis of everything The Saturday Evening Post represented. It condemned Big Business. It choked free enterprise. It abrogated individualism and self-reliance. It offered economic and social security as the gifts of a planned economy to a dependent people. In time the change which began then made all business in effect a government monopoly through direct control or controlling taxation. It became the state socialism that Lorimer most dreaded. It went beyond that. Through heavy taxation of corporations and individuals the federal government re-allocates wealth. In the literal rather than the propagandistic sense of the word, the federal government is communistic in its role as agent in the redistribution of the earnings of all profit-making labor through its maze of faceless bureaucracies.

All this negated the position which The Saturday Evening Post established under Lorimer when that position was in full accord with its times and which the Post retained when it was in opposition to the new order. The later Post supported not the *status quo* but the *status in quo erat*.

At the same time changes other than political and social adversely affected Curtis and The Saturday Evening Post. The first two decades of the 20th century saw magazines at their height in the United States. Between 1920 and 1950 scores of them, many once popular with readers and powerful as advertising media, disappeared. *The North American Re-*

view, The Century, Scribner's, Lippincott's, World's Work, The Outlook, The Independent, The Forum, McClure's, Leslie's, Harper's Weekly, The Smart Set, Vanity Fair, the *Pictorial Review,* the *Delineator* . . . a long list, all went. *Coronet* ceased publication, *The American Magazine* then at one blow *Collier's* and *Woman's Home Companion.* The few strong contemporary magazines—*Reader's Digest, TV Guide, Playboy*—are of types no one could have suspected when The Saturday Evening Post was king.

In retrospect, the disappearance of The Saturday Evening Post and the collapse of The Curtis Publishing Company were just part of an easily discernible regression. The general magazine, in particular the mass circulation general interest weekly, has lost its hold. The Post's chief competitors are as thin now through lack of advertising as the Post was in the last years of its decline. Their publishers' hurried moves toward diversification through the purchase of newspapers, trade magazines, and television facilities is further indication of the sharp decline of the mass magazine.

That particular dog seems to have had its day, and it is the turn of other dogs to bark.

By standard definition magazines exist to inform and to entertain. Television has taken over the entertainment function and much of the informative. Women may compare fashions and recipes in the Ladies' Home Journal with those in *McCall's, Vogue* or *Country Life,* but they can get everything that really matters from the gossip shows or the detergent operas. Men can get it from cowboy sagas, news and weather programs, telecast baseball, football, basketball, hockey, and roller derbies without leaving the living room and their beer. If their television set is properly equipped, they can turn off the commercials. Who needs them?

Often annoying, advertising is now as suspect as the profit motive for which it is spokesman. The country has been built. All it needs now is a little rearranging to suit everyone. The millenium has come. Maybe it went yesterday. Who knows? You don't need magazines to find out these things. Advice?

Who wants it? Who needs hemlines when you have the pill
or civil order when you have the moon or the future when you
have the atom bomb?

Even for those with a slightly different attitude the result
can be much the same. The confusion which every generation
knows has been so many times enlarged and improved that
modern man finds it and himself so much the worse confounded. Experts and specialists in thousands of fields and
small corners of those fields have sprung up in increasing
numbers because few can understand, or even attempt to
gather the materials for understanding, the larger political,
social, economic, scientific, and what else world we live in.
Most people cannot form judgments because we have no bases
on which to form them, and we cannot gather enough of
the pertinent facts to form a rational opinion. This is contemporary man's dilemma, and he knows he cannot find a
solution through the superficial foray of some facile magazine
journalist.

There is that, and there is also this.

The decline of the mass magazine is perhaps just one more
symptom of the change back from a literal to an oral way
of life. Reading and writing are no longer basic necessities.
People can, and many do, get along quite well without them.
Traffic lights are red, green, and yellow, and they know what
they mean. Television can transmit events as they occur. Actions and ideas can be recorded, stored, and recaptured by
various electronic, mechanical, and photographic devices which
obviate the task of writing and the chore of reading. Once
vital and of the moment or its vicinity, magazines now seem
vitiated and tardy.

Perhaps the explanation for the disaster at Curtis and the
demise of The Saturday Evening Post is even simpler. If, like
a person, a magazine is an individual entity, like a man or
woman it has its vigorous youth, its settled middle years, exhaustion, and old age. Many important magazines have failed
to outlive the editors whose temperaments and ideas they expressed. The Curtis magazines did for about a quarter cen-

tury, though never with the vitality infused by their original publisher and his editors.

Busier than ever and painting in a different style, Norman Rockwell said ruefully and wistfully in 1969 that he understood that people are now collecting his old Post covers as period pieces. He had put kindly humor into their photographic realism, managing somehow to glamorize the commonplace. If, he says, he thought a picture was not going well, he put in a dog, always a mongrel. If he wanted a stronger effect, he put a bandage on the dog. People would write in to the Post exclaiming over the dog without noticing the rest of the painting. They liked dogs then.

He painted his Saturday Evening Post covers, Rockwell says, when all grandfathers were lovable and mothers even got along with their children. The Post was his life. In a way, he says, it still is, but, "Everything has a length of success, then it goes. The Post was terrific, but tastes changed."

The Reader's Digest selected, condensed, and reprinted 386 articles from The Saturday Evening Post. It used 160 pieces from the Ladies' Home Journal, 56 from Country Gentleman, and 70 from Holiday while these magazines were still published by Curtis. The most successful magazine editor since the Lorimer he diffidently approached about 1924, DeWitt Wallace scrutinized the Curtis magazines professionally. Recently he said, "Practically and emotionally it was a great loss when The Saturday Evening Post ceased publication. Not only was it a dependable source of vital information and comment on subjects of wide appeal, but the Post, as it described itself, was also truly an institution in American life. I think we are all the poorer without it."

History, which has a way of doing both, made the Curtis magazine publishing empire and The Saturday Evening Post; then, helped by a few determined individuals, it killed them.

Bibliographical Note

This book is based principally on the author's experience as an employee of The Curtis Publishing Company 1946–1964 and two additional years as a book consultant to the Curtis Circulation Company and on discussions for the purposes of this writing held with a number of the Curtis principals mentioned in the text. Also used were files of the Curtis magazines; the Company's informational bulletins, annual reports, and reports of stockholders meetings; and the files of the Philadelphia *Inquirer*, *The New York Times*, the *Philadelphia Public Ledger*, and *The Wall Street Journal*. Some publishing and advertising trade publications were consulted, along with the following books:

BOK, EDWARD W. *The Americanization of Edward Bok*. New York: Charles Scribner's Sons, 1920.
The Beecher Memorial. Brooklyn, N. Y.: privately printed, 1887.
A Man from Maine. New York: Charles Scribner's Sons, 1923.
Twice Thirty. New York: Charles Scribner's Sons, 1925.
BUTTERFIELD, ROGER, ed. *The Saturday Evening Post Treasury*. New York: Simon and Schuster, Inc., 1954.
GOULD, BRUCE AND BEATRICE BLACKMAR. *American Story*. New York: Harper & Row, Inc., 1968.
GUNTHER, JOHN. *Taken at the Flood*. New York: Harper & Row, Inc., 1960.
GUPTHILL, ARTHUR L., NORMAN ROCKWELL, illustrator. New York: Watson-Gupthill Publications, Inc., 1946.
HOBART, DONALD M., ed. *Marketing Research Practice*. New York: The Ronald Press Co., 1950.
LORIMER, GEORGE HORACE. *Letters from a Self-Made Merchant to His Son*. Boston: Small, Maynard & Co., 1902.
MARCOSSON, ISAAC. *Before I Forget*. New York: Dodd, Mead & Co., 1959.
PIPER, HENRY DAN. *F. Scott Fitzgerald, A Critical Portrait*. New York: Holt, Rinehart & Co., Inc., 1965.
RINEHART, MARY ROBERTS. *My Story, A New Edition and Seventeen Years*. New York: Holt, Rinehart & Co., Inc., 1948.
ROBERTS, KENNETH. *I Wanted to Write*. Garden City, N. Y.: Doubleday & Co., Inc., 1949.

TEBBELL, JOHN. *George Horace Lorimer and The Saturday Evening Post.* Garden City, N. Y.: Doubleday & Co., Inc., 1948.

WOOD, JAMES PLAYSTED. *Magazines in the United States,* 3rd ed. New York: The Ronald Press Co., 1970.

The Story of Advertising. New York: The Ronald Press Co., 1958.

WOODRESS, JAMES. *Booth Tarkington, Gentleman from Indiana.* Philadelphia: J. B. Lippincott Co., 1954, 1955.

Index

Abbott, Lyman, 31
Abbott, Mrs. Lyman, 23, 24
Ackerman, Martin S., 272–75, 277–80
"Ad Page Exposure," 238–39
"Adventures of the Mind," 232–33
Advertising, 10–14, 26–27, 49, 61–72,
    87–88, 110–11, 113, 117–20, 123,
    128–29, 131–32, 177, 184–87,
    192, 212–13, 243, 245, 249, 286–
    87, 288
  "Ad Page Exposure," 238–39
  automotive, 69–70, 71, 77–78, 117–
    19, 226
  Curtis Code, The, 64–66
  liquor, 227–28
Alcott, Louisa M., 11–12
Allen, Benjamin, 139, 148, 198, 228
Alsop, Stewart, 264, 265, 276
American Home, 269, 275
"Atom Gives Up, The," 152
Ayer, F. Wayland, 13

Baum, Arthur, 211
Beecher, Henry Ward, 18, 19, 20, 25
Benchley, Robert, 78–79
Better Farming, 219
Blair, Clay, Jr., 246, 254, 257–58, 261,
    264–66, 267
Blythe, Samuel G., 87, 91, 104, 145
Bok, Cary W., 126, 141, 285
Bok, Edward, 4, 15–32, 81–85, 121,
    145–46
Bok, William Curtis, 126, 141, 285
Boy salesmen, 54–55
Boyd, William, 69, 110–11, 121, 155
Brain Trust, 130–31
Brandt, Erdman, 144, 150, 166, 171,
    172

Bremier, Fred, 80, 117, 118–19, 156,
    205–6
Bride-to-Be, 227
Brooklyn Magazine, The, 18
Brookman, Laura Lou, 160
Buck, Pearl, 160

Calkins, Ernest Elmo, 63
Carnegie, Andrew, 82
Cartoons, 171, 182
"Case Against the Jews, The," 153,
    168
Chambers, Whittaker, 212
Circulation, 12, 20, 26, 28, 32, 49–
    50, 52, 79–80, 83, 105, 144, 150,
    163, 174–75, 192, 212–13, 231,
    242, 250, 267
  controlled, 218, 274
"Cities of America," 211–12
City Markets, 80
Cleveland, Grover, 51
Clifford, J. M., 257, 267, 268, 270
Cobb, Irvin, 87, 91, 104–5
Cohen, Octavus Roy, 104, 138
Collier's, 29, 138, 221–23
Collins, P. S., 121
Conservation, 93
Coolidge, Calvin, 45, 107
Cosmopolitan, 18, 99, 105
Costain, Thomas B., 105, 135, 142
Country Gentleman, 58–61, 85–86,
    111–13, 136, 137–38, 165, 179,
    215–21
"Country Gentlewoman, The," 112,
    217
Country Gentlewoman League, 215–
    16

Crane, Stephen, 46
Crosby, Bing, 212
Crusading, 24, 54, 81, 104, 106–7, 113, 131–33, 140, 156
Culligan, Matthew J., 257–58, 261, 263–66, 268
Currie, Barton W., 61, 136
Curtis, Cyrus H. K., 3–14, 62–68, 121–27, 145–46, 205, 284
Curtis, Louisa Knapp, 6, 8, 9, 14, 72, 121
"Curtis Advertising Code, The," 64–66
Curtis Building, 32, 53–54, 55–57, 86, 270, 273
Curtis Circulation Company, 139, 148–49, 155, 228–30, 250, 273–74, 277, 280
Curtis Publishing Company, The
 characteristics
  through 1950's, 154–55, 201–5
  in 1960's, 257–61, 270
 debts, 262, 272, 273
 delisted by New York Stock Exchange, 273
 directors, 164, 224–25, 255–57
 founding, 23
 as integrated enterprise, 147, 172–73, 175, 196–98, 223–24, 252
 lands, sale of, 269
 as leading magazine publisher, 107–9, 110–20
 libel suits against, 262
 losses, 233, 243, 249, 256, 261–62, 266, 270, 274, 276, 279
 pension fund, withdrawals from, 276, 278
 personnel policy during the Depression, 133–34
 profits, 121, 123, 223–24, 231, 249, 270
 Research Department, 178–82, 187–87, 235–39
 Research Library, 177–78
 subsidiaries, 224
  sale of, 269, 273–75
 suits against Ackerman, 277–80
Curtis Trust, The, 121–27, 278, 280

Davis, Richard Harding, 87
de Koven, Reginald, 24
de Kruif, Paul, 112, 113, 138, 156, 214

"Department Store Lines," 75–76
Dix, Dorothy, 138
Dower, John, 155
Dower, Walter H., 90, 91, 155
Downe Communications, Inc., 275
"Dr. Spock's Talks to Mothers," 160

Eddy, Mary Baker, 30
Eisenhower, Dwight D., 211, 234
"Encyclopedia of Cities," 77

Fadiman, Clifton, 189
Farm Journal, 164–65, 220
Fashions for women, 54, 81, 162
Faulkner, William, 109, 153
Ficke, Charles, 220
Fiction, 22, 25, 28, 33–35, 46–48, 52, 101–2, 108–9, 142, 152–53, 159–60, 182, 189–90
Fitch, George, 52
Fitzgerald, F. Scott, 102–3, 106
Food and Drug Act of 1906, 29
Ford, Ann, 150
Ford, Leslie, 153
Franklin, Benjamin, 11, 38–39, 248–49, 285
Frederick, Harold, 46
Fuller, Walter D., 126, 141–43, 145, 146–48, 172, 185, 198, 226, 255, 271, 285
Fuoss, Robert M., 91, 136, 138, 166–73, 178–79, 207, 231, 232, 233–34, 244–47, 251, 252–54

Garland, Hamlin, 24
Garrett, Garet, 105–6, 107, 145
"Girls' Problems," 28
Glass, Montague, 52
Godfrey, Arthur, 212–13
Goshorn, Clarence, 155
Goshorn, Robert M., 155, 218, 220, 221
Gould, Beatrice Blackmar, 137, 156–59, 161–63, 242, 256
Gould, Charles Bruce, 137, 156–59, 161–63, 242, 256
Greenaway, Kate, 24
Gunther, John, 144, 160

Hall, A. Oakey, 26
Harding, Warren G., 89, 107
Hardy, Arthur Sherburne, 38

Harrison, Benjamin, 24
Harte, Bret, 46
Hazen, Edward W., 69
Healey, Fred, 118, 121, 134, 139, 140, 145, 146, 156, 193, 285
Hergesheimer, Joseph, 95, 101, 106, 145
Hibbs, Ben, 91, 138, 165–75, 178–79, 207, 211, 220, 227, 232, 234, 246–47, 250–51, 260, 283
Hiss, Alger, 212
Hobart, Donald M., 80, 116, 176–78, 201, 205, 238, 239
Hoffmann, Karl K., 230–31, 269
Hofmann, Josef, 29
Holiday, 183–92, 267–68
Hoover, Herbert, 82, 107, 125, 130
Hope, Bob, 212
Hopkins, Claude C., 67–68
Horwich, Frances R., 268, 269
Hough, Emerson, 104, 106
Howells, William Dean, 22

"I Will Drive Safely" campaign, 156
Illustrations, 23, 27–28, 90–91, 159, 171, 182
Immigration, 97
Irwin, Will, 87

Jack and Jill, 149–50, 230–31, 268–69
Jews, 152–53, 168
Jones, Ellen, 80
Jordan, William Starr, 38

Kahler, Hugh McNair, 98, 113, 138, 159
Kantor, Marvin D., 257–58, 264–66
Kelland, Clarence Budington, 105, 106, 108, 113, 138, 171, 217–18
Keller, Helen, 28
Kettering, Charles F. ("Boss"), 117, 153, 215
Kilpatrick, Guy, 152
Kipling, Rudyard, 22, 28, 73, 99–100
Kohler, Arthur, 194, 198, 228
Kreuger, Ivan, 103–4
Ladies' Home Journal, 8–31, 55, 81–84, 98, 111, 117, 136–37, 154–63, 240–43, 275, 285
Latshaw, Stanley, 69, 73
Laurence, William L., 152
Leckner, Myron C., 136–37

Lefevre, Edwin, 95, 106, 145
"Letters from a Self-Made Merchant to His Son," 42, 47–48
Lewis, Sinclair, 97, 113, 124
Liberty, 93, 138
Life, 139, 169–70, 184, 236, 274
Lindbergh, Charles A., 212
"Literary Leaves," 22
London, Jack, 52
Look, 139, 236
Lorimer, George Claude, 40–42, 46
Lorimer, George Horace, 40–52, 90–109, 128–35, 141–46, 166, 287
Lorimer, Graeme, 136, 137, 142, 144, 150, 154
Ludeke, Herbert C., 178–79, 182, 236–37

MacNeal, Robert E., 198–201, 203, 213, 227, 243, 247, 249–50, 252–54, 256–57, 271, 286
Mad, 248–49
Marcosson, Isaac, 87, 95, 103–4
Markets and Quotas, 79–80
Marks, Leon, 228
Marquand, J. P., 108–9
Marquis, J. Clyde, 61
Martin, Harold H., 207–11, 263–65
Martin, W. Thornton ("Pete"), 91, 144, 166, 168, 212–13
Masson, Thomas L., 105
Mayer, Martin, 153, 168
McCall's, 240–43
McManus, Theodore, 71
Miller, Dean S., 133–34
Movie-magazine pieces, 212
Muckraking, sophisticated, 261–62
Mueller, Eberhard, 203
Music, 24, 29
"My Government and I," 82

Neall, Adelaide, 91, 93, 105, 135, 143, 144, 145, 150, 151, 167
Nelson, Frederick, 168
New Deal, The, and The Saturday Evening Post, 128–40, 151, 287
"New Leisure," 184–86, 188–89
New York Evening Post, 123
New Yorker, The, 113
Norris, Frank, 46

"Old Gorgon Graham," 42

Parlin, Charles Coolidge, 73–80, 118–20, 155
Parrish, Maxfield, 56
Patent medicine, 29–30, 64
Patrick, Ted, 187–90, 267
Patriotism, 81–83, 86–88, 169, 172
Pattullo, George, 87
Payne, Will, 104
Peek, Milton L., 201, 219, 220
"Penalty of Leadership, The," 71
People's Ledger, The, 6
Perfect Film and Chemical Corporation of Manhasset, 272–74, 275, 277, 280
Philadelphia Public Ledger, 122–23
Phillips, David Graham, 104
"Pious Pornographers, The," 161
Population surveys, 76–77
Post boys, 54–55
"Post Influential" promotion, 237
Postwar (World War II) market, 182–83, 185–86
Preston, May Wilson, 145
Public Ledger Building, 122, 279
Public men, as contributors, 24, 51, 82, 125, 160, 211, 234

Radio, 115–16, 139, 164
Reader research, 178–82, 185–87, 248
Reader's Digest, The, 114–15, 139, 260, 290
Reed, Robert, 179, 215, 217–18
Research; see also Surveys
  commercial, 73–80, 117–19, 176–78
  competitive magazine, 235–43
  editorial, 178–82, 185–87, 248
Rinehart, Mary Roberts, 84–85, 87, 99–100, 145, 160
Roberts, Kenneth, 95–99, 109, 142–43, 145, 150–51
Rockwell, Norman, 90–93, 101, 169, 172, 261, 290
Roosevelt, Eleanor, 159
Roosevelt, Franklin D., 125, 130, 131, 151, 287
Roosevelt, Theodore, 30, 31–32
Rose, Ada Campbell, 149–50, 200, 230
Rose, Philip, 112–13, 137–38
Rose, Stuart, 172
Rowell, George P., 68 n
Rudderow, William, 148–49

Safe driving, 156
"Sales Opportunities," 79, 236
Saturday Evening Post, The, 33–52, 86–89, 90–109, 111, 116–17, 128–40, 150–53, 164–75, 194, 207–14, 231, 233, 237–39, 244–54, 274, 275–77, 283–90 passim
Saturday Evening Post Company, 275–76
Schanche, Don, 267–68
Scholars, as contributors, 232–33
School Plan men, 229
Schuler, Loring A., 61, 112, 136–37, 160
Sharon Hill Printing Plant, 195–98, 279, 281
Sherrod, Robert, 231, 246, 253–54, 261, 265
"Side Talks to Girls," 22, 25
Sions, Harry, 187–88, 267
Smythe, Albert, 36–37
Sommers, Martin, 136, 144, 172, 209–10, 211, 227, 259, 261, 263–64
Sousa, John Philip, 24
Spock, Benjamin, 160
Status, 277, 281
Stiefel, Frank, 203
Stimson, Henry L., 160
Stinnett, Caskie, 268
Stock market crash of 1929, 103, 129–30
Stockton, Frank R., 25
Stout, Wesley Winans, 91, 135, 143–45, 150–53, 166, 179
Strauss, Lewis, 259
Stuart, Kenneth, 91, 246
Surveys; see also Research
  population, 76–77
  on women's attitudes, 158

Tarkington, Booth, 48, 98, 100–1, 109, 145, 151
Television, 116, 205–6, 213–14, 221, 226, 231, 245, 288
Terhune, Albert Payson, 112
Texas Gulf Sulphur Company, 269
Tiffany, Louis C., 56
Tighlman, Buford, 201–2
Time, 113, 138–39, 169
"Tish" stories, 85, 99
Trade publications, 245

Train, Arthur, 101
Trayser, Lewis W., 195, 198, 228
Tribune and Farmer, The, 7–8, 9, 10
Tucker, Gilbert, 58–60
T-V Week, 227

Ulrich, E. Huber, 173, 230

Venereal disease, 29, 159
Von Tress, Edward, 228

Wallace, DeWitt, 114–15, 260, 290
Whipple, Leon, 107–8
White, William Allen, 173–74
Wiggin, Kate Douglas, 54
Wilcox, Ella Wheeler, 19, 23
Wilson, Harry Leon, 48, 106
Wilson, Woodrow, 82, 88

Wister, Owen, 52
Wolfe, Thomas, 152
Women
  attitudes of, surveys on, 158
  fashions for, 54, 81, 162
  suffrage, 32
  in work force, 24, 157–58
World War I and Curtis magazines,
  81–89
World War II and Curtis magazines,
  152, 169, 170, 172–73, 183

"Your Savings," 103

Zachary, Frank, 188, 267
Ziesing, Richard, 163
Zimbalist, Mrs. Mary Curtis, 3–4, 14,
  72–73, 126, 224–25, 256, 285